SAVIOURS AND FOOLS

SAVIOURS AND FOOLS

James Rinaldi

PENTAGON PRESS

Saviours and Fools
James Rinaldi

ISBN 978-81-8274-922-1

First Published in 2017

Published by
PENTAGON PRESS
206, Peacock Lane, Shahpur Jat
New Delhi-110049
Phones: 011-64706243, 26491568
Telefax: 011-26490600
email: rajan@pentagonpress.in
website: www.pentagonpress.in

Edited by Vibha Kumar

Printed at Avantika Printers Private Limited.

Contents

AUTHOR'S NOTE

Not long ago, I met an old friend over a cup of tea. In the late 1990's, there were only a few of us involved in active Tibetan assistance—he did his thing in Tibet and I concentrated on working with Tibetans in Nepal. We would occasionally run into each other in Kathmandu and compare notes. A book on his adventures had been released and I had been trying to make contact with him and gain some helpful advice for this project. Eventually, I found myself sitting across from him in a Washington, DC tea room, one rainy afternoon, as he told his story. Back before the time of the Beijing Olympics, literary people were parading him around to various New York publishing houses and trying to sell his Tibet-themed manuscript as a kind of political counterpoint to the upcoming games. Meetings had a recurrent "how can we market this" theme, with various publishing executives eyeing my friend's appearance from head to toe and offering what seemed to be more fashion tips than book advice. As he described this process, I could not avoid thinking that the Western world was well past its fascination with Tibet and it was only the specter of the upcoming Beijing Olympics that was forcing a bit of life back into the topic.

It would be no different for me. As the months passed, literary agents would look at my ideas and yawn about yet "another Tibet book". My favorite near-miss came from an agent who e-mailed her chief concern: "Jim, I really like this story but I'm afraid I'm going to have Richard Gere nightmares if I take it on, so I'll pass". Eventually, I found a publisher who was willing to commit to this project, but only under the condition that I re-write the entire manuscript, de-emphasize Tibet, focus on my personal development story and describe what childhood anxieties drove me towards a life of humanitarian work. What was going on here? Why was everyone

I had spoken with determined to avoid Tibet like it was a disease? I declined the offer and backed away to consider my options.

So, is this yet another book on Tibet? We were supposed to be done worrying about this years ago. What's the point? Why push this topic now if no one seems to care about it?

This book will not replay old arguments and atrocities, but it will bring to light some of the questions that have been in our thoughts over the last few years: Why does the Tibet problem still persist? Why did we in the West make it our job to free Tibet and why has this not happened? Overall, conditions inside Tibet have steadily deteriorated from the time when the first "Free Tibet" decal rolled off the printing press, until today. At the very least, we should not have presided over three decades of deteriorating conditions, or perhaps contributed towards making things worse, right? I hope this book helps you find a few cultural and moral reasons why I believe America and the West have failed Tibet, and a few arguments for why we really had no business getting involved with the issue in the first place.

And why am I doing this now? I simply had to wait. Some time needed to pass. I've had aspects of this story ready for almost 15 years but couldn't risk sharing any of it until now. Rescue tactics, locations of illegal Tibetan border crossings, the mechanisms of Tibetan movements—all the things that would give an immediate bearing to those wishing to harm Tibetans as they go through Nepal—had to be kept quiet. Hopefully, enough time has now elapsed that no retaliation or harm will come to any Tibetan, Nepali or Indian citizen because of what I have written in these pages. Even so, most names used in this book have been changed, as the real ones still belong to actual people and places still needing discretion, privacy and anonymity.

All of the stories told in this book are based on true events. These things happened. For the sake of readability, a few accounts have been compressed into a single timeframe. The events described in the chapter where I travel up to the Tibetan border and all hell breaks loose transpired over two separate trips, not one. I have been up to the Nepal/Tibet border at Kodari dozens of times, but it would make for a tedious read if I repetitively described trips where I was bored to death and nothing happened—which happened frequently. Next, the accounts of the children crossing the Nangpa-la were compiled from the numerous stories of that journey I was able to hear while working at the Tibetan Reception Center Clinic in Kathmandu.

Quite a bit of material has been left out of this project as well—for a good reason. I wanted the personal stories presented here consist exclusively of those that could be verified by some combination of direct interview, receipt, photo, e-mail or video that is in my possession; this was not fully possible with every account. We're going to make some people angry with this book, so I've done my best to see that it will be well-defended.

Lastly, I'm going to make a big assumption. I will trust that the reader has at least a basic knowledge of the politics and the tragedies behind Tibet. We will only sparingly flirt with Tibetan history here. It is old, well-trodden ground that gives most books on Tibet an undercurrent of tedium. If you are at all interested in the deep issues behind this book and the fascinating and heartbreaking events of Tibetan history, by all means, seek out more sources. Purchase almost anything with "Tibet" in the title and you will find some version of the Tibet back-story. Many of these books are boring; a rare few are indispensable. Regarding the latter, I was saddened to read of the recent passing of John Kenneth Knaus. This book leans heavily on his two contemporary political histories of U.S. involvement in the Tibetan struggle. Both his *Orphans of the Cold War* and *Beyond Shangri-la* offer accounts of the early days of Western attention to Tibet right up through the most recent efforts of the U.S. Congress to aid and, as I will argue, attempt to quiet the Tibetan Movement.

As another matter of old ground, many works on contemporary Tibetan issues focus on what "China must do" to improve the Tibetan condition—and vehemently bashing China's role in Tibet's travails has always been the default strategy of Tibetan activism. None of this is without merit or justification, but from our perspective here, China will neither be represented as part of the problem nor part of the solution; we will focus on a different pool of blood in the water.

On a non-descript afternoon in the fall of 2015, I happened to wander into a Tibetan bookstore in Kathmandu and immediately walked over to a book about an American State Department official who had penned his own ideas and philosophies about the Tibetan situation. Turning to the rear flap, I noticed that it was published by Pentagon Press in Delhi, India. After staring at the logo for a bit, lights went on in my head and it dawned on me just how short-sighted I had been. I realized, then and there, that launching this book in the U.S.—or anywhere in the world where people have burned themselves out on "Free Tibet" rhetoric—would be a betrayal of everything I had done on behalf of Tibet over the last two decades. It would no longer result in this book being used as a tool to stimulate new and creative thinking on Tibet—as I had hoped—as much as it would be about me, "The Author", my "personal journey", and about selling and marketing a profitable book. After a quick blip on the short-attention-spanned Western literary publicity scene, the ideas and perspectives presented here would fade into obscurity. By contrast, introducing this project in India—where people are engaged on a daily basis with Tibetans and Tibetan issues—would make the assertions and observations found in this memoir ring clearer and stronger.

It was a moment of epiphany. I quickly left that bookstore, headed back to my room, and spent the remainder of the evening tapping out e-mails.

Let's use this book to start a new Tibetan conversation: a conversation that involves self-reflection and a clear-eyed assessment of the future. America and the West will not approach this conversation; India is just now starting to articulate the components of it. Still, if this book accomplishes nothing else beyond triggering a much needed critique of the Western-based "Free Tibet" movement, I'll claim a partial victory and consider it the first of many steps needed to both, re-invigorate interest in Tibet and re-commit ourselves, intelligently, towards finding a more effective means of advocating on behalf of Tibetans.

I suppose, after reading a few chapters, you will begin to wonder why, exactly, I did such seemingly crazy things. Throughout the process of writing this book, I would ask myself this question, over and over. There is no clear reason for why I did the things that I did, and perhaps that is the best and only answer. Maybe there is something fundamentally human in each of us that should rightly remain beyond category, definition and questions of "why".

After a few weeks of e-mail exchanges, I met Rajan Arya of Pentagon Press. He immediately agreed to publish what you are about to read.

CHAPTER 1

PUZZLES

I bought into it as a child – they hit me early with the idea and I took it at face value. Work hard and success will come your way. Simple, but adults would tell us this as though they'd just given up a treasure map. To them, this was serious business. It was the secret formula, a sacred linearity that was lubricated by self-help speak. Tomorrow will be better. Good things happen to good people. We just need to have faith and believe in ourselves. Follow your dream. It had its intended effect on me. It also blurred the line between delusion and possibility, but I didn't care. To me, it was as though the adults were speaking of no less than the engine of the American industriousness. It was the "Great Call" to American society. We were "winners" and I was taught to be grateful for having been born on the right side of history and the winning side of the Industrial Revolution. The evidence of our greatness was everywhere, and rags-to-riches stories abounded in our cultural lore. America is the envy of the world. It is a plain fact that everyone who is not us wants to be us, and it is our duty should we find ourselves – God forbid – in a foreign country to help as many of those poor foreigners as possible convert to our way of doing things. We are special, and everything we do for the rest of our lives will somehow be of importance for the greater good of the world.

Throughout our history, the sheer force of these beliefs has compelled us to do things beyond our abilities and beyond our ability to reason. So thoroughly do we buy into this idea that we never take a step back and consider that there seems to be no accounting for luck, serendipity, cheating or a host of other factors that probably influence our success more than self-confidence and hard work. It is seldom mentioned that the formula is not a guarantee; there is no linear progression and the rest of the world does not necessarily want to be American. It's a fantasy. We were lied to as children – probably to keep us from complaining too much and killing ourselves before we turned 20.

It was late 1994 and I was tired of the "greed is good" ethos that defined the previous decade of my working life. Ten years in real estate finance had taken its toll. The worst of the first savings and loan crisis was behind me by that point, and I wanted no more of the instability and deceit that I had just survived. I was an underwriter. My job was to assess new loan applications and decide if the individuals behind these applications were worthy of the funds they requested. I looked at the borrower's cash on hand, credit and ability to repay the debt, as well as the condition of the property and the likelihood of recovering our investment should the borrower default. It was a turbulent job conducted during turbulent times, and the past few years leading up to this point had found me hopping from job to job, just ahead of some merger or the doors being shuttered. Security Pacific, Guardian Savings and Loan, American Residential Mortgage and Chase Manhattan were but a few of the companies that saw me pass through their doors in those days – Bank of America as well.

On that day in late 1994, I began to think of my time at Guardian Savings, back in 1989, when I first realised that something was amiss in my childhood indoctrination. We had just been commandeered by the federal unit – The Resolution Trust Corporation (RTC) – designed to oversee the savings and loan bailout at that time. We were told that we would all receive full paychecks, and that we were to show up at work and do absolutely nothing until further notice. Every few weeks I'd be called into a big conference room filled with strange individuals with coffee-stained teeth and asked to analyse the credit worthiness and risks involved in certain loan application packages that seemed to materialise out of nowhere. Asking no questions, I would accept the files and begin work. Most of the good financial minds at Guardian had already left, and those of us who remained were becoming murderous with boredom, so I looked forward to these infrequent little patches of intellectual stimulation and always dove into the tasks assigned with zeal.

On one such occasion, I was given a loan application package that was dead from the start. Nothing made sense. It was a commune-style complex that had borrowers with no discernable income or ability to pay for the loan. To top it off, the foundations on the main buildings were cracked and sinking into the earth and asbestos insulation was visibly protruding from holes in the walls. They wanted me to take this loan seriously? I went in to tell the head of the brown-teeth brigade the bad news.

"Listen, this thing is a disaster. Even if they were to spend the hundreds of thousands of dollars required to bring their foundation up to code and remove the asbestos, we're looking at a first-payment default based on what little financial ability I can find from these borrowers. No. It's a dog. Decline this thing and set it on fire."

I was emphatic in this, mostly because it felt good to act like a professional again, and I needed to wallow a bit.

"Well, thanks, Jim, we'll take it under advisement," clucked Mr RTC.

Something wasn't right. I wasn't used to such a dismissive tone. I gave them good work – damn good – and was expecting deeper, more technical questions. There needed to be a more thorough review, and none seemed to be forthcoming. I had a bad feeling about this.

We were trained to be critical of all loan packages, ask questions and doubt the veracity of anything too conveniently supportive in the documentation. Our jobs depended on it. Normally, a loan such as this would never have made it through the initial application process, much less be considered for funding. Who were these guys and where did they get these loan packages? Why were representatives of the Federal Government giving me these infantile, remedial loan applications to analyse?

Later, I learned that the RTC went ahead and approved financing for the loan in spite of my protestations. *My God,* I thought, *this can't be fraud. That loan wasn't good enough to be a fake.* I'd approve a Bugs Bunny cartoon before I'd approve a loan like that. If it was incompetence, then it was a staggeringly new and egregious manifestation of the term. To me, it meant the rules of good underwriting were now meaningless – my skills were meaningless. The more likely meaning was that those who comprised the various monitoring and oversight groups of the RTC had ties to the financial industry to begin with and had suddenly found themselves in charge of the loan funding mechanisms of the various savings and loan institutions they were tasked with monitoring. Too much candy thrown in front of too much of a sweet tooth probably led to this dog of a loan resurfacing and casually being inserted into the most recently funded cache of loans that was now part of a "suspect" Guardian portfolio, but was never actually originated, underwritten or approved by Guardian. Nice trick.

It was downhill for me from that point onward. I showed up for work, did absolutely nothing, as directed, collected my paycheck and went home. I demurred from helping out Mr Coffee Teeth and his RTC bunch after the dog episode, preferring to keep to my office.

I filled my days with reading anything I could obtain, and did my best to walk down through our spacious glass lobby and out into the fresh air nearly every day at noon so that I could take in a full feature movie on my lunch break. That grew tiresome and I began to crave any and all forms of mental input and devour anything that presented itself as novel or intellectual. This was an era long before one could lose oneself for days on end in front of the internet, so the print media was treasured and great interest was taken in reading deeply and thoroughly anything and everything one might get one's hands on. It was a weekly highlight when *Time* or *Newsweek* magazines arrived, and I always purchased both and read each from cover to cover immediately. One story – I think it was in a battered old issue of *The New York Times* that I had found and was ravaging through to find the crossword puzzle – would not leave my head. It seemed that two adventurers, Blake Kerr and John Ackerly, had found their way into Tibet and gotten caught in the middle of a massive local uprising. Tibetans were being killed, and the two adventurers pitched in and helped where they could. I loved the account and read it over and over. It had meaning for me. It was glorious to think that people were actually out in the world doing important things and not prioritising their earnings or leveraging their next automobile purchase. These two guys were truly alive, and I wanted to be like them and do what they did. But their world was so far from where I was sitting, tucked away in that hopeless office, that I let the excitement fade. My dream pathway that led to financial security and the nice cars and $1,000 suits that go with it was also fading fast. I believed that success in life was based on merit and skill, and none of that seemed to apply to my job anymore. I was stuck, going nowhere...and I knew it.

The one good thing that happened during this period was that I became quite proficient at completing the *New York Times* crossword puzzle – I certainly had ample time available to develop the skill. After a while, I learned quite a bit about how the puzzle works, its recurrent themes, how to use intuition, the whims of the different puzzle creators and the quirks of the puzzle's editor. (Hint: Understand that "GWTW" refers to "Gone with the Wind" and learn a smattering of Yiddish, and you've got a good foundation for success.)

As the days of RTC-mandated attendance dragged on and became more difficult to bear, I looked forward immensely to receiving, beginning and completing my daily crossword puzzle. I would fill them out in ink, magic marker or with stylised letters that could either fill the entire square or be perfectly centred and tiny. I would refuse to move onward until I completed an answer in whatever obscure pattern I'd chosen for that day: all horizontal clues in order, all verticals, from the corners inward, letters written backwards – anything. My fixation on the puzzle was such that I began to scissor out my completed works from their section in the newspaper and pin them up on the wall to the right of my desk. I looked at it as a badge of defiance. By the time all of us were eventually let go from Guardian, and probably no more than a day or so before I would have gone completely insane, I had succeeded in wallpapering about one quarter of the vertical surfaces in my office with *New York Times* crossword puzzles – completed and in ink.

I continued to bounce around from savings and loan to mortgage company to bank for a few years more. Eventually, I wound up in a prosperous, stable and growing firm in San Diego. We had our offices overlooking the prestigious Torrey Pines golf course in La Jolla. An intelligent, forward-looking upper-management team saw to it that loan files were delivered to us daily in bright, shiny metal carts that gleefully gave us more work than we could handle. This was a good thing and I relished the stressful workload. We had a CEO who told us daily how "stable" our company was, and that we would never gamble on risky loan portfolios that would trigger something as absurd as federal intervention. We were going to be the mortgage pillar of San Diego.

"We have a bright future ahead of us," he would say. "Come, grow with us, and together we'll reach a new level of service and success – oh, and did I mention how stable we are?"

After a few months of this, I began to smell a rat, and was sure that some sort of major change was in the works. Eventually, we were told that our company was being sold to Chase Manhattan Bank and that "all of our careers were safe". To me, this could only mean one thing: We were all about to lose our jobs.

*

"Jim, the vice president would like to see you in her office," said the secretary.

After 30 minutes of sitting and waiting for a conference that I had already pre-conducted in my mind numerous times before this event, I snapped out of my Guardian Savings and Loan flashback, made my way into the vice president's office and listened as the terms were spelled out. Either I could take my current salary and relocate from San Diego to Monroe, Louisiana, or I could take a nice severance package that was in the works.

It was now clear to me on that day in late 1994 just how tired I had become. I was tired of not knowing where I would be working from year to year, and tired of not being told the truth. I did not want to relocate and I did not waver in my choice – no offence intended to the good citizens of Monroe.

"For some reason, all of this doesn't seem to bother you, does it?" asked Marilyn, the VP.

Oddly, it didn't. My career on the bucking bronco of real estate finance in the turbulent early 1990s was over, and this was where I got off. Marilyn continued for a while, rattling off something about office property and access cards that needed to be turned in, but all I could think about at that moment were those two adventurers I had read about back in my Guardian days who went into Tibet and got into all sorts of trouble. I had been considering travelling around the world for quite some time, and now all I could think about was that this was the perfect opportunity for me to turn those thoughts into reality – newly emerging career gaps are good that way.

Marilyn was right, I wasn't bothered by what was about to transpire. I can look back now and say that I was strangely at peace with the whole thing. I bid Marilyn a good afternoon, cleaned out my desk and left the building smiling.

*

In the late 1980s, at just about the same time that I was admiring the next addition to my wall of completed crossword puzzles at Guardian Savings, Tenzin Gyatso – His Holiness, the 14th Dalai Lama of Tibet: the spiritual and political leader of his people – was preparing to give a speech at the Congressional Human Rights Caucus. He had been to Washington DC once before, on the political periphery, yet close enough to Washington insiders to cause a stir. Carter administration official Joel McCleary – pivotal in arranging this first visit – sat next to the Dalai Lama on the podium: He was summarily scolded by a nervous White House for the gesture. Now, here again came the Dalai Lama, about to set a precedent of sorts by meeting with US Government leaders on their turf – to the thorough irritation of an increasingly assertive China lobby.

It had been a tough 30 years for the Tibetan people. In 1956, in response to Chinese pressures, rebellion began in earnest against increased Communist assertiveness; thousands died and much of Tibet's cultural heritage was damaged or destroyed over the ensuing three years. The CIA was spoiling for a fight with the Chinese Communists during this time, and felt that the Tibetan brand of grass-roots rebellion was just the ticket they needed to harass Chinese efforts at political consolidation. They began to train small teams of Tibetans in radio operation, intelligence gathering and guerilla warfare. These CIA-sponsored and US-trained Tibetans were parachuted back into Tibet sometime during 1957. It was a grand spy effort and a grand spy plan. Unfortunately, it had very little to do with freeing Tibetans and very much to do with using the Tibetan uprising as a tool to impede the Communist Chinese.

The CIA's efforts expanded to dropping weapons and armaments to Tibetan resistance fighters. The newly armed Tibetans fought bravely, repelling Chinese troops and retaking important cultural sites. They began to feel confident in their ability to push back the Communist aggressors with the now full-throttle backing of CIA-supplied weaponry.

> ...all drops of men and equipment were subsequently made from C-130's, with their USAF markings removed. The C-130's enabled the CIA to eventually double the loads to more than 25,000 pounds; with multiple flights, sometimes three nights in a row. More than 500,000 pounds of arms, ammunition, radios medical supplies and other military gear were dropped by the CIA to the Tibetan resistance forces from 1957 to 1961.

Despite the strengthening defences of Tibetan fighters, the spectre of an overwhelming force of well-trained Chinese soldiers approaching Tibet's capital, Lhasa, the young Dalai Lama fled Tibet in 1959. He was granted asylum almost immediately by India and resides to this day in exile, with many other similarly fated Tibetans, in the mountain enclave of Dharamsala in the northwestern Indian province of Himachal Pradesh.

The US sought to capitalise on the Dalai Lama's flight as a means of demonstrating the aggressive cruelty of the Chinese Communists, but the Dalai Lama was a reluctant participant in this strategy. Still, Washington's support for the Tibet cause grew along with air-dropped weapons support.

Eventually, the scale of the operation became difficult to conceal and the demands too great. At one point, the CIA found itself somewhat overwhelmed by a Tibetan demand to "help us as soon as possible and send us weapons for 30,000 men by airplane". It was now no longer a matter of the CIA supplying small skirmish groups of a few hundred fighters at a time. The Tibetans were all in and the Chinese were regrouped, amassing large numbers of troops for their end of the fight. Tibetan commanders' requests to feed battalions of thousands of men at a time must have overwhelmed the CIA and caused a great deal of second-guessing in a Washington that was not prepared for such an escalation. A combination of a lack of secrecy and manageability due to the conflict's escalation, coupled with the fact that the Chinese were fighting back harder than imagined, and the realisation that the Dalai Lama would not be an outspoken representative of anti-Communist sentiments caused the US to abandon their plans and abandon the Tibetan struggle – it would not be the only time.

The Dalai Lama sits, waiting for his moment with the congressional caucus. He is a hopeful individual, yet this is a calculated move on his part. Under Chinese Premier Deng Xiaoping, the Tibetans had found themselves pushed into a corner, with Deng offering Tibetans a bit of safety and autonomy as long as the Dalai Lama was left out of the equation. To Tibetans, this was the same as agreeing to let breathing be left out of the equation. So they made the decision to turn their focus on wooing the international community towards their struggle – the Dalai Lama's caucus visit was to be the spearhead of this political shift. Congressman Tom Lantos, a relatively recent supporter of the Tibetans, set up the caucus visit and listened as His Holiness spoke of turning Tibet into a "zone of peace" where Tibetans could enjoy a certain amount of autonomy and, wishfully, the Chinese would stop their current disturbing practice of turning the place into a nuclear dump – the most pressing Tibetan atrocity of that moment.

It was during these momentum-building years that Joel McCleary published a thoughtful report that outlined not only the steps needed to begin the "international" Tibet campaign in earnest, but also the major concerns and stumbling blocks for Tibetans as they seek world attention.

Tribal exclusion and disunity and Chinese population transfer to Tibetan areas were among McCleary's many concerns. But this report was not intended for public use, and undoubtedly many of its practical and ground-based strategies were never brought to light. The newly emerging Tibet Movement was to move along a different path.

A few days later, on September 27th, 1987, the violent riots in Lhasa that introduced John Ackerly and Blake Kerr to the world – and first ignited the curiosities and compulsions that would consume the next 20 years of the life of a lowly underwriter in California – began. Those riots would trigger many smaller uprisings throughout Tibet. American outrage was more palpable as reports of Chinese soldiers firing their rifles indiscriminately into crowds of Tibetans began to make the rounds on Capitol Hill.

If the Dalai Lama had made a few friends with his speech to the Congressional Human Rights Caucus as reported, the Lhasa riots substantially enhanced his cachet. By October, an angry US Senate had voted unanimously to condemn China for its actions, and held up future arms sales to China until they started paying attention to human rights. Support for the Dalai Lama and the Tibetans was high, and it seemed as though real political momentum was building. Would the US finally and formally support Tibet and the Dalai Lama? Would they put real force behind their condemnations and move to sanction China?

It would have been nice to have met the Dalai Lama during those times. I would have told him what I'd learned, because it applied to his situation: Don't get starry-eyed at the freedom and self-determination speeches that we Yanks throw in your direction. Good intentions are wonderful, but they always seem to mask a greater policy goal, agenda or some individual self-interests that remain to be revealed. Step carefully and don't take what they say at face value. I wish I had told myself the same thing.

*

The State Department offered their vehement opposition to the Senate's vote, worrying that whatever benefits such a condemnation may yield for Tibetans, they were "insufficient to outweigh the almost certain damage to the U.S.-China bilateral relationship". This was an early version of the "don't rock the boat" viewpoint that would come to dictate most of the Western world's philosophy on China v. Tibet, and it undercuts anything that approaches a coherent Tibet policy today. China was to be engaged, and the Tibet issue stood in the way of effective engagement. Back in 1987, however, such a viewpoint was just that, a viewpoint. The Chinese economic miracle was still years away, and the China lobby seemed to hold no real power, for the moment, as a Washington lobby – unless you call screaming objections powerful. Because of this, legislators felt no sense of political peril and began to voice their opinion in the form of a few Tibet-supportive lines finding their way into the legislation of that day. The Foreign Relations Authorization Act signed by Ronald Reagan in December of 1987 was perhaps the prime example of this. It forwarded a strikingly pro-Tibet position by implying that Tibet was an independent country "invaded" by China.

It seemed as though the Tibet cause had finally found its champion in Washington. A dedicated group of individuals on Capitol Hill was committed to finding legislation that would provide amenable insertion points for Tibet-friendly language; and now, the International Campaign for Tibet (ICT), a Washington-based advocacy group, was forming to support the cause of Tibet on all fronts – its first president was to be John Ackerly.

By the end of 1989, the Dalai Lama was speaking again about his "zone of peace" idea; this time it was in Oslo, on the occasion of his acceptance of the Nobel Peace Prize. Things were continuing to look up for Tibet.

*

I can't say that I thought of my banking career much during the period immediately following my ascension from Marilyn's office. The next six months were spent trip-planning, drawing unemployment cheques and avoiding gainful employment. I was looking for more fundamental change. I wanted to be defined by something other than my job. I wanted to be someone else.

Being of an older school of thought, it was frightening for me to not be working or looking for employment, so I made the task of researching the upcoming trip my job, and I dove into it headlong. My girlfriend Holly was keen on going, and trip preparation became a fun project for the two of us. Not knowing where our planned world tour would take us other than Nepal, we were open to ideas. Whenever we even thought of visiting some place in the world that sounded interesting, we would buy the appropriate guide book and read all that we could. It was exciting to look at the photos in the Fodor's guides, and we became minor connoisseurs of guidebooks and their respective specialties. The Let's Go series of books seemed vague and lazily written, while the Rough Guides were much more specific to the low-budget style of travel we were planning. But the more remote the location being considered, the more obscure the desired locale, and the more the Lonely Planet guides stood out. One could tell that these people had done their homework. It seemed as though you could pick a village of 50 people in the middle of, say, Siberia, and the Lonely Planet guide would know the location of the best budget lodge in town, the price and the first name of the proprietor. I was half expecting to read "ask Yuri if his rash has cleared up" at any moment.

I had a certain level of disgust with the lifestyle I'd left behind, and I didn't want to take a nice vacation, spend my severance pay and return to start over. I wanted difference, I wanted upheaval. If I was going to commit career suicide, I was going to go into it fully engaged and looking forward. Long nights of beer with Holly produced a sort of drunken philosophical bonding on this point. We didn't want comfortable hotels and a nice sanitised experience. We wanted to live on bread bought from local markets, and travel around on the tops of farm trucks. Give me another perspective on what it is to be happy. How do the natives do it? What makes that Tunisian man so content? Could I live, raise a family and die satisfied selling coconuts on a street corner in Kuala Lumpur? Why do I need to work so hard? For a bigger house, a better car, a new washer and dryer?

I was working up a quiet foam that was no doubt leading towards something medical, so I calmed myself and realised that there were still things to be done. Mostly, there was a travel budget to consider. My severance pay was no golden parachute – it wasn't even a bronze parachute. Hard travel choices would have to be made. We decided to spend the bulk of our time in Thailand and Nepal as the budget-traveller options in those countries were numerous. Then, funds permitting, we would spend just a little time in cash-draining Europe and then head home. Based on the prices and exchange rates at the time, we figured that we could live fairly well, take cheap transportation and see lots of cool free stuff for around $500 per month. This, we felt, was a reasonable budget target, but we could get by on less if need be.

Within a few months, we had sold all of our possessions, bid goodbye to friends and family, and hopped on a plane to Malaysia.

It was late August, 1995.

Chapter 2

Down the Road

I don't actually know what snapped inside of me. I just knew that the American Dream no longer held any attraction. It was like being told that the church you belonged to was running a brothel in the basement in order to pay the rent.

It would have been easy to move to Louisiana and keep going, but now there seemed to be no point in relocating once again on the whims of the real estate industry. There hadn't been any sense of direction in my career, much less my life, that even closely resembled that great and special linear success road I was told about as a kid. Sharpening my underwriting skills and accumulating merit were getting me nowhere and enough was enough. The worst part was that I was fully aware of my spoiled brat complaints, but I was done nonetheless. I was severing all ties to my previous life and it felt good – really good. Floating, unencumbered and uncertain, frightened yet exhilarated, we boarded a Malaysia 747 bound for Kuala Lumpur. It would be our first look at Asia, and we planned to cross into Thailand immediately upon landing and spend the next 30 or so days eating cheap food and riding on the tops of trucks whenever possible.

Thailand suspended us in a state of wide-eyed wonder. Holly and I had both led lives consisting of very limited episodes of international travel, and we had never been to Asia. Just the act of buying noodles from a Thai street vendor felt ground-breaking and legend-inspiring to us. From August through to September of that year, we travelled from the southernmost tip of Thailand northward to Bangkok. We considered staying a few weeks longer, but after a tough, humid month we were getting weary of living in sweat 24 hours a day and we were burned out from spending the last week in the tourist-hustling scene of Bangkok's Khao San Road. We were itching to see Nepal and the Himalayas, and we had heard that "trekking" season was just beginning. Eager to move on, I purchased a good pair of hiking boots at a cheesy Thai tourist boutique and slept poorly that night thinking about Tibetans.

The next day, we arrived at Bankok's Don Muang Airport after a harrowing minibus ride through the claustrophobic back streets of old Bangkok. Our driver was convinced that this method would circumnavigate the morning gridlock on the main thoroughfares, and we were no better than helpless abductees on his circuitous re-tracings, so we hung on for dear life and hoped for the best.

Arriving, we thanked the driver with a *"khap koon kap"*, and gave him a small tip, hoping he'd use it to get some seat belts. No, a brake job would be better.

From there on, the day evolved into a familiar routine of Asian travel: Sit in an airport, wait and sit some more. This went on for at least two hours as our line in the Royal Nepal Airlines terminal seemed frozen in time. I had been practising some rudimentary Nepali phrases during the few months prior to our departure, but was totally unprepared for an abrupt meeting with a Sherpa woman who took very deliberate steps towards me and asked if I'd carry her 50-pound duffel bag full of God-knows-what to the counter and check it in as my baggage. Before an obvious decline, I tried out a few *namastes* on her for effect, but this woman was in no mood for tourists; she was all business. She obviously had no time for the contrived courtesies of common Western idiots and told me so in what was probably some very explicit Sherpa profanity. Now I had doubts. Had I prepared enough for this wild place, Kathmandu, which I had never seen and was a complete geographical and cultural world away from my spoiled and fat American existence? Was everyone going to be like this Sherpa woman? We were about to be eaten alive.

Our plane boarded successfully and we took off. Nepali stewardesses dressed in Tibetan aprons or *chubas* greeted us as we found our seats on a Royal Nepal Airlines flight bound for Kathmandu. An uneventful four hours passed until I realised that everyone on the plane suddenly wanted to be on the right side of the aircraft. This raised my curiosity and I asked the passenger in the seat in front of me what all the fuss was about.

"Take a look," he said.

A sea of white clouds of unspectacular variety and placement was all I was able to see from the window. One of those clouds refused to follow the rules and seemed to be standing still rather than moving with the rest of the cloud tribe. Nearing, it was clear that this was no cloud but a massive granite pyramid thrusting into the jet stream and creating its own set of clouds. It was Sagarmatha, Mother of the Universe to the Nepalis; and Chomolungma, the goddess mother of the Snows or Holy Mother to the Tibetans. To us Westerners, its name comes from the man who first set his eyes on it and decided to name it after his boss, an obscure surveyor named George Everest.

Holy Mother was appropriately descriptive as soon the entire Everest massif came into view: Nuptse, Lhotse and Lhotse Shar and eventually to the west, Cho Oyu. The sight of such imposing peaks – all over 8,000 metres in height – gave me the feeling that there would be no turning back from this point forward and for the rest of my life. I had no idea what was to come, but a feeling is a feeling and the whole experience frightened me more than a bit.

I was throwing up Thai food now, but couldn't be happier; a little air sickness was not going to spoil this moment. The Airbus tossed and bucked its way through the mountains as I went over in my mind what I had to do if and when we reached terra firma and the airport. There would be no fancy terminals, just an unceremonious tarmac and a walk under the airplane wings into a brick building. From there, it took a plan – you need one every time you land in a "third world" airport. The Lonely Planet guidebook can only help so much in a situation like this. You have to act and move sharply and look like you know what you're doing. Street touts and hustlers who wait patiently at the final door out of the terminal can sense your indecision and have you lost, confused and without the contents of your wallet in a matter of moments.

It's best to get a good running start from your seat in order to secure a prime spot in the customs line at Kathmandu's Tribhuvan International Airport. Failing this, one can be left waiting for an eternity to get a Nepal visa. We had heard from a fellow traveller in Thailand that one should not purchase a visa ahead of time so as to warrant a preferred place in the "Tourist: No Visa" line, which is invariably shorter than all other lines. Sure enough, Holly and I breezed past a group of queuing yet smug Europeans in the throes of a full smoking scrimmage, who gave me their best look of entitlement, cursed their pre-purchased Nepal visas and resigned themselves to life in a line that stretched to the back of the terminal. We gave the man our visa fees and I fumbled a simple *namaste* to the customs agent, who then greeted us warmly in return with a barrage of words that hit me like white noise.

"Thanks again and, uh, *namaste*...again," I said, tucking my new visa and my linguistic tail between my legs. Embarrassing, but at least we were clear of customs and moving briskly through the terminal. Conveniently, someone had thought to put a currency-exchange booth just beyond the visa lines, and in a few moments I made $200 look like 13,000 Nepalese rupees.

Stepping out into the parking lot, we became the immediate and passionate object of every hotel tout, tour operator and tuk-tuk wallah in the area. Some lunged for our attention, all shouted. Doing my best to not look ignorant and determined to not be taken for just anyone's fool, I set out to bargain a decent cab fare to the seedy tourist district of Thamel. Two hundred rupees seemed to be the going shout, so I stood my ground and demanded passage for 150. I was a force to be reckoned with and would broach no compromise. Fifteen minutes later, after all the cabbies had ignored me, we started out on foot towards the front gate of the airport. Someone took pity and agreed to take us to Thamel for 180 rupees, and I felt a bit better. Later, I learned that the average Nepali businessman can take the same cab ride for 35.

Always an interesting drive, getting from point to point via taxi in Kathmandu entails bouncing through potholes, swerving around cows and a pronounced prioritisation of horn usage over brake deployment. All of this is accomplished at high speed and through streets no wider than a Nebraska blue-collar driveway. After some time, the driver dropped us off at one end of Thamel so we could walk through, catch our breath and take in the sights before locating a room for the night. Smouldering garbage fires, incense and red *tika*-painted bronze idols from centuries past lurked in dark, moist alleyways; emaciated, painted holy men locally referred to as *sadhus* begged; and there were dogs everywhere – not the scabby, half-dead dogs of Bangkok, but smaller, meaner and craftier street dogs, underfed and pissed off.

It was tourist season and Thamel was bustling with activity. For a tourist in Thamel, the toughest day is the first day. That big backpack on your shoulders tells anyone who is selling anything – which is everyone in Thamel – that you are fresh off the plane, rich and ripe for the plucking.

"Excuse me, sir, you like carpet?"

"*Namaste, Dai*, your room is ready at my guesthouse, best price."

"Hello, sir. Dope? You like hashish, white, black?"

"Change money?"

"You want shoeshine?" (Even if you are wearing sandals.)

Some don't bother with the pitch, they just grab you with their outstretched hand.

Brushing aside a jumping swarm of neon fliers that screamed for attention, we found a nicely dressed and thoroughly passive hotel tout who gave us a moderate flier and directed us away from the noise of Thamel's main tourist street to our bed for the night at the Hotel Norbu Linka.

It was as clean and friendly as anything we could have hoped to find on our own, so we tipped the agent, took the first room that was offered, unpacked, gathered our wits a bit more and decided to walk around town. It was starting to sink in that we had finally made it. We were in Manjushree's valley under the protection of Lord Pashupati. We were in Kathmandu.

The streets of Thamel are the best maintained in all of Kathmandu – cranky Western tourism demands it. But maintenance is a matter of perspective in Nepal. A merchant's daily garbage is often thrown, by the mound load, into the open street. It sits there, unattended, for about a week, and once the dogs have picked through it a truck comes bearing exceedingly filthy gentlemen, who attack it with shovels, tossing the pile unceremoniously into the back of their truck – presumably to form a bigger mound in another part of the city. Yet these same streets maintain a wet sheen throughout the day as these same merchants obsessively spray water on the ground outside their modest shops in an effort to minimise the effects of trodden street dust on their merchandise.

Taking the narrow street adjacent to the hotel, which was notable for being awash with freshly butchered water buffalo carcasses and pig heads, we somehow managed to make it, gore-free, to the main *chowk*, or square, of the area, and were instantly hit by a bolt of humanity.

"Two for One Drinks" banners hung like sooty laundry across lanes of hustlers, European backpackers, Asian businessmen, Tibetans, Nepalis, holy men and sharp-eyed solicitors of all types. The day's chalkboard listings of first-run pirated Hollywood movies dotted the doorways of dimly lit tea houses: running all day and available for free if you bought a plate of noodles. Movies gave the burned-out hippies and wide-eyed trekkers waiting for their trekking permits something to do to kill the time. The old classic Thamel restaurants like La Dolce Vita, The Third Eye and KC's were running strong, like the guidebooks said, in seeming defiance of the future. Times were changing. New buildings of ghastly Indian and Chinese design had begun to replace the old red-brick, infinitely charming safety hazards that were the distinctive feature of Thamel architecture for decades. Holly and I were now in agreement that it was a thoroughly enjoyable foot tour that we had begun, and both of us stepped lively.

In order to move effectively through any Kathmandu street, it is important to familiarise yourself with the various begging schemes of the average street hustler. One creative scam involves phoney Tibetan monks dressed in phoney Tibetan monks' robes courteously asking you for money to build a phoney monastery. They also courteously produce a nice receipt for your donation. In reality, no sect of Tibetan Buddhism encourages active solicitation of money. Real begging monks simply sit quietly with their begging bowls, and are content with whatever happens to land in those bowls that day. Monks in the monasteries themselves often expect a donation to help with upkeep and so on, but you are never turned away for refusing to give. Another trick consists of a man frantically displaying a piece of paper that he claims is a prescription for medication. Naturally, he needs money immediately to take care of the problem. Forget that this piece of paper may have absolutely nothing to do with a prescription and may be ten years old, tourists think that he is sincere and throw money at him. And what about those small armies of identically dressed little Indian women wearing white saris, with identical little silver begging bowls and identical babies slung on their identical hips? They all seem to have that plaintive "woe is me" stare, which seems overwrought and over-rehearsed. It turns out that these gals hail from the south Indian state of Kerala and follow the tourist crowd around from Goa to Kathmandu. They report to a Fagin-like boss every day to turn in their booty, and the baby they haul around is usually not their own.

I didn't care. They were all part of my vision of Kathmandu and all had a place in its chaotic streets. The mud, the schemers, the noise, the smoky, dilapidated three-wheeled Vikram motor taxis, the dogs and the street children were all necessary – all indispensable.

Kathmandu can be an overwhelming and profoundly sensory place for the first-time visitor. Holly and I were immediately captivated by its odd and ancient magic. Here there were people fighting to stay alive, yet somehow happier than any humans I had seen in my 34 years on the planet. They were scratching, suffering, brawling and alive. It was indescribable, and we were both stunned by the effect. We made it back to the hotel after our walk and both of us broke down like a couple of newborn babies. We clutched each other, arm in arm, and jumped up and down laughing. Nothing prepared us for Kathmandu and no place on earth could possibly be more different from the America we had left behind. I don't know about Holly, but I could have died happy at that particular moment.

Like many who make it to Nepal, our goal was to walk the classic Everest trail. To do so, we would have to begin a preliminary journey that entailed an eight-hour bus ride to the trail head at a village called Jiri. From there, we would hike – actually, "trek" as it is known in this side of the world – across mountain ridges for seven days until we reached the village of Lukla. From Lukla, we would likely meet the wimpy "fly-in" tourists, who would land and begin their trek of the high Himalayan Sherpa country around Everest from the local airport. What we were about to embark upon is considered to be one of the toughest tourist treks in the Himalayas, and would give us some major bragging rights once we merged in Lukla with the "effete".

After paying double the going rate for a bus seat due to our decidedly tourist manner, at about four p.m. we arrived in Jiri, where we laid claim to an available room in a benign guesthouse and settled in for the evening. As is the usual custom, we sat around a communal table with other trekkers and talked about the days to come. The discussions generally centred on where everyone was going to stop the next night, what to eat and how best to treat foot blistering. Everyone seemed to have their maps out on the table, and heated debates ensued about who paid what for their map and which map had the prettiest colours.

The next morning broke to the sound of roosters. This to me was neither relevant nor theatrical, since the local dogs had been barking all night anyway, allowing me no rest. After downing a quick breakfast of oat porridge and tea, we set off towards the trail and the beginning of our Everest adventure.

According to the prettier maps, the trail head was just at the end of the pavement at the far end of Jiri, and just the simple act of walking to that point of beginning made me feel that a ceremony was in order – an awkward little prayer was all that I could muster.

"Please, God, look out for us."

Holly, not one to be moved by such things, tried her best to mirror my forced sense of the moment. This was to be the adventure of our lives. We both knew that we would encounter real physical difficulties as well as natural beauty that would be beyond comprehension. I just felt like I needed to say *something*. Confidently, we took our first strides, fully prepared to be overwhelmed by some of the most exquisite hiking trails in the world, and immediately stepped in human excrement.

It seemed the locals in Jiri were compelled to use the forests along the trail, better still the entire trail, as a toilet. *Welcome to Nepal,* we thought. As the day progressed we rose gradually through the morning mist to a low ridge where terraced, cookie-cutter shaped fields consumed the hillsides. Our days would be filled from here on with hours of constant uphill walking followed by jarringly painful descents. Previously, I had chuckled at Lonely Planet after reading that there was not a level stretch of ground in all of Nepal. I wasn't laughing now. The first day finished with a brutal two-hour climb to the ridge-top settlement of Deorali. We were moving slowly. And this was constantly being brought to our attention by the sporadic appearance of small village girls darting upwards and beyond us on the trail, with what appeared to be about 100 pounds of wheat tucked into the *doko* baskets that were secured and supported by a strap that ran across their foreheads. As the evening descended, we limped into a small lodge and the source of our laggard's pace became evident. Holly had also purchased new hiking boots in Bangkok – too new. Without having been broken in for the proper amount of time, they had cut deep into her feet during this first day of trekking, leaving her in considerable pain. Characteristically, she said nothing.

Every morning, I would have to re-bandage Holly's feet as the blisters she had acquired and failed to mention would scream for attention. She was maddening in her silence. This was one time that I would have welcomed any kind of complaint from her – she deserved to complain. Her boots were agonisingly tight and her toes and heels were torn to shreds. Early on in the journey, we were in a little village by a stream called Kenja, and I told Holly that enough was enough and to just sit in the room we'd rented, relax with some tea and read a book. I spent the rest of the day soaking her boots in a nearby stream in an attempt to stretch them out a bit. I knew that as soon as we were able to begin again, we were to encounter the most difficult stretch of the trek, where we would climb to a mountain pass at around 12,000 feet. I feared that if either one of us were to be hobbled by injury or bad footwear, it could be dangerous. After pulling the wet boots from the water, I stuffed the insides full of stones and began to smack the leather on the outside with a large rock. After an hour, the boots had softened and I let them dry in the Kenja sun for the rest of the day.

By the next morning, Holly's blisters looked better, her boots felt better and overall the world was better. I had diarrhoea.

For the most part, the next few days of walking were event-free. We crossed that 12,000-foot pass, the Lamjura, without a hitch and continued towards the Everest region. Holly's feet were still giving her considerable pain, but we felt some joy at finally seeing and crossing the Dudh Kosi river via a big steel-cabled Swiss-made suspension bridge. Crossing here is a victory of sorts, as you now get to make a big left turn and head up the Dudh Kosi valley, with your bearing now squarely set on Mount Everest. The victory part is that you are finished with the gruelling up-and-down trekking through the valleys and overpasses that highlighted your previous six days of effort. Now, the climbing itself will get physically easier, but only just in time for a new set of concerns about dealing with high altitude and its related maladies to take over.

My life changed forever after making the big left turn.

Just above a village named Puiyan, Holly and I encountered a group of about 20 individuals running down from the high Himalayas on our trail, heading to our position. Their features were Asian and rough, and included fire-red rosy cheeks. Some wore maroon-coloured skirts and shawls; they looked to have some sort of regal bearing, but really I had no idea. Some made their way along the trail in old green tennis shoes, others were barefooted. Those without shoes had bleeding cuts and scrapes on dirty red, white and black coloured feet, and looked to be in considerable pain. Being the friendly trekker that I was, I clasped my hands together as if in prayer and uttered the traditional Nepali *namaste* greeting. Strangely, there was no response. I was sure that these people had heard and understood the greeting as I was in fine voice and practice that day.

"*Namaste*, hello," I tried again.

One strong-limbed young man that I remember as having unusually large calves broke out of the cluster, turned about-face with his palms open and pointing upward, and approached me with a deliberate intent that was only partially masked by the limp in his steps. An unearthly smile broke the contours of his agony and he greeted me warmly with *tashi delek*, before turning back towards his group. I watched him kick up trail dust and labour into a trot as he struggled to catch up with his companions.

It was a while before I could bring myself to move from that spot on the trail, much less speak.

"Shit!" I blurted to Holly. "Do you know what? Those were Tibetans! What the hell just happened? How could that guy smile at me like that with his feet all messed up the way they were? Where do you think they're going in such a hurry? What was up with those women in the robes?"

I had a hundred questions about what I'd just seen, but no answers. I continued to ask myself questions for the next few days.

The questions stopped when an answer came to me in the form of one simple and clear idea.

CHAPTER 3

BACK HOME WITH A PLAN

It was to be the ultimate of all personal reinventions. A new me was to emerge: one that was the complete and philosophical opposite of the banker-me that came before. It could be done; people have done worse things to themselves and come through in good enough shape. Gone would be the pursuit of the Almighty Dollar. In its place would flow an embrace of humanity and humility dedicated to serving others – dedicated to serving the Tibet cause.

Snapping out of it, I realised that we were still on the road with a lot of time ahead of us.

Months of travel came and went, and my mind was never more than a few steps away from the images of those bleeding Tibetans. We set up house in Stuttgart, Germany, found a few odd jobs and managed to save enough money to continue still onward. By the time it was all done, we had spent over a year travelling the world and living among varied and distinct cultures. Filled with new perspectives and cultural insights, it never occurred to me that I had completely forgotten how to be an American, and when we finally landed at San Diego's Lindbergh Field, there was no sense of the triumphant return home. The unfamiliar anxieties brought on by "What are we going to do now?" thoughts, combined with the queer sensation of no longer being a part of my home town, or country, left me feeling very alone.

We managed to find a bungalow in the back of a small plot of land in small Ocean Beach, California. From my altered vantage point, the walls were too square and too white, the carpeting too clean, and dear God, was that a bathroom or a sterile research facility? It got worse: The streets I once felt were too narrow now seemed too wide and wasteful as they cut any sense of community that might blossom down the centre into separate, disengaged camps. People on these streets seemed like they would rather be anywhere but out in public. Casual conversation with strangers was viewed as plotting and agenda-driven. Human interaction was whittled down to what was necessarily transactional.

It is a rare thing to be able to step away from your culture and your biases long enough to have the memory of both stripped from your psyche. It left me bewildered and cranky.

But there was no time to seek pity. We were back home in America and we needed to find work and quickly, so I picked up a job as doorman at the newly hip and former dive bar the Aero Club, just off of India Street and next to the screaming California Interstate Five. In retrospect, it was absolutely the wrong type of job for a person who had just returned to the US and was fully assimilated into another culture. Spoiled 20-somethings were always trying to push through the doorway with the conviction that only their overblown sense of entitlement could muster; people would start a brawl over 25 cents left on a pool table; women shrieked their demands rudely at the bartenders; and above all – drowning out all – was the conversation. Not the human kind that actually tries to make a point and can be substantive, but the incessant droning, the continuous, unpunctuated blabbing that was full of words but said nothing. Was I this way before I left?

The Aero Club paid the rent and that was what mattered. It was back into the American grind where one is defined by their job, their possessions and the bills they have to pay – all else is secondary. But I had seen the mountaintop and I had plans.

Work dragged on and I began to think about keeping my promise to myself. A clear and simple idea had hit me when I had walked out of the Himalayas and it was time to see if it made sense. It was impossible for me to believe that there was no use for a knowledgeable American in a setting as poor as Nepal, and it was self-righteously clear to me that Nepalis and Tibetans needed us. How could they not? I had no doubt about the fact that I was not going back to the banking world and its intricate dysfunctions. I decided that I was going to learn enough medical and language skills to be able to become a full-time advocate and volunteer when finally I was able to return to Nepal. My willingness to pitch in and help wherever needed would be an inspirational beacon for Nepalis and Tibetans alike, and the example provided would be deeply felt and taken to heart as a supreme act of charity and generosity. It made me smile: the planned-out construction and certainty of it all. The world would be impressed, eventually, but I needed to get started.

I enrolled in a basic Emergency Medical Technician (EMT) course, hit the books and passed nicely enough. Next, I was able to wrangle a few volunteer shifts at what was then Mission Bay Hospital in San Diego. From there, once the doctors and staff saw that I didn't kill anyone, I was given a few paid shifts working in the Emergency Room (ER) as a medical technician. I was off and running.

We had options as newly minted EMTs back then. We could ride around in an ambulance with our hair on fire thinking we were hot shit, but generally be relegated to transferring elderly patients from nursing home to nursing home. Or we could try for the ER tech option. I wanted the latter because the EMT stood next to the doctors, assisted with certain procedures and saw enough medicine to make one numb to the sight of blood, gore and faecal matter when it presented itself – sometimes all at once.

Part of my job was to be the Cardio Pulmonary Resuscitation (CPR) administrator during cardiac arrest arrivals in the ER. Despite what you see on television, unless the cardiac event is witnessed and CPR begun immediately, you've got damn little chance of making it work once they get to the ER. I must have performed CPR on patients hundreds of times and seen others do it hundreds more, and not one ever came around and showed a pulse. I can't remember when the defibrillator saved anyone either, but I know it has happened. Our protocols mandated that we keep pumping on the patient's chest at around 130 compressions per minute and at a depth of about two inches. The tough part was that we were absolutely not allowed to stop unless we were relieved by another tech or were exhausted – and we were never relieved. The worst part about it was that after about 30 minutes of pumping Grandpa's chest and dripping with sweat, his sternum would give way and you'd hear the tell-tale "crack" of broken ribs. Protocols being what they were, you were instructed to keep pumping – rib fracture and all. I'll never forget that sensation, it's fresh in my mind even today.

Dumpster-diving was an invigorating sport for the drunks and homeless around Mission Bay Hospital back then. Resourcefulness combined with a bit of self-mutilation helped the crafty bum set up a comfortable night or two, a few times a month. I'll explain: A good street drunk knows that an open sore or ulceration can be a ticket to paradise. An enterprising street person would begin to dive into local trash dumpsters, not only for food but to increase the potential for both the expansion and infection of the wound. Sure enough, infection would arise, and by Friday evening a steady procession of homeless men would present themselves, drunk, happy and febrile, at the ER. We would clean them, feed them, medicate them, give them a bed for a few hours and send them on their way – Club Med for a night. Many of these drunks earned the title through years of hard work, sadly. They would show up at the ER with absolutely no ability to control their speech, temper or bowels. We would calm them with medication, place them in a bed, insert a Foley catheter, close the curtain and let them sleep it off. Therein was the problem. A Foley catheter is inserted into the penis of a patient and is designed to let urine flow into an external collection bag directly. To keep the catheter in place, the technician inflates the leading edge of the catheter tube with a small syringe. This creates a balloon inside the patient that keeps the catheter in place – it would fall out otherwise. Here comes the worst part: Our bum, after sleeping off his booze and medication, would wake up in a strange place and see a rubber tube protruding from his penis. After some incoherent shouting (always), the bum would yank out the catheter – balloon and all – and thus initiate an entirely new set of medical issues. Bums were a pain in the ass.

The other end of the economic spectrum was not immune to Emergency Room manipulation either. Friday nights at the ER were notorious for "Grandma dumping". Mr and Mrs La Jolla Country Club couple, or whoever, would show up at the ER dressed for an evening out. In tow would be "Mom", who was undoubtedly an elderly family member living with the couple and not capable of being left alone to take care of herself on a Friday night.

"Mom is complaining of pains and some other things, right, Mom?" the husband would say, careful not to let the spilled urine that someone forgot to clean up by the sink touch his sports jacket.

With that, we would start the routine. Mom, being about 400 years old, would have a bag of prescription medications that were directed at the scores of maladies old people have when they get to a certain age and have decent insurance. We would document each and triage Mom, running vital signs and asking questions. The beauty of this for the young, cosmopolitan abandoners was that at her age Mom could reasonably show symptoms of about a half-dozen ailments. We would have to look at each, spend a lot of physician time going over old ground (no pun intended) and ultimately – and this is key – keep Mom in the hospital overnight. The couple would then come back the next morning, check one fully babysat Mom out of the hospital, and be on their way.

I think if someone made a television show about what really happens in the ER instead of what happens for ratings, the show would be a colossal failure – the stories would be too implausible to be believed.

Time passed for me. I was learning. I would occasionally think back to those years when I was an underwriter with a good salary and a nice lifestyle and wonder how I got to this place where my primary task was to swab up body fluids and human ejecta from a hospital floor. I would wonder what kind of wire came loose in my head and sparked these delusions of wanting to save the world, one Tibetan at a time. If nothing else, aside from the medical knowledge, I learned that delusion is a powerful force.

During this time, I began to get more involved in the Tibet Movement as it existed in the United States in 1996–1997. I had previously shown some interest back in my old banking days during the early 1990s, and managed to make a few preliminary contacts with some Tibet support groups – but only as an outsider and only at an arm's length. Now, after actually *seeing* Tibetans in situ, I felt that I was ready to join the local San Diego Friends of Tibet group and impart my vast new Nepal wisdom and self-absorbed worldliness. We would all certainly agree to lead the nation with bold new strategies for rescuing and treating Tibetans, and I wanted to be at the forefront of decision-making and planning.

Vibrant forward-thinking was not to be a priority, unfortunately. Meetings of the San Diego Friends of Tibet were somewhat infrequent, and consisted of the usual agenda and the usual order of business conducted through the usual parliamentary procedures. One point of interest for me was that we became involved with the International Campaign for Tibet (ICT), which seemed particularly adept at coordinating all the small nationwide Tibet groups during "get the word out" efforts. I remember calling someone named Joe in Washington, who went out of his way to send pamphlets, suggestions for events and even a Tibetan flag to our little group in San Diego. Mostly, Joe and the ICT made all of us feel like we were a part of something that was growing, vibrant and making a difference in the lives of Tibetans.

Somewhere during this time, I can't remember when or how, I became conversant with John Ackerly, the president of the ICT. He and Blake Kerr, if you'll remember, were the two Americans caught in the midst of those violent Tibetan riots in Lhasa in 1987. After being frustrated at the lack of US State Department response to the report he and Blake filed concerning the riots, John formed, with the help of others, the ICT – and thus launched the modern Western Tibet Advocacy Movement. The ICT was crucial in coordinating early efforts nationwide, and John saw to it that efforts to garner support for the Tibet cause remained vital at the grass-roots level, and were inclusive of all who wanted to participate.

The 1990s represented the apex of the "raising awareness" phase of the Tibet Movement in Western countries. Movies such as *Seven Years in Tibet* with Brad Pitt and Martin Scorsese's *Kundun* were released, and we of the banner-waving pro-Tibet set were only too happy to pass out literature in front of any cinema that showed these features. Celebrities were also volunteering their time to film public service announcements such as the pro-Tibet *Why Are We Silent?* and we assisted in getting the video onto movie screens around San Diego. To top it off, actor Richard Gere leant his considerable face and presence to the movement, and became one of its principal spokespersons.

Tibet's political history and current struggles were never more in front of the American people than they were during the 1990s.

To me, the decade of the 1990s represented the "glory" years of the Tibet Movement – but not at all for the reasons you might think. I recently re-rented the film of the same name that tells the tale of the Massachusetts 54th infantry: the first all African-American unit allowed to carry firearms and actually fight in battles during the Civil War. The majority of the film centres on the struggles for respect and recognition that these men – mostly from slave backgrounds – endured just to be given the chance to fight for their freedom. Training was hard, and many took to it poorly, but they persevered. Eventually, at the end of the film the 54th is picked to lead a dangerous charge of Fort Wagner. They are cheered by their white comrades in arms as they walk through the ranks. Summoning the courage, they fight hard through a barrage of resistance. The last scene of the battle has the men and boys of the 54th on the verge of taking the enemy fort when, just as they reach the top of the battlements, a cannon goes off and they are all killed – presumably to the last man, by cinematic implication – BOOM!

By 1991, the US was thoroughly incensed by China's behaviour at Tiananmen Square only a few years before, and a handful of congressmen were spoiling for a means to give China a good human rights slap across the head. Support for Tibet among the members of the US Congress was never higher, and over the course of a few days in April, the first ever meeting between the Dalai Lama and a US president, George Bush the First, gave way to **The Ceremony to Welcome His Holiness the Dalai Lama of Tibet with Members of the Congress Assembled in the US Capitol Rotunda.** Aside from making the fellow who printed the invitations rich, this gesture allowed both houses to blow off some Tiananmen steam while thumbing their collective noses at China – and the clucking was thick. Senate Minority Leader Bob Dole summed up the mood that day as he welcomed the Dalai Lama to the Rotunda:

> Today, together, let us reaffirm this message loud and clear. As His Holiness and the people of Tibet go forward on the own great journey, we are with them. We, the people of the United States, the Congress of the United States – we stand with them, and we want the People's Republic of China to hear this message. We stand with them!

Dole's words almost sideline the Tibetan leader in their headlong rush to get China's attention. One could hear the echoes of US philosophy from the 1950s, when the CIA sought to use Tibetans as a means to disrupt the Communist Chinese.

The ICT was operating at full throttle – their influence in Washington growing daily – and their little office at 1825 K. Street in Washington was a humming beehive of activity. They were also beginning to reach out and broaden Tibet's base of supporters nationwide. Fledgling Tibet support groups knew the ICT was just a phone call away and could offer sound advice on hosting Tibet events or staging demonstrations and other grass-roots level activities. A network was forming across the US and the Western world. It was a coordinated effort of individuals and groups determined to work on behalf of Tibetans and perhaps preparing for some form of battle to come.

I had heard of groups like the ICT by 1991, but had no clue about their daily activities. Certainly, I was ignorant of the legislative wrangling and borderline subterfuge taking place in the offices and back rooms of the government in order to ensure that pro-Tibet language made it into congressional bill debates and voting. The breathtaking effort of congressional staffers, congressmen and pro-Tibet activists ensured the Tibet issue received a constant place at the legislative table in those days.

These efforts were fully realised with the passage of Public Law 102–138. It was a simple spending authorisation act, but hidden deep in its interior, section 355 emerges, boldly called "China's Illegal Control of Tibet". Never before had any piece of legislation emerged from Congress that so forcefully defended Tibet and laid down the law to China. It stated in no uncertain terms that:

1. Tibet, including the four western provinces of China containing Tibetan populations, "is an occupied country under the established principles of international law".
2. Tibet's "true representatives are the Dalai Lama and the Tibetan Government in exile as recognised by the Tibetan people".
3. Tibet "has maintained throughout its history a distinctive and sovereign national, cultural, and religious identity separate from that of China".
4. "Historical evidence of this separate identity may be found in Chinese archival documents and traditional dynastic histories, in United States' recognition of Tibetan neutrality during World War II, and the fact that a number of countries including the United States, Mongolia, Bhutan, Sikkim, Nepal, India, Japan, Great Britain and Russia recognized Tibet as an independent nation, or dealt with Tibet independently of any Chinese government".
5. "In 1949-1950, China launched an armed invasion of Tibet in contravention of international law."
6. "It is the policy of the United States to oppose aggression and other illegal uses of force by one country against the sovereignty of another as a manner of acquiring territory and to condemn violations of international law, including the illegal occupation of one country by another."
7. "Numerous United States declarations since the Chinese invasion have recognized Tibet's right to self-determination and the illegality of China's occupation of Tibet."

Money and assistance were now starting to flow towards Tibetan issues. The ICT and other groups began more nationwide organisational efforts. With Tibet support groups forming in cities and towns across the US and the world, the tent was big and all were welcomed – the crazy and the cognizant, the pathetic and the prescient. The ICT and Tibet advocacy was at the height of its growth spurt, and new groups were continuing to form. There was the Students for Free Tibet; the now-defunct Tibet Information Network, which seemed to have more of a combative, inflammatory bend; the American Himalayan Foundation; the International Tibet Network; the UK's Free Tibet, which started at about the same time as the ICT; and a few others. From Dharamsala (India), the Tibetan Youth Congress was beginning to find its voice as well. Momentum for the cause of Tibet was continuing to pick up speed. "Free Tibet" and "Save Tibet" became the bumper-sticker descriptions of our earnestness as we marched to raise awareness and raise funds. Added to that was the knowledge that the US Government was now behind the Tibetans and big advances were now anticipated.

All of this came to a peak in President Bill Clinton's office in 1993. Clinton had spoken rather harshly of China and its human rights record during his re-election campaign a year earlier, and was now looking for a way to show the American people that he meant business when it came to human rights. Tibet, and the attention it was now getting, offered him the platform he sought.

Using an Executive Order to condition China's trading partner status as Most Favored Nation (MFN) on their ability to adhere to certain pro-human rights and decidedly pro-Tibetan preconditions, President Clinton threw his hat into the Tibet advocacy ring. He would show his promised human rights credentials by sticking up for Tibet and not renewing China's MFN status until they shaped up and played nice. Within months, it became apparent that Clinton's ideas on Tibet were not shared by all – quite the opposite. It seemed that every agency, congressman and branch of government had its own ideas about dealing with China and Tibet. The Commerce and Treasury Departments began a campaign of "de-linkage" that sought to break the ties binding China's MFN status to any form of human rights-based conditions. In a broad sense, all counter-linkage efforts like these seemed to coalesce around a pro-US business strategy, and an almost single-minded faith in the primacy of economic engagement with China.

Pressure was building on Clinton to back down from his MFN linkage stance, and he was looking for a way to do just that. He began meeting with Jiang Zemin and sending representatives to Beijing in the hope of finding a space for compromise. The last and final charge of the US Government's effort to truly and effectively advocate for Tibet came in the early spring of 1994. Secretary of State Warren Christopher arrived in China, hat in hand, seeking any viable means to get his boss out of the MFN mess he had created for himself as he crested the diplomatic battlements in Beijing. Tough-guy Chinese Premier Li Peng mixed no words: "The sky will not fall if MFN is revoked." And, more to the point, in case Warren didn't catch the tone: "Human rights are not universal and China will not accept the human rights concepts of the United States." BOOM!

The longest and most persistent push to officially recognise, protect and advocate for Tibet by the US Government had ended in failure. Christopher would get no compromise from the Chinese, and he would not be able to negotiate any middle position. The Americans were solidly smacked down over their Tibet stance, and just like the CIA's abandonment of the Tibetan Resistance in the early 1960s, the Americans once again retreated from actively assisting Tibet. They would never fight so hard for their cause again. Within weeks, Clinton dropped his MFN demands and renewed China's status. The ICT and Tibet supporters put on a brave face by claiming they had at least put the issue of Tibet on the congressional map and made it a national concern. It was a shallow victory.

Overall, human rights had lost. Economics had won. China's "potential" as a trade partner trumped all. It would take the next major wave of Tibet activism, initiated by the public at large, to bring new hope for Tibetans and prod the governments of the Western world into recognising the Tibet issue once again.

During the early part of 1998, our group was holding a demonstration and banner-wave event at a cinema that was showing *Kundun.* There was quite a bit of earnest yelling of the usual "Free Tibet" and "Shame on China" when a local La Jolla yuppie in a BMW drove by, rolled down his window and blurted: "The Tibetans have sewers now because of China, why are you guys so angry?" I didn't know how to answer that, frankly. Why *were* we so angry? What did we hope to accomplish on a practical level with our demonstrations in comfortable, sunny San Diego? His words burned like a cheap Tijuana tequila. Our brand of awareness would never be raised for some people, and at that point I realised that changing the hearts and minds of individuals from different cultures and with different values, like Westerners, was not going to happen to the point where we would all rise up and demand action on behalf of Tibet. We could never get that level of actionable consensus on a foreign issue from Americans – never the necessary critical mass. We couldn't do it as a people. Tibetans would all have to genuflect and profess the supremacy of our values before we'd give them anything approximating mass support, I thought. This wasn't World War II; Yanks just don't go off marching for the sake of a cause anymore. We've got bills to pay.

What does matter, then, when one desires desperately to be of help to a person or group in need? Is it shouting for attention or simply raising awareness? Should one go back to school and get a PhD in International Relations in order to feel qualified enough to do some good? To me, after quite a bit of soul searching, it came down to the idea that one person can and should help one other person when and if they are able – that's what humanity is about. Pressuring people to change their behaviour and act on your pet issue in a sustainable way is folly. Change your own behaviour and offer that change where you can, and that's the best to which we can aspire. Hopefully, you'll do a good enough job that others will copy what you're doing and the idea will catch on.

I always think of that over-used Gandhi quote: "You must be the change you want to see in the world." *Fair enough, Mr Mahatma, that's what I will do,* I thought, and promptly gave up banner-waving from that night onward.

It was a very nice BMW, by the way.

CHAPTER 4

A NEW LEG FOR A MONK

About a year and a half had now passed since my first encounter with the Tibetan monks running down the mountain trail in the Himalayas. I was impatient to go back to Nepal, but didn't have what I thought was enough medical experience to return. That's the noble excuse. In reality, I was broke and making slow progress towards saving for the airfare to Kathmandu, which ran to about $1,500. The good thing was that I was beginning to develop a deeper understanding of why people wait until they are millionaires before committing their lives to philanthropy. I began picking up double shifts at the hospital in order to try to gather some financial momentum. I would finish a laboratory shift that started at four a.m. by one or two p.m., take a break and start an ER shift that finished after midnight. It's funny how the mind narrows during such times of singularity and focus. The most prominent forces in my life were blood, faeces, emesis, urine and expectoration – in no particular order and playing no favourites – and I invoked a journeyman's indifference with each and all.

One particular bright spot gave me some relief and renewed purpose during this time of muddle. The San Diego Friends of Tibet had agreed to pay for an amputee Tibetan monk to come to the United States and be fitted for a new artificial limb. A series of diseases had necessitated the amputation of his right leg just above the knee, and he had resigned himself to limping through life on crutches and whatever devices he could obtain for assistance. His current prosthesis was a poorly fitting post-World War II model that made the demands of his daily prostrations and meditations extremely painful in their execution. It can only be described as a breathtaking convergence of negative factors and bad luck that prohibited this monk from sitting in a position that would have allowed him to do the function that gave him his only feeling of peace and relief from his condition. His name was Karma.

Karma's arrival in America for treatment was a bit showy. I had arranged to have his initial physical exam performed by one of the orthopaedists at the hospital, and the San Diego Friends of Tibet would ship him off to a state-of-the-art prosthetics development company in San Diego for the fitting of his brand new robo-leg. The press followed Karma's every move.

"G-R-E-E-N," pronounced the orthopedist to a reporter, making sure his name was correctly rendered in the pending story as he examined Karma thoroughly.

"Well, I wish those Indian doctors had pulled a little more muscle tissue down towards the kneecap after they amputated, but this is still enough to hold the new model prosthetic we've got planned for him," Dr Green said with an element of display.

The newspapers thought it would be fun to see Karma at a San Diego Padres game – a real friar at a "Friars" game, that sort of thing. He and I went together, and were given very good seats, I might add.

Karma's mind was keen and inquisitive, and he seemed to be one of the few people in the world who understood baseball almost immediately.

"Ken Caminiti is smart and strong, yes? Steve Finley, I think, is best player because he's not too big and very flexible," he said. He even understood the importance of the now portly Tony Gwynn and his style of hitting. "Always something happen with Tony Gwynn," he intoned.

I liked Karma. People wanted to make a bit of a circus out of his presence, yet he remained happy and smiling and kept his monk-like reserve. Perhaps he realised that he'd been given a rare opportunity to see a different part of the world, and to lessen his discomfort once and for all. He gave back to the Americans. He talked about life in a monastery, his journey from Bhutan to India, the love of his father, and how wonderful everything seemed now that he had new friends in San Diego. And he constantly made himself available for questions or to show off his new leg. Working with him made me realise that my life had more purpose than collecting various body fluids in an obscure hospital. I saw the reason for the choices I'd made, and it gave me some contentment – Karma indeed.

It was nice to have a bit of a spring in my step in the weeks following Karma's departure. His visit made it easier to keep the drudgery of hospital work in a more balanced perspective – it was a means to an end. The problem was that I needed a substantial jolt in order to realise just when the "means" were over and it was time to begin the hard-earned "end" part.

Long after the euphoric effect of Karma's visit had worn off, I was plodding though another shift as a laboratory phlebotomist – about to draw a blood sample from probably my 30th patient that day. As it happened, I was familiar with one Mr Wilson, who was in a private room in our Skilled Nursing Facility (SNF) wing on the third floor of the hospital. Mr Wilson was a quadriplegic, and was currently on a respirator that helped him breathe. My skill level was up to a point where the lab director would always ask me to do the blood draws on this individual. I was proud of this as Mr Wilson's quadriplegia had left him with flaccid musculature and diminished vasculature, making a typical venipuncture blood draw nearly impossible. I do not know if it was due to a medical decision or an advanced directive, but Mr Wilson did not have a centrally inserted catheter installed for the purpose of easier blood sample procurement by the nurses. Regardless, I was usually able to find some active veins and obtain a sample. Phlebotomists don't like to waste time searching for veins as it can be painful and annoying for the patient, but in Mr Wilson's case the only noises I heard were those from the respirator.

My second trip to Mr Wilson's room that day was not at all noteworthy. We were monitoring the level of a certain medication going through his system and were used to the repeat blood draws. I swabbed the antecubital area of his right arm as always, prepared a small 5cc syringe with a 23-gauge needle (butterfly needles are for wimps), let the swabbed area dry, applied the tourniquet, prepared a gauze and tape bandage, uncapped the needle and gently inserted it into Mr Wilson's arm in an area where I'd known previous success.

"Damn it. What's the deal here? I *know* there's blood in this vein," I said audibly to myself.

After a few minutes of probing, I withdrew the needle, unbound the tourniquet and took a rest. Failure is part of the game in phlebotomy, but I was sure I'd hit his vein. I tried again. This time, I began with a tourniquet down by the wrist and massaged his hands in the hope of raising some venous presentation. At the very least, I could get enough to fill a small pediatric tube and pray I didn't damage (hemolyse) the specimen in the process. Nothing. A few minutes of massaging and slapping the hand did nothing, so I didn't try another hand puncture. Our protocols at the hospital stated that a phlebotomist could only make three failing attempts at a blood draw before they must give up, and let either a nurse or a respiratory therapist dig down deep and draw from an artery. My ego was not about to let this happen, so I didn't waste my last attempted "stick" on certain failure on the hand veins. After re-prepping the arm, I tied the tourniquet for the third time and made a determined and patient attempt to find the arm vein that eluded me on my first attempt.

"What are you doing in here?" blurted the desk nurse as if I were a burglar.

"This is a scheduled drug-level draw – what do you think I'm doing here?" My frustration was beginning to show.

"Mr Wilson passed away less than an hour ago. Wasn't the lab notified?" she replied to me as she turned to her underling nurses for an explanation.

Another convergence of bad luck. Mr Wilson was flaccid as it was, mortality did not change that. No one turned off his respirator and no one placed the little dove insignia outside his door to indicate he'd passed. His blood tests were ordered as scheduled draws that did not need to be confirmed, and no one thought of cancelling the order. This kind of thing is not uncommon in a busy hospital, but I felt a particular sense of direction now and began feeling as though there was a message in all of this.

I had been working diligently for about 15 minutes, trying to draw a blood sample from a dead person.

It was time to head back to Nepal.

CHAPTER 5

I LIE MY WAY INTO THE RECEPTION CENTRE

Not this again: Bad weather must instinctively know when I'm flying this route. It must. Deliberate, indefinable cosmic collusions, intent on fractioning my enjoyment of a pivotal event, always surface at times like these. *Not this time,* I told myself. It was just another hurdle, another distraction demanding to be handled. I knew the routine, and over time had found a sort of constancy and familiarity in its manifestations. Life is about the things that get in your way and I treated this bad weather, and its accompanying effect on our aircraft, as a member of an extended family of obstacles that had to be appeased in order for me to return to this point.

Two years now, two years of preparation for what would greet me at the end of this flight. School was out, this was it, and I was tired of waiting. Nothing was going to spoil the moment – not the weather, not the tossing plane. An odd self-assurance formed my mood as I reached for the air-sickness bag and went over in my mind one last time what had to be done when we reached terra firma. As before, a strategy was imperative and I rehearsed mine and its unusual new provisions: deniability and escape.

In my checked baggage I was smuggling 500 sterile syringes and needles: primarily as a donation, but partly as an experiment simply to see if I could pull it off. The bag was lightly marked with data that wouldn't incriminate, so it could be ignored and abandoned should trouble emerge at the baggage pick-up.

This was important. I was landing in Nepal. Disembarking foreigners who give even a hint of being involved in the international heroin trade can be thrown in a damp cell on speculation alone, and months of detention were not uncommon. The large volume of needles in my possession could not be explained away as being for personal medical use, and I had no official paperwork to explain or justify such a shipment. In the eyes of the authorities, I was bringing contraband into the country to facilitate a growing heroin market. Just picking the bag off the carousel could put me at tremendous risk.

The syringes were packed with old books and a pair of binoculars near the zippered top of a deliberately innocuous-looking duffel bag. Any thieves breaking into the bag would see the decoy binoculars and, with luck, be singularly content with a job well done in their theft and leave the remaining contents of the bag undisturbed. This was fine with me. The clean needles were more valuable at this point. I needed them to make an impression.

Breaking through a clinging brown haze, a soot-filled urban landscape aligned with our final approach. I remembered the routine: Our pilot would now be tasked with a unique landing that involves navigating through a narrow mountain corridor and praying there are no dogs on the runway. Below, I could see the old shells of hulking helicopters from the defunct Everest Air service as well as row upon row of exposed rebar jutting from the roofs of eternally unfinished concrete and brick buildings. Air sickness gone, I located the horizon out of the window to try to find more familiar landmarks as buildings rushed past, until one wheel and then another screamed in protest as they touched the runway.

I was back in Kathmandu. I was home.

Fresh from the insanity of working in an American Emergency Room and relieved to be rid of my very un-scholastic plod through my worn copy of Yankye Tsering's Tibetan Language Phrasebook, I was eager to apply my skills and efforts – such as they were – and find work with real Tibetans. I hadn't seen any in situ for almost two years and was a bit nervous about my plan. I knew from previous research that there existed a facility somewhere in Kathmandu where Tibetans went to heal after the long walk from Tibet. Asking around led me to hop into a cab and head to the outskirts of the city.

The Tibetan Reception Centre (TRC) sits in an affluent suburb of Kathmandu, just a bit northwest of the ring road and the ancient stupa at

Swayambhunath, called Ichangu. It was founded out of a United Nations mandate to facilitate the processing of Tibetans who make it to Kathmandu. Undocumented Tibetans would wind up at the TRC in a number of ways: they would take a bus and be let off near the ring road; they would be retrieved from Nepal immigration after they'd been arrested and detained; or they would just walk in – feet bloody and blackened from the frostbite incurred by days of trudging through Himalayan passes wearing nothing more than cheap Chinese canvas tennis shoes.

The United Nations High Commission for Refugees (UNHCR) maintained offices on the third floor of this facility for the express purpose of documenting these transiting Tibetans, and singling out particular individuals who may have a valid claim for political asylum or other special needs that might be addressed by the UNHCR. "Of concern" was how they labelled these particular individuals. The clinic and longer-term dormitories as well as some of the resident Tibetan staff offices were on the second floor. A big, open concrete hall and yard composed the ground level where the bulk of arriving Tibetans slept, ate, played ball and, above all, laughed. (No human on earth laughs like a Tibetan. It comes easy, and is full-throated, genuine and a bit mocking.)

Tibetans were constantly moving in and out of the TRC – some 2,500 per year back then. They were given a place to sleep, some new clothes, shoes and an unusually good level of medical care, which included vaccines. Every arriving Tibetan was banged up in one way or another, so the clinic was always overworked and understaffed. I found my opening.

Back then, one could walk freely into the TRC and mingle with the Tibetans. When my self-guided tour found its way to the clinic and I witnessed the chaos, I thought I could make my pitch while the nurses were too overwhelmed to object.

"Tashi Delek!" I said, the Tibetan greeting. *"Kosto Chaa."* (Wait, that was Nepali.) "Er...*kerang kusu debo yinbay*" – which is a crude way of asking someone how they are.

"Hello," said Tsering Lhamo, the no-bullshit, chronically professional Tibetan nurse. "Can I help you with something?"

"Oh yes, English, great. I'd like to help out here at your clinic."

"Are you a doctor?" Tsering asked.

With that, I presented my duffel bag full of 300 clean syringes as an offering and continued.

"These are from the Emergency Room where I work in the United States. We had an overstock and I thought you could use them here. Where should I put them?"

Tsering directed me to a private room that had been taken over by thousands of well-meaning medicinal donations from visitors and trekkers with left-over supplies, cheap Indian medications that had been purchased locally and box upon box of holistic, if not outright strange, concoctions from hippies and various other assorted spirit-seeking characters who felt they must do their part. I placed my hard-smuggled syringes on a creaky metal shelf with hundreds of other donated syringes, and drew a deep sigh.

"You are a physician in America, is that right?" Tsering pressed.

"Hey, what do you think? I work in an Emergency Room in San Diego, California, USA."

"OK, glove up," came her reply. "We've got the next round of 200 BCG and MMR vaccines prepped – IM for both. It goes faster, one in each deltoid."

Gulp. I followed about half of that at first. But after playing it over in my mind a few times, I knew I'd heard this stuff in the ER back home. "IM" refers to the delivery vector of the injection. For BCG, the tuberculosis prophylactic injection, it was the recommended standard "intra-muscular" injection: straight into the deltoid muscle of the arm, about an inch or so deep. For MMR, which stands for the Measles, Mumps and Rubella vaccine, IM is not the recommended way to administer the vaccine. MMR is best given through an "SC" or "subcutaneous" injection, which requires just a fraction more time and skill to administer. Briefly put, injections done in this manner are delivered at an angle, just below the skin. Since there were no substantial published procedural arguments that proved diminished efficacy by injecting MMR through the intra-muscular path, Tsering made the decision to give both injections the same IM way at the same time, one on each side, to save time and keep the line moving.

The trouble was, I'd never actually given an injection to a patient before. I was an ER Emergency Medical Technician, and while I got to do a lot of things, administering medications was strictly the purvey of doctors and nurses. Uncap, swab, load, bleed, swab the patient, dry, stick, inject, retract, gauze and tape – that much I'd seen a hundred times, and I was sure I could do it with my phlebotomy background. What I wasn't prepared for was judging the length of the needle against the diminished musculature of these emaciated individuals. At times, there was a real feeling that I would alter the needle opening by banging it against the patient's humerus, or upper arm bone.

"Go from the anterior aspect of the deltoid," Tenzin, the other nurse, told me. It was a cheap way to get some more clean distance out of the needle length and avoid hitting bone.

Halfway through that first day, the realisation hit that I was actually living in Nepal and working in a clinic that helps Tibetans. I wasn't telling people in the United States what needed to be done about Tibet and how to direct their donations appropriately – I was walking the talk. I was actually *doing* it. No one ever actually *does* this stuff, I thought; people just send donations off into space perpetually in the hope of some positive effect or an annual progress report of some kind. It was maddening to think that there I was, a nobody from the other side of the world, providing immediate benefit for someone in need. Why doesn't everyone do this?

There was always a big procedural choice to make with the Tibetan patients that came through the clinic. The usual vaccine crowd could be counted on to keep us busy for a few hours, while we gave their queuing masses hundreds of injections. They had made it through the high Himalayan passes relatively unscathed, and just needed to be prepared immunologically for India and a host of lowland diseases that could kill the average high altitude-dwelling Tibetan who seemed to carry no natural immunity to much of anything. We moved these people through the check-up and vaccine process quickly and efficiently. There was no fee harvesting, no superfluous lab testing or X-rays; the efficiency was a marvel. My co-workers were nothing more than a room full of smart people who knew when to administer what little resources they had, and when to leave the body alone to do its own work. It was "treat what is presented" medicine without the Western additive of "test in order to rule out". The sheer volume of patients left no other alternative.

On dozens of occasions, we received another type of patient: frostbite victims who seemed certain to lose toes, if not limbs, very shortly. They had made it to the TRC and our clinic, but just barely. Totally unprepared and misled by the often corrupt and profit-seeking "guides" that led them through the Himalayas on foot, these individuals had walked for weeks in poorly made canvas - wafer-thin and usually green-coloured - Chinese sneakers that were an entirely inadequate, if not an outright suicidal footwear choice for crossing ice-bound passes at 19,000 feet. They had very few possessions, and were malnourished when they arrived at our door. Intravenous catheterisation was not an option, so we gave them *Nava Jeevan* or *Jeevan Jal,* Indian-made electrolyte solution, orally. Generally, just the nourishment and the company of other Tibetans was enough to bring these particular patients back to life. I have observed that Tibetans seem to be at their hearty best when in the company of other Tibetans, and such companionship worked wonders at the clinic. But hard facts remained. Frostbite had blackened the toes and feet of some in this group, and had been the source of considerable vocal demonstrations of anguish during our initial assessment. There was just no way in hell I was going to be able to do anything about this; but I came to learn that the human body is an amazing self-preserving organism. I had scoffed at the seemingly cheap axiom surrounding frostbite treatment that said: "Frostbite in January, amputate in June." *Come on,* I thought. Some of these patients would die of infection by February if we followed that rule. But follow we did, and positive results flowed. After multiple rounds of re-dressing, all of our patients showed signs of new tissue growth and wound healing. We never had to call in an orthopaedist from Kathmandu's Bashok and Benskota Hospital to do the dirty deed of amputation, although it had been done in the past.

I looked back at those days in the San Diego ER where I pumped CPR on heart attack victims knowing full well they wouldn't begin to generate a heartbeat. Initially, I had adopted the same cynical view with my frostbite patients in Nepal. But the Tibetan nurses admonished me to keep at the task, and eventually I began to see real and tangible results. Healthcare workers in the clinic, perhaps through lack of resources, did not accelerate patients into the next possible procedure. They administered care and resources as needed and available. This taught me a lot. Mostly, I began to believe that the genius we believe exists in Western medical practice and procedure is only partially to be credited, as the human body carries its own inherent genius for self-healing – the human body itself helps us out and can cover our mistakes and misdiagnoses to a certain extent.

It was gratifying to have a Tibetan look you in the eye and smile while you treated the gaping and grotesque open wounds on his feet.

I was getting fairly proficient at the unorthodox technique that involved basically throwing everything we had at treating the wound. First, we would prepare a bucket with lukewarm water and hydrogen peroxide as a foot-soak. Into the soak we would drizzle just a bit of Betadine solution. One had to be careful with this, as while killing virtually every pathogen it encountered on the wound, Betadine was also somewhat tissue necrotic and could destroy or keep tissue from healing to an extent. Once out of the soak, we would gently swab the wound with gauze to remove any tissue residue or dried blood. In the US, since there is a ready supply of clean surgical gloves, one would just do this with the hand. But in the clinic, clean gloves were a rarity, and we would wash our hands between patients without removing the gloves, and do the tissue swabbing and blood removing with the piece of gauze firmly attached to a surgical clamp and far away from our offending recycled glove wear. One gets used to this. Visit almost any rural clinic in Nepal and you will see re-washed surgical gloves hanging from a drying line in some portion of the facility.

Finally, we wrapped the wound in loose-fitting gauze. Renewed blood circulation is paramount, so any constriction from a bandage is a big no-no. The bandages themselves served mostly to keep dust and mud out of the wound. This was an unfounded hope, as Tibetans found ways of getting dirt and contra-indicated filth into every part of our medical efforts.

On still fewer occasions, we would receive "special" Tibetans who had varied and unusual wounds and maladies. Bruises from beatings by Chinese soldiers or corrupt Nepali security forces personnel were not uncommon presentations, and nor were bullet grazing and piercing marks. Most of these individuals had a political story of some sort to tell, and were immediately whisked up to the third floor for some form of advanced classification by the UNHCR.

One day, an eight-year-old boy showed up at the clinic complaining of chest pains. He was of the unscathed and vaccine-only group at first glance, and none of us in the clinic thought too much of his complaints at first. Then we removed his light shirt for further investigation and were surprised to see a series of odd horse-shoe shaped indentations – not bruises – in the distal subclavicular area of his chest. No one could figure out the wound pattern. It was too small for a horse kick and too traumatic for a fall onto an object for a boy of his weight. Tenzin Yangkyi queried the boy. This took a few moments of shouting because Tibetans not only do not understand the speech of foreigners, but they have trouble understanding *each other* from village to village. But the story eventually emerged.

"The Chinese man in the blue coat held me down and kicked me with his boot."

Somewhere and somehow, this boy was beaten by a guard or security person, possibly Chinese, severely enough to cause him to flee Tibet. We never knew the details of his passage as he was promptly whisked up to the third floor, but we do know that the boy will carry a permanent reminder of the Tibetan homeland he fled through the cruel scars of a cruel boot heel.

Months went by and I was settling into a routine: arrive at the clinic, treat patients all morning, have a lunch of Tibetan dumplings or *tingmos*, treat more patients and take the bus back to Thamel, where I would crawl into a beer or three, stumble back to my room and fall asleep while reading.

The restaurant at the little Hotel Mona where I was staying at the time was doing poorly. On weekends, I would sit sipping milk tea and reading for hours, and no customers would come in. Guatam, the owner, was determined to boost his business and had decided to turn the place into a sushi bar. The problem was that in those days one could never get any fish to stay fresh long enough in Kathmandu to make decent sushi, so the idea failed miserably. I'll note here that the smell of that failure emanated from the kitchen for a number of weeks. I felt bad for Guatam. Every morning, I would come down to the restaurant and he would greet me with his usual: "Hello, sir. Sushi?"

Most mornings, I would head to the communications kiosks in Thamel before returning to the hotel for tea, because they were just beginning to install public computers and I liked playing with the relatively new "Inter Net" back then. Computers were just toys, I thought. Obviously, they would never amount to much more than that. One of these mornings, I received an e-mail:

> Jim, I got your name from a friend who said you worked in Nepal. My name is Joyce and I'm supposed to lead a humanitarian mission in Nepal for a group called Airline Ambassadors. I don't know where to begin but I know these people will want to go out into the rural areas, see things first-hand, and purchase what is needed. By the way, what is "trekking?".

Not quite sure of what to make of what I had just received, I returned to the hotel restaurant, sat down at my usual table and found myself at a complete loss as to how to proceed. In the corner of the restaurant, by a window – as he had been for the past few days – was a young man with thick jet-black hair, a confident bearing and a good command of English. I noticed his pattern on a few occasions: He would always be examining papers while a steady stream of young Nepali boys came, responded to his commands and quickly took their leave.

"Guatam, who is that guy? He's always here."

"Sir, that is Deepak Bhandari. He runs big trekking agency. Very good man. You want sushi?"

The e-mail from Joyce was starting to bother me. Nothing ruins a nice pot of tea and a good book more than the realisation that you are caught in that rare circumstance where you absolutely cannot get out of helping someone without sending them to their doom. This was not going to be a stroll around California for Joyce and her people; these were the Himalayas. Joyce's group was coming to Nepal without any preparation and was planning on going deep into wherever for whatever, and the result was probably not going to be pleasant for anyone. I couldn't focus on my book and I didn't feel like thinking about anything else at that point. I absolutely had to help Joyce, but what was I going to do?

"Ho, ho, *namaste*, *Dai*. I've noticed you in here before," said one of the friendliest and most assertive Nepali voices I had ever heard as I walked over to introduce myself.

"Jim from the US. How are you? I've got a bit of a problem and maybe you can help," I said in that pushy Western tone that he'd probably heard before from most of his trekking customers.

"*Bosni*, *bosni*, sit, *Dai*, have some more tea and let's relax and talk," said one Mr Deepak Bhandari of the Chettri warrior caste, and owner of Himalayan Trekking Company, Saat Ghumti, Thamel, Nepal.

The conversation over the next few hours flowed easily, and I felt a bit more freed from the sense of responsibility for the lives of Joyce and her group.

Deepak came up with a plan: We would send Joyce's group on a trek through the middle hills of the Solu region of Nepal. This was the classic Jiri to Lukla route that was known to most Everest trekkers. We picked this for a variety of reasons. First, there was a reasonable amount of lodges and services along the way due to the moderate amount of trekkers the route saw. Since we didn't know much about Joyce's group or their abilities at that point, we figured that the local lodges would be adequately positioned to be of service to both her slow- and fast-walking group members. Next, the Solu region was still relatively poor, in spite of the tourist traffic, and experienced a number of existence-level problems. It was a good candidate for whatever philanthropy was thrown its way. It was our decision to deliver basic medical supplies to any and all clinics along this route, as needed.

The trek typically took one strenuous week of effort, as the middle hills of Nepal are one constant up-and-down slog. I had walked this route before and knew of its difficulties, but did not know the number of health posts in need of supplies or what those supplies might be. I did know from my limited medical training that medications requiring a rigid adherence to an administration schedule, like antibiotics, were out. Rural Nepalis, like Tibetans, would take an antibiotic, stop immediately when they felt better and not finish the required course. This was bad. The germs that you fail to kill by not finishing the required course of administration are the strong ones, and they have now been left alive to reproduce into super-strains of the disease you were trying to kill with the antibiotics in the first place. No, we would deliver bandages, topical treatments, gloves, toothache medicines and other items that did not require repeated supervision to work successfully. But again, how much and where?

Deepak and I decided that I needed to take a solo trip to the region, pre-visit each health post, and take an inventory of supplies and medications needed. I would then return to Kathmandu with the list and we would buy the supplies locally with the donated funds from Joyce's group. With the supplies ready, we would then have Deepak's ace trekking guides and porters take Joyce's group on the Jiri–Lukla trek, and distribute the supplies to the predetermined recipient clinics. Deepak was used to this routine, and to him it seemed like just another successfully booked walk in the Himalayas. These were new and inexperienced people, and Deepak felt he had enough staff to watch over their every move, send them out on the back of a porter if need be and helicopter them out if anything really bad happened. Five porters plus a guide was our estimate for a group of about the same size.

How many could they realistically bring anyway?

The plan was set, and I felt badly in need of respite from my time at the clinic – volunteering is as big a bore as any regular job you could have. The only thing left for me to do was to make my way to the bus station in the morning and head off to the trail head some eight hours away, and I would be able to clear my head for a week or so. Deepak refused to let me pay for a taxi to the station. "No, Jim *Dai*, I will send a boy in a car for you in the morning," he said. I thought to myself that this was one classy gesture. Deepak had known me for just a few hours, and he was paying to have a car take me to the bus station in the morning. I liked this guy.

Dawn came and I waddled down the stairs with my backpack. "No time for tea or sushi this morning, Guatam. I'll see you in a week or so."

The Hotel Mona was notorious for its low front doorway, and I smacked my head on its top lintel with regularity on entry and exit. But this morning, with a last-second duck, I made it through without damage of head or diminishment in spirit. As promised, Deepak had sent a car to the door and the driver awaited my instructions.

"Good morning, *Dai*," came the cheerful chirp of a middle-aged man, who was quite proud of his Toyota micro-van taxi.

"Wow, thank you, *Bhai*, and be sure to relay my thanks to Mr Deepak for his kind and thoughtful service." I truly was thankful – thankful and flabbergasted. Nothing goes according to plan in Nepal. Nothing seems to ever get done. But there I was, staring Deepak's promise square in the face. It was unusual, almost Western in its efficiency.

Verbal genuflections complete, off we sailed through the fog of an improbably quiet Kathmandu morning. Hearing only the familiar anger of tyre against pothole, we wound through the morning rag vendors and sleeping street-children towards the municipal bus terminal near the Bagh Bazaar neighbourhood. Only a few more feet now before the morning silence would break into manic negotiations in unfamiliar tongues as yet another clueless foreigner attempted to locate the correct bus for his eight-hour journey. A self-conscious grab for my backpack was followed by an anxious butt-scooting towards the taxi door as I anticipated my impending departure. Seeing the station approach, I awaited the driver's left turn – but the turn didn't come. *OK, he probably knows a better entrance and I'll let a professional cabbie do his thing,* I thought. Unfortunately, we were now about a half-kilometre from the bus station and heading out of town. Something was terribly wrong. The cab driver, seeing the bus terminal, picked up speed and refused to stop on my command. *Damn!* I knew it. I'd fallen prey to the taxi scam. Deepak didn't properly scrutinise the cab driver he sent to pick me up, and I was about to get royally fleeced. It's a common scam for cab drivers in Kathmandu to pick up speed and refuse to slow down and stop until their unsuspecting foreign passenger forks over a few hundred extra rupees. I'd been had.

"OK, knock it off, you dick. How much do you want?" I was about to pay the guy first and then tear his head off the moment he finally let me out, when he turned around and responded, totally filling me with shame.

"No bus for you. Mr Deepak said for me to take you the full trip to Lukla."

"Are you kidding me?! Holy shit!"

Deepak did not want to put me on the bus and surprised the hell out of me by paying his driver to take me all the way to the trail head at Lukla – a seven-hour, $200 cab ride. My shame evolved into speechlessness.

Fortunately, the driver's command of English vernacular was non-existent, and he didn't catch the "dick" part. So off we went, happy and laughing at Mr Deepak's classy gesture and life's occasional good fortune.

God himself in the form of an American jerk was sitting in the back of a micro-van that day, as legs accustomed to surviving this journey through a permanent eight-hour coil at the mercy of a bus seat stretched out in perfect leisure. *I could get used to this,* I thought. The name of my driver escapes me but he was certainly not a "dick". "Jesus" was more like it, as his abilities with the tiny vehicle saw him navigate safely through avalanche-decimated lanes that dropped off into oblivion, full, rushing stream crossings and screaming head-on stalemates with trucks the size of Cuba.

We were travelling through the rural foothills of Nepal now, and the autumn harvest was in various stages of enactment. It was amusing to watch the local farm-girls spread their crops along the road in search of a free threshing at the hands of a speeding set of tyres. But this was not farm country – not like most people know it to be; there is very little level ground to speak of in these foothills. Nepalis solve the problem of arable land by creating it. They cut terrace after terrace into the sides of impossibly steep river gorges, until the landscape is consumed by cookie-cutter-shaped mini plots stacked one on top of another for hundreds of metres up the steep hillsides. The drive to Lukla is nothing more than a series of grinding climbs and descents above these little terraces and into massive gorges.

"*Dai,* I get out now," said Jesus with purpose.

"Wait, wait. Where you going? What's up, another tea break?" I asked, fully aware of the Nepali aptitude for spontaneous relaxation.

The driver's-side door was left open as we found rare adequacy in a cliff-side parking spot, and Jesus trotted towards the trunk of the cab. The clang of tools and the sound of pounding under our rear axle had me curious, and I went to check on the commotion.

"What happened; did we get a flat?"

"No, *Dai*, steep coming, change pads," Jesus said. And with that, he proceeded, as a simple measure of precautionary maintenance, to quickly and expertly change the brake pads on the rear wheels. It seemed we were coming to a noteworthy stretch of dangerous downward curves and Jesus just wouldn't broach the thought of our demise – so new brake pads it was. Amen.

Within a few hours we reached Lukla, and the memories of my first visit here with Holly and the inadequate little prayer I offered just as we were heading out on the trail to Everest returned to me. This "scouting" trip for the stewardesses was to cover many of the same trails that we took during that first trip, and my spirit was already getting syrupy and nostalgic at the thought. The trail out of Lukla was our last adventure together, and vivid memories of Holly watching me reach a personal changing point in my life – one that was also to change our relationship – still haunted me. As I threw my bag onto the pavement, I invited Jesus to tarry a while with a beer and I looked back on how far I'd come.

Two years ago, I'd stood with Holly in this same spot: a burned-out asshole of an ex-banker looking for adventure in the Himalayas. Holly was cheerful, trusted my judgement and carried high hopes for our future. Then something turned, twisted. The visions of Tibetan suffering witnessed along this very trail flipped a mental, maybe human, switch in my head and everything changed. Perhaps it was the desire to get as far away from banking as I could that catalysed my actions from that point forward. As much as I revisit that time in my mind, doing so doesn't shed any light on my underlying motivations; but I gave up everything for these people, these Tibetans. It probably would have been for the best had I returned to America and written a nice cheque to the Tibet Movement and left it at that. But there I was again, in Nepal after two years of preparation, and thinking now that I'd made a terrible mistake with my life. Certainly, some good was being done through my volunteer work at the clinic, but I was not necessary to its success, and at times, my "help" seemed entirely incidental. There was no pattern and no reason to what I was doing in Nepal – I was just there. And now, for some reason, all of my preparation had led me full circle to this spot, to repeat a familiar hike and make a note of clinic locations so that airline flight attendants would have a nice photo-op with poor, rural Nepalis. Why was I here? Was this just another extended vacation? *Goddamn Tibetans,* I thought.

The next week was spent in an agonising slog through the Solu region of Nepal. My bright idea was to bring school books and canisters of powdered Gatorade on this trek as a goodwill donation so that the clinic operators would let me see their stocks of precious (and highly pilfer-able) medicines for my inventory. Unfortunately, the sheer weight of the donations made the endless climbs and descents of the region unbearable as my over-laden backpack dug deep into my shoulders and hips.

Deeper meanings and crossword puzzle answers often don't reveal themselves on the first pass, and while I was wallowing in self-pity one day on the trail, I discovered the monastery at Ghandruk, above Jubing. I learned it was at the end of a secret and exclusive trail that the Tibetans had adopted since my last visit. No more walking the main trail near Puiyan for them, it was apparently too dangerous now.

There was a little clinic at the monastery that displayed no Western medicines of any consequence, but a pleasant and diminutive nun, working as a nurse, opened her cabinets and proudly showed off what looked like row upon row of malted dung-balls. It was traditional Tibetan medicine made from traditional compounds. I had read about this stuff, but seeing it for the first time, I wasn't so sure I would reach for it in a medical emergency. She then rattled off the usual series of needs I'd heard a dozen times by that point: bandages, gloves, ant-fever medicine, toothache reliever, Betadine and more bandages. I promised to return with a pile of wide-eyed Americans and deliver it all.

More importantly – something I had no idea I would discover – I had gathered specific and useful information on how Tibetans move through the area, which would lead to how ultimately they might best be assisted. It felt good to have a bit of logistical data that I was sure no one else possessed. Ghandruk was a major halfway house for fleeing Tibetans. And if we all could keep quiet about it, we could keep that specific function vital for a long time.

A lot was gained from that trip, and about a dozen local clinics and health posts were visited and inventoried for Joyce's impending supply-drop trek. But it was the partnership I formed with Deepak that became my greatest, most enduring treasure.

I knew that the trek might ultimately still wind up a disaster for these flight attendants regardless of my scouting, but at least I was out of Kathmandu's smog for a bit.

I was feeling pleasantly warm and drowsy when the delicate thump of the Twin Otter's tyres on the paved runway of Kathmandu's Tribhuvan International Airport abruptly broke the spell. It was time to get back to work at the clinic.

CHAPTER 6

THE KATHMANDU WAY

Back in Kathmandu again, I was feeling mildly ready to assume my duties at the clinic. The trek through the Himalayan foothills of Solu had left me exhausted and broke. Stretching my small budget in order to maximise my time in Nepal was now paramount, and I thought of various schemes to achieve that end. One evening I walked downtown and purchased a bicycle – an Indian "Ranger" – that had beach-cruiser sensibilities about it. My thinking was that I could save money in the long run by buying this cheap bike and riding the four miles to the clinic each morning. The savings in bus fare would be small, but I could always sell the bike when I was done and come out ahead.

Smug with my new purchase, I headed out the next morning towards the ring road that encircles Kathmandu, and is the main route west from Thamel to the clinic in Ichangu. I wove in between monstrous Indian Tata heavy-load trucks with their basketball-sized rear differentials and local buses spewing out thick plumes of black Asian toxicity. I dodged mounded buffalo-dung leviathans sculpted mid-lane as well as porters carrying full refrigeration units on their backs as I made my way westward. The tell-tale Tibetan prayer flags strung across the road near Swyambhunath – the Monkey Temple – meant that I was to make a sharp exit to the right and head down a muddy gravel road towards the TRC and the clinic.

"What happened to you?" Tenzin asked as only a nurse could.

"Good morning. I'm trying to save a little money," was all I could muster as I spat up the first of many charcoal-grey expectorations I was to see that day. My eyes had become swollen and red from the journey and I couldn't seem to complete a full breath without coughing up something; plus, I stunk of sweat, street grime and cow manure – lovely.

"Jim-la, you have some tea and clean yourself up. You cannot work like this today. You will make the new patients sick." Tibetans are nothing if not brutally honest.

This bicycle routine went on for the remainder of the work week, at the end of which I realised that I'd had enough. I was killing myself driving through Kathmandu's toxic air and homicidal traffic just to save a few dollars. It wasn't worth it and I decided that my bicycle experiment was over. I still needed to find a new way to stretch out my budget, and if I was honest with myself, I knew this could only be done if I left Thamel, which was nearly impossible. Not only was I a resident of the Hotel Mona, but I was a part of Thamel culture. All my friends lived there, and it seemed as though all of them owned bars or restaurants. I kept the Thamel economy humming with my purchases, and no one appreciated this more than Sudesh Shrestha.

*

I first met Sudesh in 1995. Holly and I went up to his dusty, well-worn and hidden yet brand-new bar (a Kathmandu phenomenon without explanation) on the second floor of an old building in Thamel. His easy be-bop-era jazz demeanour made me like him immediately. Guitars were hanging on the walls and we eventually pulled them down and jammed until dawn. It was the old, and now legendary, Blue Note bar, and a new and vibrant music scene was about to take off from this epicentre and spread throughout Kathmandu. Sudesh adorned the place simply, but with significance. John Coltrane photos as well as Miles Davis, Dexter Gordon and a host of other old jazz greats had pride of position on the walls and left no doubt that the proprietor knew his stuff and loved good music. My memories come and go on this, but I do remember returning again and again to the Blue Note for Sudesh's hospitality and some damn fine jam sessions during that first year.

I never forgot those experiences and on this trip, before settling into the Hotel Mona, before doing much of anything, I made a beeline for the Blue Note bar to see my old friend. This was before e-mail was used significantly in Nepal, so Sudesh and I had maintained no contact for the past two years: I was eager to catch up.

The Fire Club? What the hell was something called The Fire Club doing in place of the most intensely cool bar in Kathmandu? Where was Blue Note?

"Down the street, new place," I was told.

Sudesh had relocated down the street, to my relief, and had renamed the place the New Orleans Café, but that was not what I was thinking about at that particular moment. The boy from the Fire Club who gave me the information had a tone I'd not heard before, and was perhaps the most arrogant and rude Nepali I'd ever met. I didn't think such a response was possible based on my previous encounters, and I was knocked askance for a bit. Later I learned that this was the new wave of Manangi tribe, gang-owned clubs in Thamel. It was the beginning of a new era where violent little boys were opening new nightclubs, pouring cheap booze and pissing people off. The Fire Club was just one of their new style clubs, and its purpose was to extort money from foreigners and split their heads open with a beer bottle if they complained. The Underground, the Tunnel Club and a few others whose names escape me were also notorious in this respect.

Sudesh had managed to secure the business rights to a little courtyard in an alley across from Pilgrim's Bookstore. It was partially outdoors, but the old jazz photos and the ability to retain some of the Blue Note's charming seediness remained. No one knew it back then, but the New Orleans Café would be the centre of music and musical innovations in Kathmandu for the next ten years, and I had no idea that I was to be in the middle of it with perhaps the best seat in the house.

From about 2000 to 2007, the New Orleans was packed full of people every night during tourist season. We routinely played music for 200 or more people at a sitting during those times. The best musicians from Nepal enhanced their careers by playing at the New Orleans. Names like Anil Shahi, Mukti and the Revival, Robin Tamang and others often graced the venue. International acts from various parts of Asia and the world would make it a point to stop at the New Orleans when in Kathmandu. It was just a ton of fun. I was a guitar player with a reasonable blues background and usually was able to sit in on any session, but my jazz chops were all but non-existent. I did try faking it by sporting a goatee and Dizzy Gillespie glasses for a time, but after one night when someone yelled, "Hey, those glasses are phoney," I gave up the routine.

The beauty of Thamel was that its main streets were intimate and narrow, so if one was looking for a place to sit and enjoy the evening, all they had to do was take a walk and find the music of their preference wafting out of one of the clubs, and the immediate proximity of the experience would compel them to follow their ears towards a table near a bandstand. It was fun for us as well. We'd play a blues-raga fusion set (don't ask) at the New Orleans, pick up our instruments and head down to the Bamboo Club for a jam with Robin, the owner. We'd later hear of a house party where a couple of great *tabla* players were hanging out, and go and see what we could make happen. Golden-age stuff, now that I look back. You get into these situations and they seem normal in the context of their moment. It's not until years later, and well after the fact, that you realise just how magical those times were.

The big thing was that everyone in Kathmandu in the early part of that decade seemed to be a music fan. Everyone came to the New Orleans; everyone means Nepali politicians, Tibetan activists, ambassadors, aid workers, spies, US marines, Indian embassy workers and diplomatic types of all flavours. I met, schmoozed, lobbied, slept with, drank under the table, conspired with and argued with each and all.

All of the contacts I made eventually became friends, or at least trusted acquaintances. I spoke with Keshap Sthapit, the mayor of Kathmandu, during that time, and he said: "You could have asked me anything after what you just played with those Nepali musicians." Such was the power of pulling off a good set. In all candour, we played an equal amount of bad sets, but were able to avoid sitting at important tables after such performances.

Art and the struggle to communicate could be found everywhere. Daily, someone would present a new painting, poem or an arrangement of a blues fusion tune that would challenge everything you knew, and would demand a response – a hunger to express the human condition like nothing I'd experienced. Teenage boys could mimic the most intricate of Western guitar riffs with ease on their cheap Chinese instruments, and old people would take the greatest care in positioning their hands and feet just so while reconstructing an ancient and highly erotic dance, their faces beaming with memories.

Inspiration was everywhere – inspiration to create. I fell into a minor period of expression through drunken poetry and would spend hours in candlelight mining the deepest sentiments I could find – after a dozen beers. I nearly passed out on this one:

Kathmandu

Squalor and soil, leap the rat
Serve the gutter thick cultural corpses.
A baby's shaved head begs rupees for Fagin,
Elbows of soot seek a Visigoth's salvation.

All night, hounds in their pus

Eyes of the prophet's peer from dark thoughts,
staring as children they retract, violated.

Bottle of urine, turgid quagmire – paraffin air.

Sell, if you will, your jewels and soul white;
Acid-tongued vendors buy sex, sell the night.
Indiscriminate black-outs jest of social defeat.
Sedative chaos, slapped flies, melted conceit.

Dust be brickwork; street rain, mud:
Lights incandescent, in candle, in blood.

All smirking and pious, hell's choice to be first,
will you cool me, decant me, thoughts pagan, perverse?
Foul waters love me, puke helpless, fall headlong

Kathmandu coughs, laughs aloud.

But Kathmandu often betrays those who love her. There is a debt to be paid. She often recoils and asks her price in blood. It was impossible to live in Kathmandu – in Thamel – for any length of time as a young man without finding some trouble in those days. The most exciting places to go on any given evening – the Fire Club, the Underground Bar, the Tunnel Club and a few others run by those gangs of young boys from the Manang region of Nepal – were too tempting to resist for many foreign visitors, and their evenings there often ended in violence.

The Manangis had found favour with the king in the old days and received some sort of special economic and international travel privileges that allowed them to reap significant advantages over other groups. A tribal mountain people from the Annapurna region, they were given access to all that their new-found wealth could buy. That distorted the identity of the Manangi people and the way they viewed themselves. To us, they were rich, rough brats who didn't take any shit from anyone.

Here was Thamel in, say, 2001: bars jam-packed with European tourists who couldn't hold their drink and Manangi boys who ran the most interesting clubs, enjoyed European girls and couldn't hold their temper. It was music, art, sex, violence and strangers coming up to you in the middle of the street demanding you try their hashish. What's not to love?

It all came to a head for me during one of Sudesh's promotional parties at the New Orleans Café. It was "Danish Night" and people from Denmark got a special price on drinks. Sudesh's soft spot for Danish girls undoubtedly played the most prominent hand in this, but why quibble? Long rows of plastic tables and chairs were added to the brick courtyard of the New Orleans in anticipation of the huge, festive groups that would soon arrive. Lots of people were watching the preparations – some we didn't see.

Sudesh's brother was an ex-policeman in Nepal. Solidly build with thick, powerful legs, he was generally jovial but had a gruff, abrupt speaking style that tended to rub people the wrong way. That evening, he had apparently offended some Manangi boys and they were looking for a chance to make their concerns known to him, directly and personally. As Danish Night evolved, all the Danes present appeared to be happy and well-cared for. I was a bit groggy and considering poetry when I looked across the room and saw Sudesh's brother in a heated discussion with a young man. Nothing unusual there, but in a few moments the young man became three young men, then five. *Shit, here we go,* I thought to myself, and I went over to the five boys, who now had their quarry surrounded. Fast, loud Nepali was being spoken and the boys began to reach for beer bottles from the surrounding tables. *This is going to hurt.* I grabbed one of the boys and held him to the floor.

"Stay put, down, stay," and I showed the boy my hand for emphasis.

Crack! I felt a bone in my temple give way, and the next thing I knew I was crawling through a pool of blood towards the restaurant office. Danes and those not as tall made a mad scramble for the exit just as a dozen more Manangi boys descended from their pre-planned positions on the roof awnings of adjacent buildings. It was a masterful plan. By the time it was all over, not one bottle or piece of glassware was intact. Half the staff was beaten bloody, and every table and every chair in the place was flattened into a splayed monument to teenage mob testosterone.

A very cute girl who worked at USAID named Carolina found me in the office and seemed as surprised as I was that I never lost consciousness. Carolina knew of an all-night local doctor, and off we went in a cab to get my temple and a wound in the back of my head stitched up. It was good to get in front of a doctor, but his level of craftsmanship saw to it that the visual reminders of that evening would remain permanent. The damage done internally would be more difficult to gauge, but let's just say that I was rather stupid for about a year after the Danish Night. To this day, friends and acquaintances alike dispute my estimate of the duration of that effect as being rather conservative.

My head was throbbing the next day when I arrived home from the clinic. I settled into my beer at the Mona and considered my options. Like any working stiff, I was happy to be home, watching the sooty sunset drop behind the Thamel tenements and crawling into a glass of the local battery acid, when I started paying an unusual amount of attention to my glass and its contents. *How many of these things do I drink every night, and how much does that add up to over the course of a week?* My mind was racing now. Guatam had annoyed me into paying his current guilt-free rate of around five US dollars per night for a room, and would also occasionally wrestle me into his sushi trap for another five. So I began to think as only a man with two or three 600-millilitre bottles of poorly conceived beer could.

"God, I'd save the cost of that goddamn bike in a week if I just got out of this place," I blurted out loud.

A head injury can catalyse a reality check when one is needed. There was no way my budget – or skull – would survive if I continued to stay in Thamel. I finally faced up to the fact that I was here to volunteer and not drink and brawl until I was broke and stupid. It was time to get out.

Guatam was genuinely sad to see me go. He understood my financial situation, finally, and on this occasion didn't try to sell me any sushi. I was going to a cheaper, more spartan guesthouse, within eyesight of the clinic, and would not be a beer-swilling Thamel rat any longer. Thamel would always be a part of me and I was sad to leave, but I had to go if I was to have any hope of making my meagre budget stretch out for another nine months or so. *Time to begin again,* I thought, and I headed out of the Hotel Mona for the last time – promptly smacking my head on the doorway.

I gave my bike to a new employee of Deepak's, who was having some trouble getting to work on time and needed some reliable transportation. After my beer revelation, I was not about to quibble about money and squeeze the poor fellow out of his rupees, so I just gave him the damn bike and wished him well. "*Dai*, I will kill anyone for you. You just ask," he responded in violent gratitude.

*

It was a small guesthouse of a nondescript nature. If it was noteworthy at all, it was for the fact that it supported a massive and probably never-illuminated neon sign of roughly 80 feet in length that someone was hoping would one day proudly exclaim to the entire Kathmandu valley, KATHMANDU VIEW AND PEACE GUESTHOUSE, in two metre-high lettering. It was to be my new base of operation, and in my current mood I hoped that no one would throw the neon switch. The "KV", as it needs to be called here, for sanity, was located above the far northwest corner of the ring road, up a hill and yes, overlooking Kathmandu to the southeast. It was in a non-tourist section of town and no bars, music venues or brawling opportunities were anywhere in the vicinity. This would do nicely, I thought. I told Jyoti, the proprietor, that I would take a room on the top floor and wanted absolute quiet. She looked at me like I was nuts, said "OK" and gave me a key. This single room would be my home for the next few months, but for the moment, it was time to do some shopping and complete the set-up necessary for the personal reinvention I had conjured for this phase of my Kathmandu experience.

Head injuries can be cathartic. Mine was more like a warning. Now, I wanted nothing more than to explore a more solitary perspective and see if I might be able to figure out a few things spiritually. I gave myself a plan: I would get by on as few things as possible and would live in silence when I wasn't working at the clinic. Furthermore, I would set up a little Buddha shrine complete with candles and incense, just like the real monks do, and crawl into my new identity of quiet humanitarian spiritual seeker and loving accepter of all things. During a clear-headed moment, I realised the possibility of my mind not being able to accept the rigorous demands of Buddhist meditation, and it wasn't much of a stretch to see that I could very easily wander towards thinking about naked women if I didn't do a little preliminary research on the subject. Fortunately, Kathmandu overflows with volumes of information on Buddhism and Hinduism. Every type of analysis, statue, ritual, primer, teaching text and painted image can be easily accessed by those who look. Over the next few days, I spent hours in cavernous bookstores looking for some guidance before settling on a few very thin and very simple texts on meditation basics. From these, I felt that a foundation could be laid for some reasonable contemplative competence that would at least keep the naked women at bay. All that was needed now was the Buddha himself.

Buying a Buddha statue might be the easiest thing one can do in Kathmandu. Tens of thousands of cast bronze renditions of all sizes exist, priced anywhere from a few dollars to thousands of dollars. I settled on a modestly priced, three-inch-high tourist model Buddha that seemed to have a pleasant demeanour – for a statue. They were always odd, these little figures. The most primitive casting techniques seemed to be employed in their manufacturing, but the local monks and craftsmen would take great pains in depicting the facial features of each Buddha in white, blue and gold with a single horse hair for a paintbrush. A good effort was always wrapped in soft cloth and managed to fetch a higher price for the painter's craftsmanship.

I loved the impermanence of the whole Buddhist experience during these times, especially when I remember the philosophy around buying such statues: "You can never own a Buddha image: You can only rent one."

After complementing my philosophical rental with some incense and gloriously pure paraffin Nepali candles, I headed back to the KV. I was determined to use the time and the circumstances that were presented to me to do some personal seeking. I was about to turn inward for the first time in my life. It was frightening and I couldn't wait.

The Buddha statue was placed with the candles and incense on a glass shelf in one corner of my room. I had no idea how to start my new, quiet life or which mechanisms were to be involved, so I turned to one of the books I'd purchased: the Dalai Lama's sympathetic primer called *Cultivating a Daily Meditation.* In it, the Dalai Lama explained how those who wanted to find peace through Buddhist meditation could follow some basic structures and invocations, and have quite the introspective experience, apparently.

I gave it a shot for a few weeks and...nothing. Not one damn bit of peace and certainly no sense of enlightenment. I didn't like the structure of the crossed legs and the hand positioning, either. I'd seen a lot of phoney-looking American Buddhists displaying themselves with open-palmed forefinger-to-thumb poses, but always felt they had a self-possessed sense of display.

I did try it, but I failed to reach any mental state other than frustration.

The life of silence part was coming together rather nicely, however. I'd finish a day at the clinic, and walk through a few muddy fields and directly up to my room – human interaction successfully minimised. In the mornings, I'd awaken and head down the hill to a microscopic and grimy Nepali tea house for my morning cup and a few potato *parathas*. From there, it was on to the clinic where I allowed myself to speak – always a good idea when treating patients.

A nice balance was taking shape between the quiet simplicity of my evenings and the chaos and anguish of treating traumatised Tibetans during the day, but I found myself looking forward to the quiet, ascetic life I'd invented for myself more and more as time passed. Days at the clinic were unpredictable. One could never tell when a group of 100 Tibetans would show up and need treatment. We were never warned of any mass arrivals – we just had to be ready. Mostly, the days drifted along with little excitement.

One particularly slow day, I took it upon myself to arrange and catalogue the ceiling-high donations of Western medicine that were thrown randomly into the storage room. This wound up taking three days to complete, but at least I had something to do that was reasonably useful. Antibiotics were thrown away as Tibetans would quit taking them at the first hint of improvement and possibly develop resistant strains of whatever it was that predicated the need for antibiotics in the first place. Bandages were sorted, soiled donations tossed. We liked topical creams, especially hard-to-obtain burn ointments, as well as surgical gloves that were generally found after digging through a backpacker's mini first-aid kit. It was rare to find a full unopened box of gloves unless it was donated by a large expedition or trekking group. Anything we could hand out in a small container for a Tibetan to use later, such as eye drops or a nasal spray, was sought out and moved to the main clinic directly. The golden ticket, and that which was most prized, was splinting material. Weeks of walking through Nepal left many of the Tibetans who presented themselves at the clinic with sprains and pains of all types. Anything we could offer to give the injury some relief and immobilisation was always appreciated. Metal, plastic – whatever was rigid and available was pressed into service for the task when proper splinting was unavailable.

The feral-looking backpacker section of the donations enlivened the sorting task considerably. What were these people thinking? Countless herbs without labels had to be sniffed and ultimately discarded, along with piles of unsalvageable socks and underwear. I was pleased to find a bag full of tennis balls, and not so pleased to find a bag with a voodoo doll and a broken hash pipe. Huge bottles of hair gel and some odd-looking Kama Sutra oils rounded out the episode for me, and I found shelf space for all.

On no day in particular, I was feeling low and burned out as usual – the glamour and prestige of helping Tibetans had long since worn off – when I happened to find something that nurse Tenzin said amusing to the point that it made me laugh for a bit. Looking through the glass of the treatment area and out into the hallway, I noticed a group of young Tibetan nuns – shaved heads and all – returning my laughter with considerable interest.

"Tenzin, what's up with those little nuns?" I asked.

"I don't know, Jim-la. You don't smell very bad today, so that can't be it."

And with that, Tenzin headed towards the nuns to see what was so amusing.

Returning, she offered that the nuns weren't laughing at me and no, it was confirmed, I didn't stink. So I asked Tenzin about what she'd learned. What the nuns said didn't make my day, it made my year.

"He smiles like a Tibetan."

Evenings came and went in self-imposed silence in my little room at the KV. Each night, I would prop myself atop a few pillows, cross my legs and make yet another attempt at meditation. Each night, I would fail. Invariably, I couldn't shake the imagery of self-absorbed Westerners making crossed-legged poses and circles with their fingers. It was as if they didn't care as much about the deeper aspects of meditation as they did about the appearance they gave off while meditating. Was it all a big act? I didn't know. One part of the ritual that involved no imagery, however, was the pain I felt after sitting for a short time with legs akimbo in the "lotus" position, and it didn't take long before the small recitations and mantras I'd been chanting under my breath were overtaken by the demands of an egregiously numb foot making me lose all concentration.

"Oh, to hell with this," I yelled one evening, after a particularly painful cramp had started to set in to my leg. If meditation is to be a calming of the mind and is to involve mental training and mental discipline, what difference does it make how you sit or position yourself? I mean, theoretically, you should be able to have the discipline to reach enlightenment while reclining in a hammock, right?

The lotus position as well as the circled fingers or hands cupped in the lap were designed as practices to help calm the body so the mind could do its work. These are ancient positions and ancient ideas. Sure, the positioning is supposed to align or awaken "chakras" or whatever, but those concepts are so distracting to a beginner that one seems to spend most of the time worrying about alignment and not concentrating on quieting the mind. Even the monks I saw at various temples around Kathmandu didn't have perfect posture, and they sure as hell didn't make those silly shapes with their fingers while meditating. What was I missing?

Looking through *Cultivating a Daily Meditation* again, I came across the concept that all the exercises and mantras you recite are just pathways that help condition the mind for the serious contemplation of nothingness to follow. It was the same with the physical stuff, I thought. Buddhist meditation is not about following a strict set of rules and practices, it's about finding the tools that work for you and that get you, the individual, to your contemplative destination. Wow. You start to think like this when you spend a lot of time alone and are able to get inside your own head a bit.

It was then that I decided to completely let loose of the constrictions of Buddhist regimen, as mandated at probably every Buddhist retreat or camp in southern California, and quit trying to follow someone else's ideas on effective positioning and posture. It changed everything.

So, here's the Buddhist practice that seemed to work for me: Get comfortable in any position, sit upright on a bunch of pillows and make sure your lower back is supported. The whole bit about crossing hands in the lap is comfortable and feels natural, so try it if it works for you – none of that circle-fingered crap, though. Next, if my mind is completely haywire that day, I use the breathing exercises. Put simply, breathe slowly and concentrate on nothing but the aspects of breathing in and out.

Try it. Try anything that quiets your mind and gets you out of your stressful day, and I'll call that Buddhism for the Western mind.

I've always had trouble with those people who feel they must copy religious practices to the letter if they want to be considered practitioners. I've noticed that most of the world's faiths spring out of the needs and myths of the cultures where they originated and don't seem to travel well. I can't stand to see white people forcing Jesus down the throat of African tribesman just like I can't stand to see Westerners walking around an airport with saffron robes and shaved heads. It's cultural mimicry to me. Religions are defined by what they mean to their originating culture. What is effective Buddhism to a New York businessman then? Do we call him incomplete just because he refuses to wear a robe and shave his head? I'd like to believe that our New Yorker can simply apply the ideas of impermanence and quiet patience to his daily life without impinging on his ability to be a Wall Street tiger. Buddhism provides a little benefit to any culture, but can and should reflect different things on different cultures.

It was not long after this epiphany that I lifted my self-imposed experiment in asceticism. What started out as a minor spiritual quest evolved into the realisation that I was just trying to imitate the practices and methods of the cultures that I admired. I would take a bit of Buddhist practice with me for the rest of my life, but on the whole, I was mostly just fine the way I was.

*

It was almost a daily annoyance at the clinic: An overly officious young woman would poke her head in the doorway and demand some set of obscure reports from Tsering Lhamo.

"Get the reports up to the third floor immediately," she would bark.

Ah yes, the third floor of the TRC: the Ivory Tower. It was the place where the United Nations High Commission for Refugees (UNHCR) staff had their offices. They spent their days examining and interviewing each undocumented Tibetan who arrived at the clinic and making determinations vis-à-vis their "status". Most Tibetans just received authorisation to travel onwards to India, where they would be met, each and all, by the Dalai Lama himself. After they were through crying and generally being overwhelmed by this event, the Dalai Lama would promptly tell them that there was no future for them in Dharamsala, and that they would be better off going back to Tibet – more crying.

"Miss Susan", as she was known, was a UNHCR protection officer and she was obviously not enjoying her stay in Nepal. The compassion of the Buddha was not entirely present in my visage on the day that I blew my top at her for her arrogance.

"Listen, you little witch, these people are working their asses off to take care of the medical needs of these people. You back off a bit and maybe you'll get your goddam reports, got it?"

It was not clear at all whether she'd ever been addressed in such a manner since she had come to her position in the UN hierarchy, and she was decidedly taken aback.

"Well, yes, OK, but I need those reports," she replied with less edge than before.

Miss Susan seemed somehow different in attitude and tone to everyone in the days following that incident and began to take a noticeable interest in my presence and function at the clinic. I was sure she'd discussed our confrontation in a meeting or two (or more – she worked for the UN, remember), and was initiating the mechanisms to have me removed from my volunteer position at the clinic when she caught me in the hallway one afternoon.

"You want to go for some lunch tomorrow? It's my day off."

A blur of time soon passed where lunches with Miss Susan became dinners, and dinners turned into all-night drunken passion brawls – reports from our clinic, it seemed, were not the only thing Miss Susan felt she needed immediately. All of which was followed by morning recovery periods on the spacious and sunny terrace of her compound.

"Hey, how do I get your job? Look at this place," I said, focusing gingerly one morning.

Susan had a huge, walled-in complex with a four-bedroom, three-storey house; a private car with driver; a *didi*, or older sister/housekeeper; and a gardener. As a protection officer she was also pulling in an unholy monthly salary from the UN, which went almost exclusively into her savings as she was afforded a considerable expense account during her stay in Nepal. To top this off, the UN had paid to ship all of her furniture from her last posting in South America to her new digs in the plush, diplomatic sector of Kathmandu.

Something wasn't right and I couldn't figure it out. I couldn't understand the logic of why people from the UN needed to come to one of the poorest countries in the world under the pretext of "aid" and live like insulated princesses in walled compounds surrounded by luxury. Did they not care about the context and environment of their mission? Surely they would want to be more informed, unless they didn't care in the first place, right?

After a while, the sight of the compound's opulence and Susan's place among it began to annoy me. Some hard questions began to come into my brain and they were starting to take our relationship down a path from which there would be no recovery, no redemption and no reconciliation. I knew that soon the fun would be over and only a purpose-driven game would remain: Susan was now a resource and I needed to find out more.

"Wait a minute, how much did you say you make per month?"

"You get how much for expenses?"

"What is it exactly that you do up there on the third floor anyway?"

"So, what you're saying is that those reports you wanted so badly from us were never used?"

"Are you telling me that Tibetans can still get to India regardless of your authorisation?"

Over the course of the next few weeks, I picked my questions even more carefully:

"OK, I know you guys are supposed to go up to the crossing areas where Tibetans come through and not only monitor the situation but also direct transport efforts to Kathmandu, right? Well, how come I never see the UNHCR do that?" I asked one day.

"Ah, that," Susan said dismissively. "The fact is, Tibetans wind up at our facility anyway, one way or another, and no one in our office wants to go up to the border and be cold for a few weeks, that's all."

I was starting to believe a fantasy I had created in my mind about the UN being just a shell, a presence in Nepal with no real function other than to be a presence. If any progress was going to be made on the Tibet issue and its relationship to Nepal, it most definitely was not going to come at the hands of the UNHCR or any other UN agency. It brought to mind a joke I'd heard at the New Orleans Café in Kathmandu. A young Nepali guy came up to me during a discussion about foreign aid and said, "*Dai*, don't you know that you can't spell the word 'unnecessary' without 'UN'?"

Susan and I wound down our time together until we eventually lost track of each other. It was a bit sad, but I didn't mind. In a practical sense, I was able to stay connected to her copious UN expense account for a few months and spend almost no money, and for that I was exceedingly thankful.

It was a thief's good fortune to be able to stay and volunteer for a few months longer because of a brief fling with a UN protection officer, and I laughed at the notion that Kathmandu had taught me well. It wouldn't be the first time I was to say thanks to the UN in Nepal, however: Much more theft and gratitude was to come.

CHAPTER 7

THE GREAT VACCINE SMUGGLING CAPER

We had been working consistently at an exhaustive pace at the Reception Centre Clinic. Anywhere between 50 to 250 Tibetans were passing through our doors on any given day, getting what they must have thought was a bewildering medical experience via injections, urine samples and completely undignified physical exams. I was gratifyingly exhausted. Every dumb foreigner's dream of helping out in the world contains some component of working yourself to death in a foreign health clinic of some sort. I'll quote every adventure memoir that has ever been written right here and say I was "living the dream" in that respect.

The big routine was to get the younger Tibetans, say roughly under 16 (many had absolutely no idea how old they were), into our treatment room for a series of vaccinations. Measles, Mumps and Rubella (MMR) was the standard along with the somewhat controversial Bacille Calmette–Guerin (BCG) injection for tuberculosis (TB). There was some professional doubt in Western circles over this vaccine, as its efficacy had never been proven to be above 80 per cent, and this figure dropped dramatically as the patient grew into adolescence. Yet, I came to learn this was far preferable to the Direct Observation and Treatment System (DOTS) that was the usually administered treatment. The big problem with DOTS was that the patient actually had to become symptomatic with TB first; then, one had to give a series of medicinal dosages over a period of six months, which entailed *directly observing the patient taking the required medicine.* This was impossible for

Tibetans. The minute they felt better, they threw away their medications. Combine this with the fact that they were not predisposed to see a health care professional on a regular basis for any reason, and you get the point of why BCG gave a better chance against TB. It's also the reason I cringed whenever well-meaning Westerners delivered a case of antibiotics to the Reception Centre: same concept, potentially worse results.

We were running low on BCG and I was itching for a change of atmosphere. One day, after seeing absolutely my last festering, pre-gangrenous toe, I asked Tsering Lhamo about the BCG problem. She said that the government of Nepal had their shortages as well, and that they couldn't spare any extra to help us out here at the clinic.

"Well then, what do we do?" I asked.

Tsering said that all she knew was that the vaccine came from Delhi, and was delivered on the whim of the Serum Institute of India – which had an ample supply.

There it was: my chance to help out a bunch of kids who would be highly susceptible to TB in a new, foreign land and, more importantly, my chance to get out of that smelly clinic for a few weeks. I immediately told Tsering that I would go to India and bring back a new batch of BCG, and that all would once again be well in our small clinic. I had a plan, but what I received was an education.

Still consumed by my usual assortment of hero delusions, I boarded a bus for Delhi and, true to pattern, had no idea what I was going to do when I got there.

It stunk. India, especially Delhi, was awash with high-powered touts and an almost unbearable stench. Kathmandu was Club Med in comparison. Heat, pollution, human squalor and a manic intensity of existence ruled the day. Americans have this idea of personal space: Talk at a distance, respectfully do not touch others (immediately at least) and allow others to speak. I was totally unprepared for completely well-intentioned Indian males holding my hand and speaking less than an inch from my face. Culture shock was a frailty I thought I'd mastered, yet the physical assumptions made by these complete strangers were disconcerting. It was a culture both nuanced and rapacious, and I was definitely a fish out of water. This was my first trip to India, and it took me years to get used to this treatment. Over time, you realise that it's just part of the game with Indians – they know it as well.

Always a big fan of the Lonely Planet guides, I found a cheap hotel room from their India guidebook. It was in Paharganj, the big Western tourist ghetto. After walking through a nondescript entryway, I was greeted at the front desk by a guilty face with greasy hair, and was shown a room. It seemed Asia-normal until I found a window opening near the bed with water and rats streaming through it. "No, that's where I'll draw a line on this trip," I said to myself, and off into the Delhi night I went.

I had no idea what to do at that point. The only other bit of advice I knew came from Tsering, who told me to stop by and visit the Tibetan settlements near the river: Budh Vihar and Majnu ka Tilla. With no particular preference for either, I hopped into a motorised rickshaw with a hole in the floorboard, and headed down a speeding motorway towards Budh Vihar.

Tibetans are grateful for the help that India provides. Since 1959 when the Dalai Lama first arrived and asked for asylum, there has been a great friendship and caretaking aspect to India's treatment of Tibetans within its borders. Tibetans, for their part, have not squandered India's magnanimity by acting the part of hopeless refugee. Tibetans in India can often be found as vigorous, competitive and successful businesspeople who labour hard to contribute to Indian society. For my purposes, it would have been enough if the Tibetans living in the tiny settlement of Budh Vihar would just help me find a room for the night.

Immediately on arrival, I found myself in some administration facility. Apparently, word of my coming had spread, thanks to Tsering, and I was looked upon as some sort of political and humanitarian curiosity. Understand that in those days Budh Vihar was housing Tibetan activists, abused refugees fleeing persecution and various Indian merchants and opportunists. It was a tightly enclosed souk of markets, monks and machinations covered in canvas and plastic tarp. My presence seemed to imply some larger meaning to them, and I was uncomfortable. I did some cursory questioning about the availability of vaccines and quickly made my exit. Budh Vihar was a bust, on to Majnu ka Tilla I went.

The white walls surrounding the entry to Majnu ka Tilla were inauspicious. This is a generous word. "White" is also generous, as I witnessed a procession of seemingly idle young Indian males urinating on those white walls. It didn't matter. I needed a bed, and this was my last option before returning to the rat highway in Paharganj.

A light was flickering over a doorway down an inconspicuous alley in this nondescript place. "Hotel Wangchen" in small blue letters fought for recognition and to keep the evening moths at bay. Green and white marble floors highlighted polished, mahogany-stained banisters once one committed to an entry. *Oh my,* I thought, *we can't let word of this place escape to that tourist ghetto of Paharganj or they will be overrun with screaming Euros begging for muesli.* Clean is the first and only thing you care about when picking a cheap hotel in Delhi. I didn't expect to add style and comfort to the list, but here they were. Tibetans are masters of the hospitality business; I was learning this point quickly.

Tea and *chapati* and I was out the door the next morning. There was work to do. I walked a few steps to a small Tibetan clinic and asked the attending caretaker, Tashi, about how to get the BCG vaccine.

"Yes, we can give the injection here. I can do that," said Mr Tashi with authority.

"I need 3,000 doses and I want to smuggle them into Nepal. Can you do THAT?" I shot back.

The most astounding thing about that little exchange was that Tashi never blinked, never looked at me like I was nuts, and he most certainly didn't laugh. What he did was turn and look over his shoulder at his rather nervous-looking nurse and start a rapid-fire exchange of questioning in some of the oddest, most vernacularised Tibetan I'd heard.

"This is very difficult. Serum Institute is in old Delhi. You need signature of Indian doctor for that much supply. We know doctor who will do this. He is at the university. Take a taxi. Dr Singh: easy to see, Sikh, big turban, you know."

I gave thanks to Tashi for the direction and bid him a good afternoon. Now, the chase would begin to find enough BCG to supply the TRC clinic until more supply could be found elsewhere. It would probably see them through three months at least.

Next morning, I found a friendly tuk-tuk driver at nine a.m. at the gates of Majnu ka Tilla, and we proceeded to weave through the morning rush-hour traffic towards Delhi University. The driver spoke no English and I had zero command of Hindi, so we spent the next half-hour buzzing around the campus trying to make sense of Tashi's handwriting and find Dr Singh's room. Gestures, pointing and more gestures from a student led to a door on a second floor with the correct number on it.

"*Namaskar*, Dr Singh! Hello!"

After a few minutes of tea and some scribbling on Dr Singh's coffee table, the prize was won. We had our signature. Now, off to buy vaccines. Dr Singh refused any type of payment or gratuity for trusting total strangers with his medical credentials, and I came away from that apartment thinking that Sikhs must be the most human of all human beings.

Off we sped towards the heart of old Delhi and an annex of the Serum Institute of India, where the main supply of BCG vaccines for this part of south Asia could be accessed and purchased. Winding the little tuk-tuk past row upon row of single-roomed offices stacked three stories high and passing under dense spider-web clusters of black electrical wires, we asked, pleaded, gestured and eventually found the correct finger on a gentleman who used it to point us in the correct direction, towards a bleak opening in an unpainted concrete building. We worked our way through a damp hallway that had suddenly turned black from a power outage just as we entered, and felt our way up a flight of stairs (my tuk-tuk driver was really getting into this and had decided to follow along). I stepped on something alive but managed to keep climbing until we reached a door with the correct markings. There it was. In candlelight, the Serum Institute of India Annex conducted its business behind a long glass partition that pushed into the lobby so thoroughly that customers could not turn around effectively in the small sliver of corridor allotted for their comfort. Dr Singh's hard-won endorsement landed abruptly on the counter and we announced our intentions.

Taking extra time to admire the curves and flourishes in Dr Singh's signature, the tiny man behind the counter looked up. He was earnestly preparing to say something, but instead he plunged his head downward again and began a thorough re-examination of Dr Singh's handiwork. A full minute went by before he looked up again. Silence – silence and time.

"OK, pal, don't start a pattern here – can I get this order filled?" I had to break his rhythm.

Horror stories abound about Indian bureaucracy, and my mind was replaying each one I'd heard in an endless feedback loop. All of these accounts involve the simplest decisions being held up by the most meaningless signature or piece of paper that is not to the liking of the bureaucrat of the moment, that hurls the petitioner into months of Kafkaesque procedures and endless waiting. This guy would have given anything to be able to look at Dr Singh's signature a few more times, but I threw him off his game and he was compelled to speak.

"Yes, we can fill this order."

"What, that's it? No Kafka? You guys are great. I take back every improper thought I've fostered about Indian efficiency. Thank you. Thank you." I could barely contain my joy.

"You are most welcome, sir. Oh, wait, you want 3,000 doses? We have only 500 here."

There it was, I'd been waiting for it: the hammer drop. It was too good to be true. I had always believed that every Indian conversation with a foreigner leads to a sales pitch – they can't help themselves. Where they continue to fool all of us is by varying the time it takes to get to the closing line. It could be one minute, or you could develop a deep friendship over many months with an Indian only to have him ask you to sponsor his daughter at an American university.

"Let me guess, it will be at least a month before you can get the rest, right? And, oh, I'm sure there's a price to fix the problem, eh, pal?" I said.

"No, no, sir, no extra. Vaccine is not here, but I will send our boy to the cold storage facility and he will come right back: only a few minutes."

I was being a jerk again, ready and willing to accuse this poor man of some form of corruption simply because he didn't meet my criteria for expeditious service. Anxiety and deadlines: the American way.

Contrition is not my strong suit but I gave it my best: "I'm so sorry. Please let me apologise for the misunderstanding. Yes, I will sit here and wait until the boy comes back with the vaccines."

"That is not possible, sir. We close now."

"Wait, you just told me that it would only take a few minutes?"

"It is lunchtime now, sir. You come back late this afternoon and order will be ready."

Perched on a patch of concrete kerb between two rickshaws outside the Serum Institute of India, it occurred to me what it was that I hated about Delhi: the stench, pushy charlatans, rats and garbage, sure, those were visceral. But sitting there, watching a toddler throw an apple into a stream of black gutter sludge, retrieve it and then take a bite, I could not understand just how, at that particular moment, I found I was actually enjoying myself.

Being tucked as I was into Indian urban working-class culture, there was none of the screaming pressure to consume or give your full attention to someone rushing up to your nose to sell you something like there was in the tourist splat that was Paharganj. I noticed that I was being left blissfully alone among Indians going about their daily business. That was it. That was why I hated Delhi. It was because Delhi didn't want me to like it. More specifically, it was about the way Indians treat those outside of Indian culture – those that don't belong. It's not violent, it's the power of their raw humanity that they use against us. I see it in the way adults laugh and encourage their children to torment tourists for money. It's a kind of national defence – a firewall. Perhaps it was because I was now inside that firewall and being given the briefest of glimpse of what it must be like to be a part of the fabric of Indian culture that I felt happy. Sitting on that kerb, I felt protected – I felt Indian. I didn't know it yet, but it was that sense of familial humanity, of inclusion, that resonated with me and helped inform my perspective on the Tibetans in India's care, their cause as viewed through the Indian lens, and the ideas and strategies that fill the latter chapters of this book.

Full immersion in my internal debate over Indian national character would have to wait; the afternoon was ripening and I had to pick up my vaccine order. My tuk-tuk driver seemed genuinely disappointed when I turned him loose after the morning adventure, but I felt a more substantial piece of iron was needed to haul these precious vaccines through Delhi traffic. I flagged down a classic white Ambassador taxi for the job, and asked for the driver's patience while I made my way back up the stairwell to the Serum Institute. The lights were now on, and whatever it was that I stepped on earlier seemed to have left for safer ground. So, good time was made in picking up and paying for my cargo.

"Sir, wait," came that familiar voice.

"What is it now, my friend?"

"BCG must be kept cold or it will lose its efficacy. No warmer than two degrees Celsius during transport."

"Wait, wait, what are you telling me?" I was beginning to inflate and deflate at the same time. "Are you saying I've got to keep these ampoules at just a few degrees above freezing from now until I reach a refrigerator in Kathmandu? It's 90 degrees outside!"

The little man behind the counter was having his turn. Pausing an inordinately long time before speaking, he languished over my frustration before presenting his next offering.

"Yes, sir. I suggest you get a cold-chain monitoring thermometer to check temperature in box at all times."

"Fine then, I suppose I can't take these until you give me some ice. Do you have ice for this?"

"Very sorry, sir, we have no ice to lend. But we have a box. You can get ice at the market. We will not charge you for the box."

The Ambassador taxi was still waiting; I caught him just before he was about to give up and drive off. Into old Delhi we crept. The usual gestures and pointed fingers this time led us to a man sitting by the side of the road, who proceeded to reach under his table and unfold layer upon layer of old burlap sack remnants to expose a two-pound block of ice.

"It will do," I said and we took our purchase – now wrapped in newspaper – and headed back to the Serum Institute, where we packed the ampoules in the free box with the ice and then sprinted back down the stairs to the taxi.

Arriving some time later in Majnu ka Tilla, I noticed water from rapidly melting ice softening my free box. I hurried.

"Sorry, our freezer is broken," said Tashi. Taking my precious cargo in hand, I sprinted down the tiny street and headed for my last option.

"Sure, we have room in our freezer," came the reply from Sonam, the cheerful and well-groomed desk clerk at Hotel Wangchen. "You can leave it behind the frozen mutton for the night."

With that, the box of glass ampoules containing desiccated cellular fragments of tuberculosis were placed delicately behind slabs of frozen lamb scheduled to be used on the next day's menu.

It was now time to go shopping. Amazingly, I never had to leave Majnu ka Tilla to find the remainder of what I needed. The first key item was a duffel bag procured from the local outdoor-cheap-duffel-bag stall. It looked okay; it even had a pretence of being water-resistant with its plastic lining and zippered cover flap. Fine, now for a bundle of cheap Chinese towels: Remember, we were making a big, insulated pillow for a small box about a third of the size of a DVD player. Check. I got those at a little Tibetan Catch-all market. I disregarded the neon-green duck patterns; these wouldn't be hanging in any sane person's bathroom. They had one and only one function: insulation. Next, I found a surprisingly good digital thermometer at a mini-pharmacy. I'd place it in with the vaccines and read it when I got to Kathmandu. In all probability, the reading I got when I landed in Kathmandu would be the warmest of the journey, so I'd call that a poor man's "cold chain monitoring".

Finally, it was time to work on logistics. I made my way to the formal wood-trimmed offices of Tibet Travels, just across from the duffel-bag stall, and made a phone call to Tsering Lhamo, telling her to be ready at the airport tomorrow for a pick-up – that I was on my way. I booked the first available flight to Kathmandu, reserved a cab for the morning and bid the agent a fond *"kale shoo"* as a goodbye.

BCG is a perishable vaccine that has to be kept cold at all times. We would have been sunk had there been a power outage at the Wangchen – the mutton would not have fared so well either. The refrigeration in Delhi was not that great to begin with. Our "freezer" storage was barely more than a cold refrigerator with bad insulation. Daytime temperatures were reaching 90 degrees Fahrenheit, so it was going to be a race against time, poor refrigeration and the rising daytime heat to make it to Delhi airport first thing in the morning with our vaccines maintained at a cool temperature. To top it off, BCG is a "live" vaccine. It contains a strain of Mycobacterium bovis, which is a bacterium that causes tuberculosis (TB) in cattle. The idea is that this is supposed to stimulate your immune system to make you resistant to TB and fight it off naturally. Transporting such vaccines requires following a myriad of prohibitive rules. The US Center for Disease Control doesn't even like to think about transporting live vaccines across state lines in the US, and probably combusts into a pile of goo when they hear about it happening. For me, I felt like I was off the hook: There was absolutely no research available and no guidelines to follow that addressed the illegal, purposefully disobedient smuggling of live vaccines across international borders. So as far as I was concerned, this should be easy.

This is probably be a good time to say that the only thing stronger than personal delusion is willful disregard.

Morning arrived. Blur ensued. I packed vaccines, ice and the thermometer in obnoxious Chinese towels and stuffed it all into the new duffel bag. I wrapped the whole thing a few times with duct tape to deter quick-snatch thieves. The bag was tagged "Ram Chettri, Kathmandu" so I couldn't be readily pinned to the bag if it was confiscated.

The taxi driver, true to his word over the phone the preceding evening, was waiting at the gates of Majnu ka Tilla at seven a.m. An uneventful drive to the airport followed. I reached my terminal within an hour and located my flight on the departure board. The tragedy of 9/11 was still a few years away, and overall security at Indian airports was a seemingly confused display of nonchalance at the time; still, I spent a few minutes watching some of the nearby gates and their ad-hoc security procedures. This was informative. Seeing that carry-on baggage was subject to at least two more security checks than bags that were checked in, I chose the check-in. But I still had to clear that one check, and I dreaded feeding my bag through the X-ray machine. After gently placing my new duffel on the conveyor belt, I stepped out of line, tied my shoe and stepped back into line – considerably out of sequence so that anyone looking could not quickly associate my face with the suspect bag.

I was still in line when my bag cleared. The conveyor stopped. A man behind the X-ray counter (damn these little men) called for his supervisor. It was my bag they were looking at. *OK, I'm done here. I'll just get through this line and board the plane – they got the bag,* I thought to myself as I cleared the security check.

Turning around, I watched them run the bag through again. Whispered conversations followed. I feared the worst for the vaccines. Eventually, the bag emerged and took its place on the ground, next to all of the other bags cleared and ready for transport to Kathmandu.

Thoughts began to swirl in my mind. *They knew it! They knew there were glass ampoules of white powder in the bag and they let it go anyway!*

Perhaps somewhere in those whispered conversations someone decided that holding up the line, searching the bag, filing out the forms and bringing the whole story to light was not worth the potentially career-derailing show of individuality and personal initiative that was required, and an agreement was reached to just wave the whole thing through. My shipment was in the clear. Now it was just a matter of a one-hour flight to Kathmandu and a simple pick-up at the other end.

Thankfully, it was Kathmandu. Security checks could be voluntarily bypassed by travellers in a hurry, and security people back then didn't seem to know much about security anyway. I took full advantage of this. Picking the bag off the carousel, I felt a cold, wet sensation on my knee. My water-resistant duffel did not perform as advertised, and I was trailing a visible stream of melted ice water through the terminal as I left.

"No, I don't want a goddam rickshaw!" I barked, as my eyes located the purple Tata Land Cruiser that belonged to the TRC. Another 30 minutes, and we would be safe and in the presence of real refrigeration.

"Jim-la, you look exhausted," were the first words from a bewildered-looking Tsering Lhamo as I dropped the bag on the floor of the clinic. The vaccines were removed and placed in the tiny cooling unit sitting no more than a metre from where the bag landed. The light cardboard shell that kept the ampoules separated and in order in their little box had disintegrated into a watery mud. From Indian freezer to Nepal refrigerator, it had taken roughly four hours to smuggle the vaccines, and yes, I was exhausted – exhausted, dehydrated and emaciated from what I'd just been through.

"Jim-la, you want this?" asked a nurse as she held up a small plastic box.

"Hey, give me that thing. That's my thermometer, let me see that."

Peering down at the black numbers on the display, I smiled.

Three degrees Centigrade: *I'll take it.*

In the months that followed, I wrote down the entire sequence of events and procedures that needed to be followed so that the entire process could be repeated and executed by anyone from the clinic travelling to Delhi in the future.

Lhodup Dorjee, the director of the TRC, was impressed by the results and decided to try the whole thing himself. I caught up to him a few weeks after he had returned and asked him how it went.

"Ha! Jim-la, you didn't tell me it was so easy."

Photo Gallery

Jiri 1995.

First trek in 1995. Photo taken near Pangboche.

Lukla Airstrip 1995.

Monk

Prosthesis will make difference in his life

Continued from E-1

San Diego, which has about 650 members.

"Several of us wanted to help. At first, I thought we'd get measurements of his leg, have a prosthesis made and send it back to him. But we learned that it's a little more involved than that."

Karma, whose father serves one of the most revered lamas (or Tibetan Buddhist leaders) among those who escaped Chinese oppression to live in exile in India, had his cancerous right leg amputated above the knee in November 1996.

He was given the best prosthesis available in his small community in India, a crude, ill-fitting, pre-World War II era peg-leg made of wood and leather that Karma must support with his right hand in order to walk.

"His faith requires sitting cross-legged in meditation for hours at a time, to walk for hours over mountainous terrain and to lay prostrate in prayer — none of which he can do now with his incredibly primitive prosthesis," said Richard Greenfield, an orthopedic surgeon at Mission Bay Hospital.

Greenfield is part of a team at the hospital that examined Karma, helped with the design of his new leg and is overseeing the weeks of therapy necessary to teach walk with it —

JOHN GASTALDO

A fan: *Tibetan Buddhist ... Rinaldi watch the Padres play the Expos last month.*

Karma has tried

legs can still play sports.

The immediate goal is walk efficiently with his

Karma and I at a baseball game. Photocopied San Diego Union Tribune article.

My first job as an emergency room Tech.

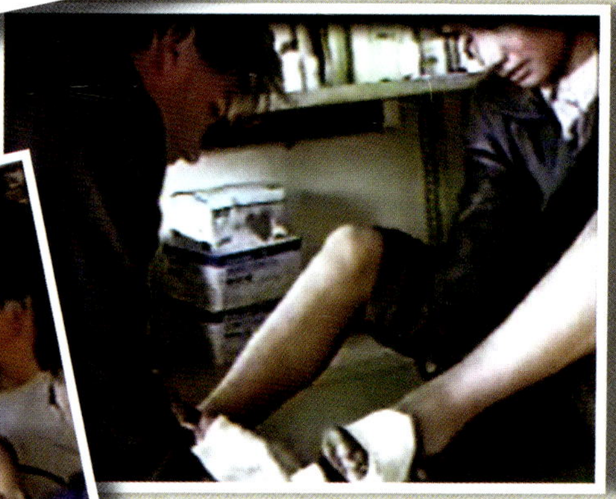

Treating frostbite at Reception Centre Clinic

A Tibetan nun receives a vaccination at the Clinic.

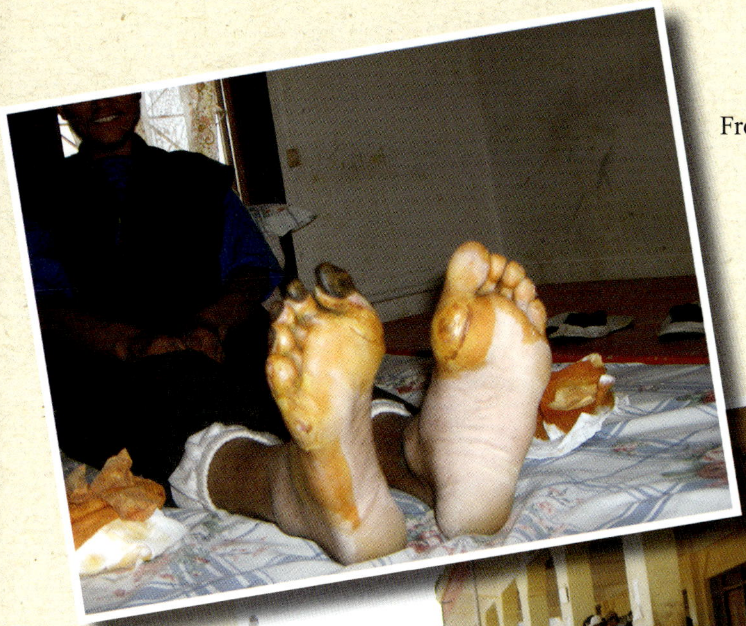

Frostbitten feet.

Tibetan Reception Centre: circa 1998.

Sudesh wears a Santa cap behind the bar: New Orleans Café Christmas party, 1999.

Deepak and James, 2006.

Music with Sudesh at the New Orleans Café: 1999.

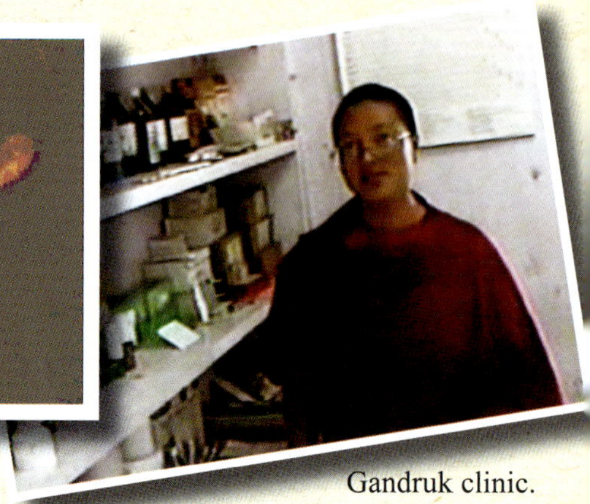

Gandruk clinic.

Serum Institute of India.

Delivering BCG vaccine. Small box is cold-chain thermometer.

Chinese agent on Friendship Bridge. This is the guy that followed us back into Nepal.

Nepal Immigration Tatopani.

Tibetan at immigration desk in Nepal: the last photo I took before getting hauled off and beaten.

Pema interview: Lhasa, 1999.

Khampas at the Barkhor.

Working on our next trick: circa 2003.

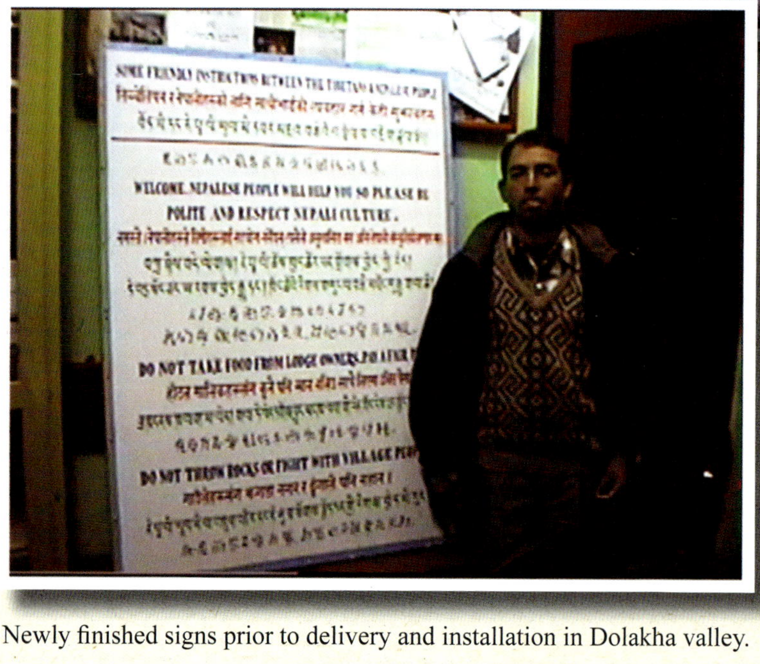

Newly finished signs prior to delivery and installation in Dolakha valley.

Ram nails up a sign at Siguti bridge.

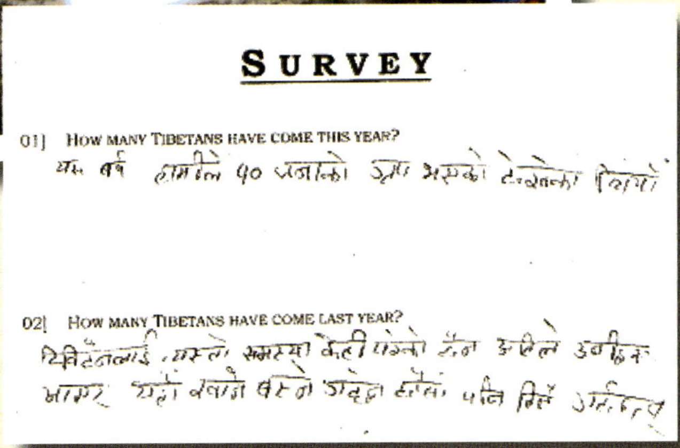

SURVEY

01] HOW MANY TIBETANS HAVE COME THIS YEAR?

[illegible]

02] HOW MANY TIBETANS HAVE COME LAST YEAR?

[illegible]

Survey from Gorkha. Typical of open surveys we used for fact-finding.

Survey in progress.

Namche Bazaar: circa 2003

First ever known photos of this Chinese base near the Nangpa-la.

Typical herder's shack near the Nangpa-la.

Checkpost
Kodari.

HCR - UNHCR

Haut Commissariat des Nations Unies pour les réfugiés
United Nations High Commissioner for Refugees
Section de l'Information — Information Section

March 1, 2004

To: Immigration Officials, Border Police and Army Personnel
From: The United International Independent Commission (UIIC)

It has come to our attention that policies adopted by His Majesty's Government of Nepal and the Office of the Foreign Minister of Nepal regarding the forcible return of Tibetans to Tibet have been violated.

According to the Policies of Nepal and the International Community, you are to follow these rules immediately, and without question:

1. Do not return captured Tibetans to Tibet. Contact the Tibetan Reception Center or the UNHCR for Tibetan transportation to Kathmandu.
2. Do not release captured Tibetans into the hands of any police or immigration officials from other nations.
3. All captured Tibetans are to be kept safe from harm until transport arrives.
4. You are to act according to the policies of His Majesty's government as outlined in the enclosed letter from Foreign Minister Acharya, and articles 13 and 14 of the Universal Declaration of Human Rights at all times.

We will be visiting your facility soon to insure compliance.

UIIC Representat

Les communiqués sont destinés à l
For use of info

Case postale 2500
CH-1211 Genève 2 Dépôt
Téléphone: (022) 739 81 11
Télex: 412 972 REFPI/CH
Télégramme: HICOMREF, Genève
Téléfax: (4122) 739 84 49

Checkpost
near Banepa.

Actual copy of letter used to fool Nepali checkpoint officials.

One of the last times I played with Sudesh at the New Orleans.

With APF IGP and friend at APF headquarters, Kathmandu.

नेपालमाथि दबाब : पैसा जुटाउने रणनीति

गुणराज लुइँटेल

काठमाडौं, ३ मंसिर : तिब्बती शरणार्थीलाई सुरक्षित प्रवेशाज्ञा नदिए नेपाललाई सहयोग रोक्ने अमेरिकी कंग्रेसम्यानको चेतावनीका पछाडि शरणार्थीका नाममा खुलेका संस्थाहरूले आर्थिक सहयोग जुटाउन गरिरहेको राजनीतिको हात रहेको टिप्पणी एक प्रभावशाली अमेरिकीले गरेका छन्।

अमेरिकी कंग्रेसम्यान फ्र्यांक उल्फले तिब्बती शरणार्थीलाई सुरक्षित प्रवेशाज्ञा नदिए नेपाललाई सहयोग रोक्ने चेतावनी दुई साताअघि दिएका थिए। भर्जिनियाबाट प्रतिनिधित्व गर्ने रिपब्लिकन प्रतिनिधि उल्फले भनेका थिए, 'उनीहरू (नेपाल सरकार) यो गर्न चाहँदैनन् भने हाम्रा मान्यतामा उनीहरू सहमत छैनन्। हाम्रा मान्यतामा उनीहरू सहमत छैनन् भने हामी हाम्रो डलर बाँड्न चाहँदैनौं।'

झन्डै २० वर्षदेखि 'तिब्बती शरणार्थीलाई सुरक्षित रूपमा नेपाल हुँदै भारतको धर्मशालादेखि अमेरिकासम्म पुऱ्याउन सहयोग पुऱ्याइरहेका ती अमेरिकीका अनुसार कंग्रेसम्यानको यस्तो भनाइ आउनु दुर्भाग्यपूर्ण हो। चीनसँगको सम्बन्धलाई समेत असर नपर्ने गरी नेपालले वर्षौंदेखि पुऱ्याउँदै आएको सहयोगलाई बेवास्ता गर्दै दिइएका यस्ता अभिव्यक्तिले तिब्बती शरणार्थीलाई कुनै सहयोग नपुग्ने उनी ठान्छन्।

'नेपालले वर्षौंदेखि शरणार्थीलाई सहयोग गर्दै आएको छ', सीमापार शरणार्थीका गतिविधि र त्यससम्बन्धी मुद्दामा अनुसन्धान र अभिलेखन गर्दै आएको गैरसरकारी संस्था हिमालयन एडका अन्तर्राष्ट्रिय निर्देशक एवं अमेरिकी कंग्रेसनल ककस वासिङ्टनका सल्लाहकार जेम्स रिनाल्डीले अन्नपूर्ण पोष्टसँग भने, 'केही तिब्बती सहयोग समूहले सहयोग जुटाउन (फन्ड रेजिङ) का लागि यस्तो रणनीति अपनाएका छन्।'

'शरणार्थीहरूले आन्दोलन गरिरँदा चीनको दबाबका कारण नेपाल सरकारले थप सुरक्षाकर्मी परिचालन गर्नुपर्ने हुन्छ। त्यसैलाई देखाएर सहयोग जुटाउने काम हुन्छ।'

—जेम्स रिनाल्डी

सल्लाहकार, अमेरिकी कंग्रेसनल ककस वासिङ्टन

उनी नेपालले शरणार्थीका लागि बाटो दिइरहेको र तिनलाई संयुक्त राष्ट्रसंघीय शरणार्थी उच्चायोग (यूएनएचसीआर) सम्म पुग्न सहजीकरण गर्दागर्दै पनि सहयोग नगरेको भनी अनावश्यकरूपमा काठमाडौंमा शरणार्थी आन्दोलन चर्काउँदा नेपाललाई थप असजिलो पर्ने ठान्छन्। 'शरणार्थीहरूले आन्दोलन गरिरँदा चीनको दबाबका कारण नेपाल सरकारले थप सुरक्षाकर्मी परिचालन गर्नुपर्ने हुन्छ। त्यसैलाई देखाएर सहयोग जुटाउने काम हुन्छ', रिनाल्डी भन्छन्।

उनका अनुसार पाँचछ वर्षयता शरणार्थीका नाममा आउने सहयोग निकै घटेको छ तर शरणार्थी सहयोगका नाममा खुलेका संस्थाको खर्च भने निकै बढेको छ। 'यसले यो मुलुकमा ठूलो क्षति पुऱ्याएको छ', उनले भने, 'यस मामलामा तिब्बती समूहहरू गलत छन् तर नेपालले धेरै राम्रो काम गरेको छ।'

उसो भए अमेरिकाको विदेशी सहायता-सम्बन्धी हाउस एप्रोप्रिएसन कमिटीका सदस्य उल्फले नेपाललाई सहयोग रोक्ने धम्की किन दिए त? रिनाल्डीले भने, 'नेपाललाई धेरै अप्ठ्यारो छ। अर्कोथरीको आवाज चर्को हुनु नै समस्याको कारण हो।'

कंग्रेसम्यानहरूले तिब्बती शरणार्थीहरूलाई सुरक्षित बाटो प्रदान गर्न यूएनएचसीआर र पश्चिमी देशहरूसँग नेपालले 'भद्र सम्झौता' (जेन्टलम्यान्स एग्रिमेन्ट) गरेको बताउँदै आएका छन्। त्यस सम्झौताअनुसार यूएनएचसीआरले नयाँ शरणार्थीलाई भारतसम्म लैजाने काम गर्छ।

रिनाल्डीका अनुसार यस्तो कुनै भद्र सम्झौता नेपालले गरेको छैन। नेपालको तिब्बतसँगको शताब्दीऔँ लामो सम्बन्धका कारण मानवीय हिसाबले मात्रै सहयोग गर्दै आएको हो। यसमा नेपाललाई अनावश्यक दबाब दिने हो भने उसलाई चीनको पनि उत्तिकै दबाब हुन्छ, जुन शरणार्थीहरूकै निम्ति घातक हुन जान्छ।

'चीनले नेपालबाहिरका समूहहरूको प्रभाव रहेको बताउने गरेको छ', रिनाल्डीले भने, 'दुःखका साथ भन्नुपर्छ, चीन सही छ, तिब्बती समूहहरूले नेपाललाई प्रभाव पारिरहेका छन् र तिनीहरूमाथि दमन गर्न नेपाललाई बाध्य पारिरहेका छन्। प्रत्येक पटक तिब्बती समूहहरूले भन्छन्– चीनले नेपाललाई दबाब दिने गरेको छ।'

अमेरिकाले पनि एक चीन नीति नै अख्तियार गरेको छ। नेपालका प्रत्येक सरकारले एक चीन नीति दोहोऱ्याउँदै आश्वस्त पार्ने गरेका छन्।

रिनाल्डी भन्छन्, 'नेपाललाई अरू दबाब दिने हो भने सीमा क्षेत्रमा नेपालको काम अरू कठिन हुनेछ। नेपालले विद्यमान परिस्थितिमा तिब्बती शरणार्थी मामिलामा सकेसम्म राम्रो काम गरेको छ। नेपालले थप काम गर्न सक्छ र गर्नु पनि पर्छ तर हामीलाई थाहा छ, उनीहरू दबाबमा छन्। फ्र्यांक उल्फले सीमा नाघेर अभिव्यक्ति दिएका छन्।'

Article from Annapurna Post given during "Gentleman's Agreement" controversy.

Arrested Tibetan nuns demonstrating inside detention facility, 2011.

CTA Presentation.

Lobsang Sangye being forced to wear a San Francisco Giants hat, 2014.

His Holiness, the XIV Dalai Lama, 2015.

CHAPTER 8

BLAME IT ON THE MIST

You could see them from the city. They called to you, just out of reach: fields of terraced barley bathing in the moisture of rising ether. Spring had returned to the foothills of Nepal, and with it, the morning mist.

I was edgy and impatient. The sight of the hills intoxicated and lured, and the thought of another day spent brooding and rudderless in a squalid downtown café filled me with memories of wasted efforts and lost opportunities.

A pot of masala tea arrived to break my numb half-watch of newly arriving tourists chattering by our window. In a few weeks, they would be driving me mad with their holidaying neediness, but for now, it was good to see them again – it had been a long winter.

We'd had no word of any Tibetan movements for weeks, and with no real agenda, we were left to wallow in the toss of bad idea and discounted rumour. Each day, Ramesh and I sat at the same table and created options. Each day, we left undecided.

An hour passed before a story we'd heard earlier in the week returned to the conversation. It was just another rumour, but we couldn't seem to clear it from our thinking this time around. The audacity of the account was so disarming that we found ourselves unable to consider all else. Yes, it could be done, but would they dare? Unbelievable – those damn arrogant bastards.

Ramesh began to intensify the conversation with animated talk of logistics and possibilities. This particular rumour would not be discounted like the others – not this morning.

Months ago, talk had surfaced that for the first time Chinese agents were travelling deep into Nepalese territory for the purpose of corralling and forcibly repatriating any undocumented Tibetans who had the misfortune of being captured by bribable local policemen. Once back over the border in Tibet, the Chinese would beat, imprison or run over the ankles of the runaway Tibetans with a truck to prevent them from trying such a stunt again.

Ramesh and I had no idea if the accounts were true or how to go about documenting such a thing, but if someone were to verify the presence of Chinese agents snooping around unauthorised deep in Nepal, it would be a big prize for the Tibet Movement, and would bolster the claims being made in Washington of increased Chinese influence on the Government of Nepal. Without any technical support or resources, our chances of proving such stories were remote; but for now, it didn't matter. Any rumour that led to a good road trip would qualify at this point.

Our minds were made up. A dismissive shuffle of cup and chair announced our hasty departure, and I meet Ramesh's fatigued Toyota in an adjacent alley a moment later.

"You sure we want to take this?" Not the question I'd hoped to be asking this morning, as doors creaked open and weary suspension slowly caved under our weight.

Ramesh offered silence in response – he does this occasionally. I'd insulted him again. *Apologise, breathe; let it go,* I thought, in fear of ruining the moment. We were leaving Kathmandu and heading north, that was all that mattered – north to fresh air, north towards the Tibetan border, into the mist.

The very fact that we were getting out of the city seemed purpose enough for the time being, and even Kathmandu's rancid atmosphere smelled of possibility, now that we were finally hitting the road with a sense of mission. But a few things needed to be determined or this whole adventure would turn out to be just another nice drive in the countryside. How in the world were we going to approach this? How would we be able to verify any Chinese activity, much less active evidence of Tibetan repatriation?

Eventually, we agreed to spend the bulk of our time gathering whatever information we could from the corrupt and suspect Nepalese police post in the riverside village of Barabise near the Tibetan border – an easy four-hour drive from our abandoned teapot. It had starred prominently in our rumour, and was the place where we would most likely find something useful. We would ask a few questions, sneak a few covert photos and perhaps learn something about the nature and frequency of the rumoured Chinese incursions in the process. If all went according to plan, we'd be back in Kathmandu drowning in cheap cocktails by mid-evening. It seemed simple and clear, as half-baked ideas go, and we made our way along Kathmandu's ring road towards the edge of town with the feeling that we just might pull this thing off. Visions of being a hero to the Tibetan people, addressing a congressional hearing and having official people call me "Mr Rinaldi" floated through my head as Kathmandu's haze faded in the distance. But first, we had to make it to Barabise, an eventuality not guaranteed.

Out of Kathmandu the Kodari highway, Nepal's main artery of commerce with China and our chosen thoroughfare, begins its meandering course through the central foothills. Serpentine, unmaintained and often less than one lane in width, our pace and passage along this route were dictated by lines of massive Indian-built Tata long-haul trucks that repeatedly scraped hillside boulders into pavement obstacles with their elephantine ploddings. Fleets of local buses, filled to over-capacity and rocking with uncertainty from roofs teeming with dozens of passengers clinging to every possible handhold, vied for position with gravel trucks that strained under loads of dripping rock, piled high and topped with families trying to get to the next village. Early on, our side-mirror was sacrificed to one of these gravel behemoths as a penalty for passing too closely.

"You're out of practice, friend," I said, half-laughing, as I watch Ramesh lament the loss of yet another piece of his Toyota to the road gods.

Not one moment of relaxation was allowed while driving the Kodari, not one moment's distraction. Hyper-vigilance was the only thing that increased the odds of a successful journey. The rest was in the hands of the deities one chose to invoke first thing in the morning.

Ramesh and I welcomed the end of our first hour of driving by gently coasting past a mound of undefined moist garbage and over sheaves of wheat purposefully laid flat across our path in anticipation of a free threshing from our tyres. Slowing to a crawl for a mid-street Communist youth rally near Banepa caused us to question our chances, and we wondered if this was to be our pattern for the rest of the trip. Climbing up and out of the Kathmandu valley, we traversed cliff-faced tracks barely one vehicle's width, honking violently as we approached each blind corner. The smell of burning brake shoes was our constant companion as we plunged from cliff side to river valley, the little Toyota shuddering almost sideways as we bounced through countless stretches of potholes and savaged pavement.

An eternity later, after the morning mist that had started this whole thing had long abandoned us to the heat of the day, we made a big right turn and headed over the Bhote Koshi river bridge. On the other side lay Barabise and our goal – four hours and just seventy miles from where we had begun.

So far, this had not turned out to be the liberating and joyously jaunty road trip that I'd envisioned, and as we rolled the old Toyota to a stop and exited, stretching, an unexplained foreboding began to dominate my mood. We had fought hard to make it this far. Taking to the streets of Barabise on foot, I was hit with the feeling that there was more to come.

Difficult journey or not, I needed this trip. After a few years of "monitoring" refugee conditions for the ICT and photographing their plight in every imaginable configuration, this was a rare chance to achieve something significant and potentially game-changing – some red meat.

"There it is." Ramesh pointed to an official, rather mildewed-looking structure a few hundred yards ahead.

Barabise had struck me as a charmless, unfriendly town during past visits, and as Ramesh and I walked its streets I found no evidence of any redemptive qualities that would now raise it in my esteem. As we approached an iron entry gate, a cold blue sign offering no welcome for road-frazzled travellers shouted its warning for all to see. Just for luck, I give it a light pat on the "Municipal Police Post, Barabise" portion, and gingerly walk past its concrete moorings.

The police at Barabise were infamous. Constables stationed here were known to be opportunistic profiteers, and the accounts of their brutality were no rumours. Oddly, we entered their lair unmolested and this freshened our confidence – a bad read. Instantly, we picked up the sound of boot-scuffed bare concrete floors amplifying an authoritative slam of a metal desk drawer and were aware of deliberate steps being taken in our direction.

"What are you doing here?"

The emphatically spoken Nepali came from behind, and we turned to greet two business-minded constables in the process of raising their antiquated but unmistakable Sterling police carbines into firing position. The commanding staccato in their voices rendered us breathless and immobile. This was not a good start.

Some preliminary calming words that passed through a not-so-calm Ramesh were returned with shouts. From what little I gathered from the exchange, it sounded as though Ramesh was struggling considerably in his attempt to massage our difficult situation into something resembling détente.

Eventually, gun barrels lowered and wary introductions followed – handshakes were not offered. Like an idiot, I plunged immediately into questions about the rumour we'd heard: *Do the Chinese come here? Do you give them Tibetans? How much do they pay?* The word "Tibet" seemed to trigger something in the constables, and a cold silence entered the room. More chairs shuffled, more footsteps.

It was a bad idea – I should have thought this out more thoroughly. I'd tipped our hand, and now our presence was beginning to draw more widespread attention.

"This does not happen. Who told you to come here?" An angry man approached with all the markings of a superior officer. His suspicious eyes led to wary movements, and the air began to thicken with tension and testosterone.

Certain now that we had gone too far, I felt a burst of fear shoot through my body. We were on the verge of provoking perhaps those very officers who had turned over captured Tibetans to a painful Chinese fate for no more than a few rupees and some cheap whisky, and I had completely forgotten the hidden camera mounted in my shirt pocket. It would give these crooked cops more than enough excuses to detain us in a dank cell, perhaps indefinitely, if discovered. Local police acted with impunity at these remote posts. They had been known to throw foreigners into jail for no reason, without food and water, until the mood hit that they should notify someone in Kathmandu. That would be bad enough, but there was something else. My small act of subterfuge represented more, much more. It would put me in the major leagues. To these constables, it was espionage and we could be jailed as spies or worse: beatings, deportation, international scandal. And my, wouldn't the US embassy be pleased by all of this? I needed to pivot, and pivot fast.

"No, no, no, *maph garnus* (sorry). I was looking for my Chinese friend, nothing else. He left Dolakha yesterday and was coming this way. Chinese:

you know, red hair, glasses. Have you seen him?" I threw out this opening gambit.

"...and he might be lost, carrying lots of hashish, by the way." Oops.

"You will go to jail for hashish in Nepal," the commandant of the group belted out.

"Not me, *saathi. Maph garnus.* No hash for me. Find him and tell him I went to Kathmandu, OK? *Jaani ho.* Bye. That's right, Chinese...red hair..."

It took a painstaking amount of artifice to appear casual as we strolled out of the facility that day. I turned to Ramesh, who now seemed to be looking in all possible directions at once, and offered my fool's opinion.

"Well, that was worthless," I said once out of official earshot. "Worthless and scary."

"Jim *Dai*, can we go back to Kathmandu now?" Ramesh's voice told me that he had seen enough for one day. He hadn't bargained on this type of confrontation and was probably wondering about my sanity, but I could offer him no words of comfort.

It was not time to go home, though, not yet. I was full of myself and feeling that manufactured type of invincible feeling that one feels after surviving a dangerous encounter, and I wanted to try my luck again. More importantly, the idea that Chinese agents could enter deep into Nepal and get away with grabbing Tibetan detainees from another nation's sovereign soil didn't sit well with me. I was determined to find some evidence of this practice. Surviving that encounter left me wallowing in self-righteousness, and I was now convinced that the Chinese were in Nepal and up to no good.

"Ramesh, I don't want to waste the trip. Let's head up to the border crossing and see what we can find."

Once again silent, Ramesh kept his gaze glued to the ground. He knew that if we tried to pull our little Barabise stunt up at the Tibetan border in front of internationally trained security forces, we could be in real danger – lethal danger.

A handful of terse words passed, but after a few moments of persuasion and dirt-kicking, Ramesh, a cautious and thoroughly calculating Nepali from an old and legendary warrior caste, gave in to the stupid foreigner.

"*Dai*, you want this. OK, but no trouble," he said. His driver's-side door closed with a decided tone. He was disgusted, and it would be an hour before Ramesh uttered another word.

I hated seeing him this way and it was my fault. It had been a tough couple of minutes, and the entire exchange had been uncomfortable. Underneath Ramesh's slight stature and politely submissive tone lurked the quick temper of a pissed-off tiger, and I had nearly provoked him towards something ancestral. I felt like a cheap tourist for imposing my travel plans on him, and I vowed to make it up to him someday. But for now we just needed to leave, and I silently prayed that our car would find a working gear that facilitated this need. Moments later, with no more guns pointing our way and Barabise successfully fled, the Kodari's jarring impassibility greeted us again like a lost friend. We were off, northward, to the Tibetan border.

The little Toyota protested in pain after failing to miss a large pothole just beyond the lowered gates of a Nepal army roadblock. We needed to stop and locate the trouble, but security detachments and check-posts were now emerging every few kilometres, and the simple act of stopping our car to inspect possible damage would draw unwanted scrutiny. The roads were lined with too many patrols, containing too many fingers, too close to triggers. The scraping sound that was now emanating from our right front tyre would just have to be ignored. The only decision made was to speed up.

Just ahead, tightly gripping the wheel of a massive Tata overland freight hauler, exhaustion personified was now betting his schedule on quickly manoeuvring around a herd of goats that was dead set against leaving the centre of the road. Just beyond, Nepal customs and the Tibetan border awaited the delivery of his shipment. Impatient to hand off his load to the next driver, he could almost taste the well-earned glass of Chinese beer that would soon sit cold in his hands. A small patch of muddy pavement had other ideas.

"He's not going to make it." Ramesh had a tone of resignation in this, but it was good to hear him talk again and I anointed myself forgiven.

Goats, being smart, elected to monopolise the road nearer the hillside. The driver, being in a hurry, made his move along the road's cliff-side edge and overcompensated with panic as fragile road fringe began to give way under the weight of truck and cargo.

"Other side, you watch," said Ramesh, confident in his physics.

Truck and a now fully alert driver swerved wildly away from the cliff and, mercifully, killed no humans or livestock as they landed nose-first in a hillside ditch. These type of scenes always seem to mandate chicken feathers flying in all directions – big, messy rural truck crashes invoke such things. But no feathers were present, just mud – mud and goats, laughing goats.

This was going to take a while to resolve.

At least we weren't the only ones having a bad day, I thought as I picked at a patch of rotten door upholstery and tried to get comfortable in anticipation of a long wait.

I was good at this – finally good at *something* in Nepal. Being from southern California, I would show these locals how it was done. Watch me: *This* is how you sit in a traffic jam.

Twenty minutes passed, then thirty. Nothing was going to get this damn truck out of the ditch. And with just a few kilometres to go, it was beginning to look as though we would have to turn back. The afternoon was approaching and our plans for the border, such as they were, began to slip away. Ramesh and I discussed paring down our agenda to what we thought we could reasonably finish before dark, should we find ourselves freed in the next hour. It had to be a one-shot effort – staying the night at the border would be too dangerous. Thinking and waiting...all the time in the world; plenty of time to mentally replay our disastrous visit to the Barabise police station just an hour before, and to wallow in the homesickness induced by being stuck in traffic.

This entire thing is absurd, I thought, taking up the conversation in a subconscious self-scolding. *Back in the States you were frustrated, sure, but you still made a decent living. Now look at you: hobbling towards a foreign border 9,000 miles from home and throwing yourself into danger for people who don't even know you exist. You almost got yourself arrested as a spy back there in Barabise, for Christ's sake. What are you trying to prove?*

My doubts were winning and would not back down. What was I doing here? Was I taking some life-changing heroic path that would save Tibetans, or was this just one big, extended yuppie holiday? I had given up my career and my life seeking self-awareness and humility along this path, but I wasn't feeling more enlightened and didn't appear to be learning anything – just the opposite. Rather than give in to the journey and accept my new reality, I would often catch myself slipping back into old habits and defences: purposefully asserting my American obnoxiousness whenever I could in order to find some benchmark from my past that would give me an identity, and a bit of relief, from this frighteningly unfamiliar Nepali way of life. If

I was learning anything, it was how to retreat back into my cultural comfort zone.

And who really cared that I was here trying to help Tibetans anyway? My doubts mounted and were affirmed in the accumulating cacophony of automobile horns outside my window. I didn't have the answers, but that didn't stop the questions coming, and it looked like there would be no relief and no escape from my thoughts for some time, thanks to this tired freight driver and his bad judgement.

The big Indian truck had managed to negotiate an impossibly perpendicular orientation to the road during one of the driver's many futile attempts to free it, but now he seemed determined to make another attempt as scores of onlookers were enlisted to help push. Our conga-line of impatient drivers watched in earnest as one of India's largest feats of overland transport engineering finally rocked out of the mire and back onto the pavement. Laughter and handshakes were evenly distributed among the small contingent of mud-covered locals who stood smiling by the side of the ditch as they waved traffic through.

Clear road opened before us and we were on our way at last. We would soon be at Nepal's contentious border with Tibet, and with ample, clear daylight to spare. The day's frustrations had sapped our energy and waiting interminably for the driver to free the truck had only added to our souring mood, but at least we could console ourselves with the fact that we were finally moving again – dispute between goat, mud and Tata soon to be handily in our rearview mirror.

It would be the only time in my life when I would come to regret being free from a traffic jam.

I remembered Kodari as a border settlement of odiferous bustle and commerce. None of that had changed since my last visit. On the far north end of town, the Chinese-built "Friendship Bridge" still spanned the gorge high over the Bhote Kosi river and linked Nepal to Tibet and mainland China. On this day, three maroon robe-clad Buddhist monks stood in front of the gates to the bridge, having a colourful exchange with a Nepali border policeman. All seemed normal – almost.

I couldn't help but notice that something was wrong with a few of our old friends. They were among the many operators of numerous tea shops along the last few hundred metres of Nepali territory leading up to the Friendship Bridge. In the past, we would sit, laugh and talk about Tibetan movements with these people. Not anymore, apparently. When we stopped to chat at a favourite stall, my friendly questioning was met with an unusually curt evasiveness. What was up? Peering from the doorway, I noticed a handful of plain-clothed Chinese agents patrolling the street, and I caught myself nodding with realisation. There was truth to the rumour. From what we were observing, the Chinese seemed to be moving freely in Nepal and creating a lot of tension for the local merchants. Did this have to do with Tibetans? I needed to keep my questions to myself for the time being – I was putting this poor shop owner at risk.

He checked his view of the street before confirming my suspicions. "No Tibet," was all he said – it was all he needed to say.

It wasn't long before a few of those on patrol began taking an interest in my decidedly foreign presence. The glance of one individual my way displayed a level of seriousness I hadn't previously experienced in this part of the world, and the shop grew tense as he neared the door. This needed to be diffused somehow, and so without giving Mr Serious a chance to enter the tea shop, I approached him with a carefree smile and offered a poorly pronounced *Namaste* for a greeting. Ramesh, familiar with this ploy, followed immediately: Map in hand, he proceeded to enquire as to the best way to reach the hot springs above Tatopani. All of this was met with a scowling silence, save for a low mumble that was barely audible as our new acquaintance turned from the tea house and offered one last cold stare in our direction. We smiled and waved in return, and then laughed, ordered a plate of Ramen noodles and sat quietly until the curious bad guy moved on. The "dumb tourist" routine: works every time.

"This is getting creepy," I whispered, uncomfortable with the idea that those serious gazes were just outside and might be tipping us off to a more direct encounter to come. "We need to keep moving. Ramesh, let's get out of here and walk around on the bridge."

The Friendship Bridge, China's gift of goodwill and trade for the people of Nepal, was more than likely constructed as a means of ensuring quick and easy access to the Indian subcontinent by Chinese military forces, should the need arise. Walking out mid-span – exactly halfway between Nepal and China – I gently confirmed that the mini hidden camera that was peering out through a hole in my shirt pocket was running and in fine form. I made a couple of 360-degree turns to give it a full panoramic view, and was instantly surrounded by a squad of Jackie Chans who approached, brushed within inches and never made eye contact. Two young Nepali boys, who looked to be fully bribed thugs-in-training, swept by as well. Finally, a big bald mainland Chinese guy who didn't seem to be taking too well to the Himalayan air passed a few metres from our position, and fixed his eyes like a laser on my front pocket. Ramesh hadn't figured it out yet, but a quick mental inventory brought me to the conclusion that this was most definitely a tight spot. We were being encircled by Chinese agents in the middle of diplomatic no-man's land, and were about to be caught with a fully functioning spy camera purring away from an intentionally concealed location inside my pocket. Déjà vu, Barabise style.

"Ramesh, the key to this thing is that these secret guys always want to get one good look at you. If they come by twice, it's time to get off the bridge. That will have to be for your future reference since we're well past that point here, so let's go."

But the bald man appeared to find motive in our retreat and seemed to be gaining ground as he followed us back into Kodari. Did he notice my filming? He was closing, fast. I had to do something. I kept a decoy disposable yellow Kodak tourist camera for emergency situations that resembled the one we were in now. Removing it from my pocket, I turned on my pursuer just as his hand was reaching for my shoulder.

"*Nie hao.* Can I take your picture? See? Easy, I'll take your picture, OK?"

Caught off guard, the big guy fumbled for a response. "No, no. Picture not allowed. No camera," he said, or something to that effect.

Funny...if I had asked a Nepalese border policeman, *in whose country we were standing at that moment*, if we could take pictures, he probably would have held the camera for a group photo and bought the first round of whisky after the deed was done. Who did this guy think he was, standing in his arrogance and giving orders in someone else's country?

Baldy seemed to sense the situation and he backed off a bit, giving me and Ramesh some time and space to retreat deeper into Kodari. Our relief was short-lived.

"Jim *Dai,* Chinese man following again. We go back home now. Bad Nepali boys coming too – look."

There was noticeable fear in Ramesh's voice. I began to worry a bit as well, since Ramesh had been driving his Toyota all day like a monkey on acid and didn't appear to be afraid of anything – at least not on this planet.

But he was right: people were converging on our position, quickly. New faces were in the mix now, ones I hadn't seen on the bridge – sinister-looking faces. Being caught would mean arrest, detention and whatever else these guys could think of.

"OK, we can go, but let me see if I can get a few quick pictures of these Tibetans arriving at the Nepal immigration office. Maybe we'll get something useful. Just a few seconds more. I'll hurry, Ramesh. Get the car ready – trust me."

The Nepal Immigration Office was just a few feet away, and I was pushing hard to catch something of substance on film so I wouldn't have to label the entire trip as a failure. But having struck out earlier at Barabise and now, having potentially stirred up a hornets' nest here at the Tibetan border, I wondered if this exceptionally ill-timed choice was a good idea. I made a dash for the door: Good judgement be damned, I thought – I wasn't using it anyway.

That was my problem, unfortunately, as once again different forces took control – irrational, blinding forces. I was determined to be a big shot. In my mind, I had harboured fantasies of capturing something important on film that would not only prove once and for all how poorly the Tibetans were treated at the hands of the Chinese, but also result in my being summarily lauded as a hero to the Tibetan people. It was all planned quite thoroughly, down to the last delusion, as I burst through the door of the immigration facility and looked for my big chance at the brass ring.

"God, what kind of place is this?"

My heart sank and the deflation quickly brought me back to earth as I surveyed the almost meditative serenity of an office doing its business as usual. Not one activity, event, tableau or sneeze stood out above the numbing monotony of this room filled with Nepalese bureaucracy, and I lamented the realisation that photographing the mere stamping of travel permits would not make me a hero. I had gambled precious seconds off our escape for the sake of my ego, and now our safety was in jeopardy. Still, maddeningly, I felt compelled to find something, anything of substance, and I ran deeper into the room – I couldn't let it go.

Breathing rapidly and out of time, I pushed my way behind the main counter to photograph a Tibetan who had turned animated and was screaming at the clerk about some issue. Through the camera lens, I caught a glimpse of a few individuals running past the doorway, and within moments the back of my head felt a jarring, blunt force and began to throb with an intense, searing pain. Instantly, my perception of the counter began to close in with a white haze and I felt my mouth hang open and my feet being lifted off the floor. I was dragged for a few moments and flung into a metal chair: My bad day was up to bat again, and was now determined to win.

What was going on? Why was I in this room?

"*Namaste*. I'm a foreigner. Did I do something wrong?"

"Who tell you come here?" asked a rather authoritative and not Nepalese voice that I determined came from no particular direction.

The new room I found myself in seemed to be rotating and resetting and rotating again. My right eye was beginning to shut down from the pain. This was not good. The sounds of rapid footfalls filled the tiny room, and more people seemed to enter. But nothing was certain; I was not processing clearly – not myself. The only thing I could think of doing was to hold out my yellow decoy Kodak camera to the first face that came into focus. Quick fingers greedily snatched my offering and I received another strike to the head for the gesture.

Swallowing too much now, metallic taste – blood. Breath was catching in my chest – breathing bubbles.

More questions. None registered with me and I gave no answers. The blows started to arrive with more regularity, and I began to realise that these were not Nepalese police. I was in deep shit here. My "dumb tourist" routine was not going to get me out of this one – they'd already drawn blood, and were not hesitating to draw more. I lost track of time and couldn't seem to remember why I'd come here in the first place – nothing I could do anymore, nothing I could say. A vague playground memory from my childhood entered and quickly exited my thoughts.

My earlier failure at the Barabise police post was meant as a warning I should have heeded. There, I had walked directly and confidently into a coven of corrupt constables, demanded information on Tibetan conditions and nearly been imprisoned as a spy. I should not have tried my luck again, not here, not with the Chinese. Now it was too late.

Everyone was shouting now, everyone was hitting. This was it. It looked like I would not be the big shot. Probably wouldn't be missed much either. Bad choice, bad luck. Strong arms hoisted me to my feet. I mentally reviewed every part of my body: nose, hands, old scars, shoulders – everything. I wanted to remember myself, take one last inventory. Affirm that I left this world all in one piece – that I existed.

Abruptly, the questions stopped and the beating ceased. All quiet now. No more shouting. I knew from the movies that this was when the pistol came out and the whole thing was done. *Fine,* I thought, *I suppose I'm as ready as I'll ever be – just don't miss, you Chinese piece of shit, or whoever the hell you are. Get it over with and do it right.*

The group closed in and I braced myself for the inevitable. I took one last blow to the head for good measure and suddenly felt myself being dragged across the room and unceremoniously thrown onto a pile of garbage just outside the building.

What's this? I'm out? That's it?

Unable to make sense of what had just happened and not particularly in the mood to return to the room and thank my new friends for the wonderful time, I rose to my feet and began shuffling towards the sounds of traffic. I *was* out – somehow – of that terrible place. Eyes refusing to focus, and shaking with fear, I made my way through an unfamiliar environment. Almost immediately, the terror that had consumed me began to give way to fatigue: a profoundly unfamiliar type of fatigue. I wanted to fall asleep. I absolutely needed to fall asleep. Using another garbage pile for a pillow, I stretched out and relaxed. Good. I was comfortable now, in fact more comfortable than I'd ever felt.

I'll just lie here for a bit.

Why does this feel so odd? Something's not right. I'm not going to get up from this place, am I?

A flashing image from a Jack London story hit me like a cattle prod and I shook off a bit of delirium and rose to my feet again – I needed to get moving.

A reflection of the setting sun offered no help and it hit me directly in my one good eye as I picked my way through the refuse, squinting, until I found the main road and my patiently waiting driver.

"*Dai,* you are bleeding," Ramesh said in a tone that suggested I'd merely cut myself shaving.

"Yeah, yeah, I know. That Chinese guy got me pretty good in the nose – I think he used his shoe. By the way, you're right, we need to go."

"No, *Dai*, look at your shirt," he said, pointing to my collar, which was soaked in blood.

Somewhere along the line, I'd been hit on the back of the head with a fairly substantial piece of equipment. Perhaps it was that first strike at the immigration counter, or just prior to my ejection; there were more than a few blows and I was still too foggy to remember.

Ramesh dumped a pair of used brake shoes out of a rag he'd found in the trunk of his car, and held the cloth to the open wound, which was still bleeding warm life from my scalp. It was an oddly comfortable, almost womb-like warmth, and I would have gladly succumbed to it just a few moments prior. But now it just needed to stop or I'd be in a different kind of deep shit.

I was safe now and under Ramesh's watch. With time to gather my bearings, my sense of the big picture was starting to return. Thoughts were coming back, frustrating thoughts. This was now the second time I'd been beaten senseless in the last few months, damn it. What was Nepal trying to tell me?

Chapter 9

To Lhasa, for a Friend

During one of my restive periods in San Diego I had become quite friendly with Kelsang, one of the few Tibetans in San Diego at the time, who took great joy in ridiculing my attempts at spoken Ü-Tsang Tibetan. He mentioned that at one time he was a translator for the Dalai Lama, but jumped at the chance to come to America when the opportunity presented itself. He had a sister named Pema who lived in Lhasa, and he had lost touch with her and had not heard a word about her whereabouts or condition in 30 years. I told him I planned to go to Lhasa on my upcoming trip, and that I'd be happy to see what I could find out. He scribbled down her full name and the neighbourhood in Lhasa where she lived, and that was that. Kelsang never mentioned it again.

I wanted to go to Lhasa to see what kind of trouble I could get into. I was going to be like Blake Kerr and John Ackerly, standing in the breech, documenting atrocities and saving lives, by golly. Furthermore, I promised myself that I was not going to take any shit from any repressive Chinese policeman or agent, thank you.

Back in 1999, the world had very little video documentation of contemporary conditions in Lhasa, and I thought it my duty to provide an update. I carried an eight-millimetre video camera that was about half the size of a loaf of bread, in an over-sized fanny pack with a removable flap at one end. My thought was to turn on the camera inside the pack, drop the flap and surreptitiously film all things relevant and political in Lhasa. While I was filming, I would deploy a decoy: my usual yellow, single-use, disposable Kodak camera that I would overtly and theatrically use in public in the hope of confiscation. My theory was that if a cop came after my camera, I would yell a bit and surrender the Kodak while the video was still humming along undetected. Yes, this was very dumb.

In Kathmandu, I practised walking up and down the streets of Thamel, turning the camera on and off in the pack and raising and lowering the secret flap.

"Hey, you got a camera in there?" a street kid chirped. Not good.

It's difficult to book an overland trip to Tibet. It has always been this way, and the process will probably continue to frustrate travellers long into the future. The Chinese are always either closing the border to tourists for one neurotic reason or another, or opening the border but changing the visa and travel permit requirements in order to include yet another meaningless and byzantine hurdle. Our particular package of annoyance stipulated that our travel permit must have five individual travellers listed, and that they must be escorted by a Chinese guide and a Chinese driver.

The courtyard of the Kathmandu Guesthouse is famous for the grand billboard where all travellers and trekkers who are seeking anything can post their requests and leave contact information. I was looking for four more people who wanted to go to Tibet in order to fill out my travel permit, so I posted a notice on the board. Within a few days, a very young and very rich Swiss couple joined in, as well as a cranky German girl with a crew-cut and a Japanese guy who spoke no English and seemed to drift in and out of consciousness from time to time. Perfect! We were ready to go. We would be the first car allowed into Tibet after the Chinese lifted their most recent border closure, which that time was due to the 40th anniversary of the March 10th, 1959, Tibetan uprising in Lhasa.

The plan was to take a Nepali bus to the Tibetan border at Kodari, cross the Friendship Bridge, meet our Chinese guide and driver just over the Tibetan border at Zhangmu and begin our journey to Lhasa. It was March 20th, 1999.

On a personal level, this trip was not the most enlightened of conceptions. I had been in Asia for about eight months at that point, and things were beginning to accumulate. For starters, my head injury was still giving me fits of pain. And a trip to the high-altitude Tibetan plateau – with no immediate means of descent should an altitude-related malady present itself – was probably foolish. Next, I was still considerably exhausted and emaciated from my vaccine-smuggling trip to India, and didn't possess the defenses to fight off a mosquito bite at that point, much less an aggressive Chinese official.

Our little tour bus waddled out of Thamel at eight a.m. Myself, the Japanese weirdo, the young Swiss couple and the spoiled German girl with the shaved head would make it to the Tibetan border in half a day – I would be at the Friendship Bridge once again.

The chaos and persistent, badgering danger of the Kodari Highway met me once more like a lost uncle begging for booze money. I tucked into my seat and prepared for its familiar, uncomfortable rhythms. Rolling past overturned Land Cruisers and local paper-making industriousness by the river's edge, it was a strangely peaceful journey, and all of us were caught up in its enchantments. We left a small village full from a lunch of *dal-bhaat* (lentils and rice), and were at the town's outskirts before we realised that we had forgotten our Japanese guy. An inordinate amount of debate took place before our driver felt compelled to swing his bus around and locate our lost charge.

By mid-afternoon, we had cleared what seemed like a dozen army check-posts, and were entering the border town of Tatopani. The pain in my head quickened as old memories and traumas began to resurface. I found the door of the immigration office intact, as it was during my last, very violent visit, and tried to pick out the exact garbage cluster onto which I was unceremoniously tossed after my beating a month before, but with no luck. It lived only in my clouded memories now.

The little Nepali tour bus stopped at the Tibetan border and would go no further. Our orders were to walk across the Friendship Bridge and meet our Tibetan guide on the Chinese side. Our guide's orders were for him to stick to us like glue and make sure we made no trouble during the next three days of travel to Lhasa. His name was Somdup.

All of us were now stuffed into a Land Cruiser, and we made our way the short distance to the Chinese immigration post near Zhangmu. After a few hours of ignoring screaming Chinese immigration officials who detained us for no appreciable reason, we were off and on our way. The Tibetan plateau was now ours to behold. It was upward and onward as our Land Cruiser wound along a gravel road past landslides and water erosion – this was the frontier: Road maintenance and road safety were low priorities.

By the time we reached our bunks at our lodge in the town of Nylam, my head was splitting with pain. *I cannot get altitude sickness here,* I thought, and feared dying before I could descend to a safe level. Diamox, traditionally a glaucoma medicine, had been proven to stop the onset of altitude sickness effectively. I had brought along a small cachet of the drug, and immediately popped two tablets into my mouth as I watched a grainy black-and-white kung fu movie on the lodge's dining-room video screen with a group of Tibetan guides. The idea of going to sleep and perhaps not waking up the next morning due to altitude sickness left me willing to burn the ears off of my movie compatriots with conversations that ran long into the night.

The next day, I was feeling much better and I spent the morning hours re-sewing the secret flap in my camera bag into a less noticeable configuration.

"Hey, you," Andrea, the German girl, said from the front seat of our Land Cruiser, which she'd been hogging all trip. "Going to take secret pictures, eh? Well, I will tell you now that most of my rucksack is full of chocolates that I am fully prepared to give to the Tibetan resistance when we arrive."

I needed to compartmentalise Andrea's chocolate revelation and put it on hold for future scrutiny, as uniformed security forces and an ominous-looking red-and-white gate rolled into view. It was checkpoint time. Police checkpoints were popping up with increasing frequency now that we were deeper into Tibet. Some waved us through immediately, others seized our passports and held on to them for hours with no apparent purpose. Checkpoints didn't even seem to need a physical presence. One surly Chinese cop in a convertible Jeep with a Tibetan prostitute – sporting the usual Kabuki white face and rosy-red rouge – demanded 700 yuan from us for no definable reason. He didn't give a hoot about tourists and their intentions as he made a deliberate show of fingering his Chinese copy of a Tokarev Soviet 9mm pistol. Those of us who were Caucasian and Land Cruiser-bound were incensed at this bold-faced display of frontier larceny. Oh, the injustice of it all! Somdup, having seen it all before, showed the Chinese cowboy that our papers were in order and we had a time schedule to keep, and that we'd given up most of our money at the last checkpoint – he let us pass. Perhaps the lure of the tragic caricature of beauty sitting by his side gave him just enough pause, just enough distraction.

A few days of checkpoints, hookers, dust and noodle soup later, we reached the long valley that held the city of Lhasa. Jutting high atop its promontory, the palace of the Dalai Lamas for centuries, the Potala was unmistakable and commanded attention. Seeing that grand edifice from miles away and for the first time made me impatient and I wanted to be at its doorstep immediately.

"Let's eat," said Somdup, as we approached the eastern edge of the city. If nothing else, this journey convinced me that Somdup was on the payroll of every noodle house from Kathmandu to Lhasa, and he was never going to miss an opportunity to collect a commission any time he could lure us into agreeing to stop. "Let's eat" became a trigger phrase for us that meant we would get fleeced if we agreed. Unfortunately for Somdup, we caught on to this scheme early on, as no human in his right mind would want to stop for noodles every 30 minutes, so we politely told him to shut the hell up as we gaped in awe at the massive expanse of the Potala, still miles away.

First impressions of Lhasa underwhelmed. At the far west end of the city stood an exceedingly unnecessary police checkpoint, where Chinese guards said and demanded little but froze our Land Cruiser into an interminable wait. We would be in their clutches for nearly an hour before anything resembling movement returned to our itinerary. It seemed a deliberate gesture designed to make visits to Lhasa difficult and inhospitable to foreigners venturing a try.

Chinese influences were gaping and ubiquitous. Most noticeable were the bold red and gold Chinese characters that were slapped arrogantly over Tibetan signs and architecture, and an odd type of ceramic tile square that seemed to coat the exterior of every other shop on every street, giving the look of hundreds of bathrooms that were somehow turned inside out and on display for all to see. But this was the newer, "modern" section of Lhasa and we wanted no part of it. Our goal was the classic grey stone buildings of the Tibetan old city.

Finally, we were dumped rather unceremoniously into the courtyard of the Yak Hotel and given strict orders not to leave town, break any rules or incite any Tibetan towards anything, and to meet back here in ten days for our transport to the airport. Somdup had been told by his Chinese handlers to escort us everywhere and report anything suspicious that any of his running-dog Western aliens might get into, and so, in typical Tibetan fashion, he promptly ignored his orders and left us all to fend for ourselves in Lhasa for the next ten days – glorious!

Immediately, I made a beeline for the Barkhor square, the spiritual and cultural hub of Lhasa. Essentially a large open-air market space, the Barkhor is built around the Jokhang Temple to the east end of the square. The Jokhang was encircled by a narrow lane filled with merchant stalls and crowds of slow, clockwise-walking Tibetans. Here, giggling girls and bullhorn-wielding Tibetan men pitched everything from shoes to false teeth in the hope of making a sale among the hordes of Tibetan pilgrims that made their way to this holy site from all corners of Tibet. I was eager to see the site where John Ackerly and Blake Kerr filmed Tibetans rioting and monks jumping down from balcony porticos back in 1987; I wanted to be where I thought the "action" would be.

Pilgrims who came to circumambulate the Jokhang Temple represented diverse groups: There were merchant women from Amdo with wide-brimmed white cowboy hats who walked with business-driven purpose; sharp-eyed city hustlers looking for their next mark; plain-clothed Chinese cops who may as well have been wearing a uniform as they all seemed to favour the same dark turtle-neck sweater and Western sports jacket; and tall, fierce Tibetans from Kham with their long black hair wound and braided with bright red yarn. All were unified, for whatever purpose, by this place. Those of particularly high devotion marked the distance around the Jokhang by falling headlong and prone to the ground, arms stretched forward, rising, walking forward the exact distance of their prostration and beginning the entire sequence again. Some had chosen to travel the entire distance from their village to Lhasa in this manner, and sported hard yak-leather mittens and knee pads to keep the flesh from wearing away on their over-taxed hands and knees.

This was to be my home for the next ten days, and I relished the thought of falling into the same repetitive walking rhythm with these Tibetans whom I admired so greatly. I would not see another person from our Land Cruiser group for the entire period. Later, tales would emerge of the Swiss couple sneaking out of town for a monastery visit, and Andrea being chased from the grounds of Lhasa's notorious Drapchi Prison; but I was content to walk, sit and talk with the Tibetans of the Barkhor. I wanted to feel their culture, wanted to know what made them tick. For me, it was of the utmost importance that I discover the collective mood of these people and their increasingly constricted way of life. No more news, no more Western propaganda about the Tibetan condition: just truth from the Tibetans themselves.

The Pentoc Guesthouse was a small backpackers' hotel, located a few hundred yards from the Jokhang. I managed to secure a closet-sized single room for a reasonable price when we arrived in Lhasa, and after a few days I was spreading out my maps and reading material on the small bed I'd been given when a knock came at my door.

"Japan guy is missing," said the familiar and always happy-looking Somdup as he entered my room. How he found me is anyone's guess, but it was good to see the face that always gave off good cheer, even when delivering bad news.

"We have to find him or we will be in big trouble with the police when we leave," he went on, trying to be officious.

This was a common occurrence for some odd reason. Lone Japanese tourists seemed to make a habit of disappearing without a trace into Tibet during those years. Somdup now risked going to jail, and all of us who remained present in the flesh could be detained until our escaped tour member was found. I took a bit of false comfort in the lack of worry Somdup seemed to exude, and let my concerns dissolve. To this day I don't know what became of our Japanese guy: he didn't come back with us.

"By the way, Somdup," I said, remembering my mission, "my Tibetan friend from San Diego gave me a name and a partial address for his sister here in Lhasa. He's had no word from her in 30 years, so I don't suppose this is worth anything really, but have a look."

"Jim, I know this place," Somdup beamed as he looked at the tiny slip of paper I'd just given him. "I will look around. But this kind of thing is very dangerous."

Over the next few days, I did my best to live as a Tibetan. Rising early, I'd down a thoroughly awful cup of the Pentoc's Nescafé instant coffee and head down the stairs and out to the Barkhor for my morning *kora*, or circumambulation around the Jokhang. Usually, it took just a few laps before the repetitive, devotional nature of each Tibetan footfall and the trance-like nature of their chanting took hold of my consciousness, leaving me wanting to do nothing more for the rest of my life than walk in clockwise circles with these people and in this city. We moved as one, as time and distance seemed to disappear. For hours, I continued on without interruption, save for the occasional avoidance of a sporadic Chinese cop deliberately and antagonistically walking through the crowd in the opposite direction. Here I was, in one of the most culturally repressed and tense cities in the world, and yet I had never known such personal peace of mind. It was impossible to get past the irony.

The evening market opened up at dusk and displayed an entirely new set of vendors and offerings. One could purchase a full-sized blue-and-white Tibetan ceremonial tent at a reasonable price, and I toyed with the idea of such a purchase; but just how such a massive canvas structure would fit in the baggage compartment of an Airbus 319 and the extra fees that process would incur gave me considerable pause, and I walked away tent-less. The prostrations remained the same during the evening hours, and I began to take notice of a more fervently devotional group crowding the front door of the Jokhang with their in-place kneeling, stretching and praying. Impossibly old women would bundle sprigs of juniper branches outside the temple, light them in brass censers, and chortle and tease each other as they watched the fragrant blue smoke rise skyward.

Wandering the Barkhor became my vocation and I was never late for work. I was entertaining ideas of dispatching daily e-mail reports from a terrace-level café that sat directly across the square from the notorious police station where a Tibetan monk had defiantly escaped Chinese capture after being badly burned. Ironically, the café near this volatile site had free and open internet access. Apparently, the forces of Chinese censorship had yet to understand the power of the internet, and for a brief period in 1999 a loophole existed. I did manage to send a few "live" reports to the San Diego Friends of Tibet, and thought the whole process to be a groundbreaking exercise in real-time journalism. But in reality, this just amused the faithful back home in the US, and the reports went nowhere.

A few days later, a familiar knock came once more at the door to my room.

"Jim, can we come in?" It was Somdup again, but why was he whispering?

He was escorting an elderly woman whom he led deferentially into my room. She sat delicately on the end of the bed.

"I found her," he said. For the first time since I'd known him, he was visibly nervous.

"Shit! This is Pema? Somdup, how in the hell did you...?" The words stuck in my throat. Somdup had found my friend's sister in a restricted and police-monitored city, and led her through the back alleyways of Lhasa to my room so she could hear word of a brother she had not seen for three decades; she did not even know whether he was alive or dead.

In reckless haste, I uncovered my video camera, switched it on and pointed it at the confused, frail Tibetan woman. I was able to mention that Kelsang wanted me to find her and tell her that he loved her very much. Somdup eased her confusion by telling her to talk into the machine, and that her words and the image would be sent back to her brother in America. For the next 20 minutes, she poured out her soul on camera to a brother on the other side of the world, while Somdup repeatedly left the room to check the reception area of the Pentoc for any signs of police activity.

Pema told of the difficulties their young nephew was having finding work and how he was forbidden to get any type of professional training. All Tibetans were feeling this very direct type of repression, and their frustrations were beginning to mount, she went on to say. Tears began to well in her eyes as she spoke of her chronic heart ailment and how she was going blind.

"My eyes are going but I still see my brother clearly," she told the camera lens in her now halting, emotional Tibetan.

Months later, after I had returned to San Diego, I triumphantly presented the video to Kelsang, who plugged it into his video player immediately and begged me to sit and watch with him. I expected questions and emotions to flow freely, but Kelsang simply sat in stony, stoic silence as the interview with his long-lost sister was played. In a matter of months, he would leave his American wife and head back to Tibet.

CHAPTER 10

LIVING IN A PIGEON COOP

There's a love/hate relationship that exists with those who joust with the *New York Times* crossword puzzle. By design, the puzzle creators increase the difficulty of the task as the week progresses. You can finish a Monday puzzle in minutes and feel like an intellectual hero, but by Friday – and especially Saturday – the damn thing is nearly impossible. I would spend an hour going through a Saturday puzzle and come away with nothing. Not one word, letter or idea on how to precede – a total blank.

*

Back in Kathmandu, a few hours was needed for me to visit the Japanese embassy and tell them that one of their citizens had disappeared in Tibet – they were not amused. I left their company after signing my name to a few cryptic documents and headed into the Kathmandu evening craving a beer and a shower. The trip to Lhasa had left me drained and confused. I imagined how wonderful it would have been to stay in the old Tibetan section at will – possibly indefinitely. I had prepared for a more militant atmosphere and was left entirely bewildered by the warmly welcoming sense of community I felt. There was a bit of a hip village vibe about the Barkhor area that seemed to thoroughly cloak the deeper resentments and repression that had been so well documented. It was oddly diverse and internationally flavoured – I didn't know what to make of it. The Chinese hadn't quite figured out what to do with the place either, so they left it relatively alone for the most part. All of that would soon change. It would have been nice to have kept an apartment in Lhasa, and I was angry at the realisation that this would never happen.

I boarded the plane for Kathmandu and I was actually looking forward to its filth, its warmth and the increased oxygen, one last time. In the days that followed, I managed to drop by the clinic and lend a hand, from time to time, but the refugee season was past its prime by late spring and there just wasn't much going on at the facility. Eventually, I bid goodbye to my friends Tsering Lhamo and Tenzin Yangkye, made the obligatory exchange of phone numbers that none of us would ultimately use and headed out of the compound. It was with a full heart that I left. In all likelihood I would never be in a position to offer so much uninterrupted volunteer work for the clinic again. The nurses knew this as well, and it was hard for all of our eyes to meet during those awkward final minutes. I knew that leaving the clinic symbolised the end of my long journey in Nepal. What had slipped my mind during those moments was that one more task awaited.

*

Day by day, flight by flight, they arrived. Not the small handful of airline workers that Joyce had implied in her e-mail months earlier, but droves of flight attendants, all eager and with no clue as to what they were getting into, arrived to begin their "humanitarian trek". Some came from Miami, some from San Francisco, the rest from all points in between. By the time we began, there would be 27 flight attendants in all, 30 porters, a *sirdhar* and a few guides. We would be the longest train of tourists anyone could remember seeing on any trail east of Kathmandu since the days of Edmund Hillary.

The two buses Deepak had chartered to take us to the trailhead at Jiri were filled to capacity with medical supplies to be donated and 27 tourists and their individual bags filled with their individual necessities for Himalayan survival.

"Monique, are you sure we can't just get you some iodine tablets? It's no big deal to filter water along the way, really," I said, oozing patience.

"No, no, I've hired my own extra porter for this, thank you," and off strode Monique to check on her new porter, who was to be dedicated exclusively to hauling the ten cases of bottled water she had purchased for the journey.

Shepherding the last of Joyce's crew onto their respective buses, I wondered just how bad this idea had become and what other "Monique" type surprises lay in store for the group. Still, there was some relief in finally getting the entire show on the road, and I immediately immersed myself in the slow plod of Nepalese bus travel. The old and familiar Kodari highway now brought back memories of my trip with Holly just four years ago, and I seemed to remember every turn in the road, every terraced field and every child with a basket-load of threshed wheat hauled aloft with that improbable strap that ran across their forehead. It never failed to be very fresh and very beautiful for me, but as I looked down the aisle of the bus, the level of disengagement I noticed in my group was unfathomable. Their gazes never seemed to stray from the centre aisle and their conversations were incessant, chattering, cloying: American.

"Here, try some of this citrus spritz I brought."

"Oh my God, I hate that flight. You do it regularly now?"

"Can we pee? Have the driver stop at a clean restroom if you will."

Just about the time that someone had finished declaring that "pink is the navy-blue of India", a huge Tata truck sheared off our driver's-side mirror, causing the entire assembled gaggle to shriek in terror. I thought of Ramesh and smiled.

Over the course of the next week, our massive train of porters, flight attendants and citrus spritz made its way on foot from Jiri to Lukla – just as Holly and I had done. All totalled, the group delivered over two tons of medical supplies to the clinics I had scouted months earlier. It was slow going at first. Moaning complaints began almost immediately, and we were chronically behind schedule.

At Shivalya, on the first day of the trek and a relatively flat few hours of walking from our start in Jiri, I pulled up and stopped everyone for an early lunch. All I really wanted to do was take stock of our situation. The next stretch would begin their initiation into the Himalayan foothills with a gruelling climb to the pass at Deurali, and I wanted everyone assembled so that I could identify and assign guides to assist the stragglers who would undoubtedly reach the pass after dark, at the rate they were going.

"Monique, you made it – good!" was my greeting as she and her tiny entourage crossed the bridge and entered Shivalya.

"That's it? These are the Himalayas? she prattled. "That was too easy." And with that, she wasted little time in telling everyone in earshot how disappointed she was with the lack of sport in the whole affair, and then turned herself and her bottled-water haulers around to head back to Jiri.

"You can find a local bus that will take you back to Kathmandu tomorrow morning," I shouted. "That should be enough to impress you. Good luck."

When a difficult, repetitive task like trekking in the Himalayas is undertaken – particularly by a group of people who have never pushed themselves in such a manner – it is always interesting to see "The Turn". It is the point where the whining stops and people begin to change, both physically and mentally.

Marco from Miami hated this trek. He hated everything about it and wasted no opportunity to remind me of that fact. For the first four days, he was a constant annoyance. "Jesus, airlift me out of here," he would say at just the right volume to ensure that I heard. On day five, however, the previous days of constant climbing and descending started to work their magic, and Marco made The Turn.

"Jim, I'd like to walk up front with the fast guides. Where is the next clinic?" he said, and that told me change was in the air for him and for the others.

Like clockwork, four days of trekking had awakened the spirits of the group – with the exception of one woman who paid $50 to have a local farmer escort her up the hill on the back of his horse – and they began to feel the rhythm of walking and the peace that a slower pace and time for reflection can bring. Some had realisations that were more profound than others; some showed me more about myself than I was prepared to see. I was talking with a young doctor named Larry who had come along with the group, and as we walked along the trail just west of Junbesi, I began to wonder out loud:

"What do you think, Larry, a few good health posts would sure go a long way out here, don't you think?"

"Jim, what I think is that we need to learn how to leave these people alone," he replied.

That stopped me in my tracks. I knew he was right and I also knew that I was nowhere near the point in my personal journey where I was prepared to hear it. Larry was telling me that my newly chosen way of life in which I would impart my wisdom on all needy humans was foolish, wrong and possibly damaging. But what was I to do? I was all in, fully committed to doing humanitarian work in Nepal for the rest of my life. Was that so wrong? How dare this Larry guy interrupt my grand plans with the truth. But if one professes to be contemplative, a thinker, one is forced to conclude that even the best conceived of our Western plans for assisting these gentle and resilient people will remain culturally incompatible with the centuries-old patterns they have established for themselves. We come to change cultures, not enhance. It would be years before I would fully realise this truth and pattern my actions around it. As for Larry, his words of wisdom never left me: I reference them to this day.

The grand medical-supply delivery trek, sponsored by Airline Ambassadors, was nearing its end. It was nice to see the relieved and happy faces in our group as we crested the last hill and Lukla Airport came into view. But it was more than that for me. These people had changed, and I'd led them to that change. It was a difficult trek, and now all were in unison at the Khumbu Lodge in their joy at its completion. Floorboards rocked and the little wood stove in the centre of the room shook with the sound of Americans singing along with *madal* and *sarangi*-playing Nepalis. I savoured the experience like none before. I knew what was coming next, and I didn't want to think about it. I wanted to stay out there in the Himalayas, triumphant, forever.

*

E-mail was new, but it wasn't exotically new back in 1999. It was not so new that one couldn't find a computer and respond to something in one's inbox. The fact that I couldn't seem to get Holly to respond to my e-mails was disturbing. More so because of my aching head injury – I needed to hear something stabilising from the US. But I must have missed something – most men do in these instances. When I did finally get in contact with her, our conversations fell into the usual "he said, she said" pattern: She felt she was losing track of me and I felt I wasn't getting enough support. Who knows? Ultimately, I can tell you that any relationship will have a good bit of trouble surviving when one partner picks up and leaves for a nine month stay in Nepal that doesn't seem to benefit any elements of that partnership. All of this weighed on my mind as the US customs desk awaited my declarations after this, my second return from Nepal.

I was back in America. Things and my perceptions of things had changed after my nine months abroad, but I knew the drill from my first return. Once again, the roads were too wide and the people were too fat, but I began to notice deeper differences this time around. The usual American caution and distance shown to strangers now seemed arrogant and rude after the behaviour of the all-welcoming Nepalis that I had come to know. I was struck by the perspective: Americans seemed to triangulate their lives rather than live them. The simple pleasures, values and company I'd come to love in Nepal were replaced with the positioning, bargaining, compromise and effort it took to maintain one's place in America. Fine. Live large and prosper. It's the US, it's my country, and I understand that, but I was feeling less acceptant of this philosophy, and I knew my future would not lie along its path.

Chip on the shoulder firmly in place, I arrived at my home in Ocean Beach, California, and spent some time reacquainting myself with Holly. Not good – ultimatum of marriage laid down. I declined. Split decided. I got no furniture. That was that after seven years. She was free of me and I was abruptly on the streets.

I had a buddy in San Diego who was sympathetic, and showed me one of his rental properties off El Cajon Boulevard out by San Diego State University. Wow! What a palace for a despondent friend who seemed a little weird from all that "Asia shit" he had just experienced – hardwood floors, breakfast bar, garage. Nice. I called him on his mobile phone:

"Matt, I don't know what to say, bro. This place is fantastic! It's going to represent a new start for me. I can't tell you how grateful I feel."

"Jim, nothing but love here, but did you get a look at the unit in the back? The front house you saw is already rented. I figured I'd be able to put you up in an old storage facility in the rear of the property. Actually, it was a pigeon coop a few years back. Sorry for the misunderstanding. Let me know if you want it."

In no place to quibble about anything, I accepted the offer. Nine months of one-room living in Kathmandu would probably make this transition to an American pigeon coop easy. For the most part, it was not that bad. With just a sledge hammer for some demolition and a Milwaukee reciprocating saw for the "precision" work, I extended the coop to accommodate a kitchen, bathroom and dining area. It was hermit-like and Nepali, and I couldn't have been happier. An odd sort of superiority came over me, like I'd just discovered the key to the universe. I was living in America without a dollar to my name, in relative squalor, and was as happy as a clam. I was vindicated. I'd be all right and survive quite well by my own wits, thank you. Pious and smug at that moment, I would have readily called my parents liars for instilling in me the non-compromising, constantly upward-striving ideology that affixes blinders so firmly to most Americans that they can't see the depth of the hole they've dug into their humanity. But then again, all of this could have just been my head injury talking.

The thing that kept me going was the idea that what I was trying to do somehow transcended American ideas about success. There had to be another path. By most standards of measurement I was becoming a lousy American, but I thought I was actually on the path to becoming a fairly decent human being for the first time.

Unfortunately, reality is always at work and it has its methods –most of which are quite sufficient to snap anyone out of self-congratulatory wallowing. I had survived two trips to Nepal now. In my mind, they provided epic adventures beyond my imagination. Events unfolded with miraculous fortuity, and there was a tangible sense that something positive and permanent was possible through my efforts. All of a sudden, this universe was thrown into upheaval and I was back in America and back to square one – wham! All the wind bled out of my sails and my focus was on obtaining food, clothing and shelter. It was as though my Asia experiences never existed, never counted. A few moments in contemplation of this could make a guy with a head injury lean towards the bitter and antisocial.

My big desire to change my life after my first trip to Nepal way back in the 1990s had resulted in my acquiring some practical and employable medical skills. After arriving back in the US, I picked up a laboratory job at Alvarado Hospital and dug in, determined to finance my next humanitarian exploit in Nepal.

I had also developed some good friendships over the years at Downtown Johnny Brown's bar on the Civic Theatre concourse in San Diego. My big joy after returning from various trips to Nepal was to sit down and have one of their huge burgers and shoot my mouth off about what I had just done overseas. A gracious group of drunks, all of them, they humoured me and actually asked questions about Nepal when the mood hit and the planets were aligned just so. That was the best of it. Now, as the effects of my second re-immersion into American life wore on, I would find myself at the bar just trying to drown out something that happened during work at the hospital, and in no mood to chat.

After one particularly nasty night of phlebotomy, I drove down to Johnny Brown's and had Brian set me up with a small cavalry of Miller beer bottles. I was happy to see John Brown himself in the room that night – a gregarious presence whom everyone loved.

"Hey, Jim, I'm thinking of heading out to Nepal to do some trekking up by Everest. You know anything about that?" This was his usual giggling line of bullshit, of course, as he was sporting the spoils of all my Nepal trips on the walls and ceilings of his establishment. (No other bar in San Diego had a metal, hand-painted sign from Nepal announcing: "Tiger, Extra-Strong Beer".)

A few hours later, after my beer cavalry had dwindled to a small detachment, I agreed to help John and his friends. I would handle all the legwork and logistics needed for an Everest trek, provide a materials list, give an oral presentation to his group, lead them on a "training" hike and guide the Everest trek myself in exchange for the airfare to Nepal. He also promised to help financially with some orphanage work I knew of that needed to be done. He was happy with the arrangement and I was bouncing off the walls, knowing that in a few months I would be back in the city that both filled my heart beyond words and ripped it uncaringly from my chest: Kathmandu.

It was no easy task, asking a bunch of heavy-drinking beach guys to not only sit through a presentation on the do's and don'ts of Nepal, but to physically accompany me on a little training hike up Mount San Jacinto near Palm Springs just so I could get a look at them and tell whether or not they'd be killed instantly in the Himalayas or figure the whole thing out like most people.

The key to this whole episode was that I'd learned something from John Brown. It took his individual, kind effort to bring me out of my funk and give me a bit of hope again. Maybe it was luck; maybe John Brown noticed that I was slipping and running out of options. Maybe I needed to dump the hermit routine, stop being a jerk and rejoin life again. Mostly, I needed to quit analysing and just be grateful for the rescue.

*

Jordia manis Sagarmathama roughly translated means "Drunks on Everest". That was our theme and that was what I had silk-screened on the T-shirts. We landed at Tribhuvan International Airport in Kathmandu and sprinted from the plane to the appropriate line at customs. We picked up baggage, exchanged currency and dodged a security check by going through the big-shot tourist "Green Lane" for no apparent reason other than that we were acting like big-shot tourists. I made a point of letting John's group lead us out into the airport parking lot.

"Hello, sir. Taxi?"

"Please, I take your bags."

"Hotel Namaste, number one. I take you now."

"Hey, you must pay 500 rupees to leave this airport."

"Hello! I love you! Fuck you!" (In the same sentence.)

"What you want? Hashish? Black? White?"

"I need milk money for my child."

"Excuse me, sir. Dope?"

"Come rest at my dance bar. Young girls. Shower."

I let it hit them, full volume. It's one of the few joys I get when I bring people to Nepal for the first time. That "holy shit!" moment when they realise they're not in Kansas anymore.

"C'mon, you guys," I barked, "let's get going. I'll show you what polio looks like on an adult who's never had treatment." I just loved that part. Their eyes were as wide as saucers, and I could see them looking for the nearest point of reference and safety. I didn't have the heart to tell them more of what I knew.

Nepal is one of the poorest countries in the world. For a while, the per capita income of the average Nepali hovered at around US $250 per year. There are pockets of life-threatening, critical poverty in rural areas and in Kathmandu. Back then, selling one good stolen pair of American hiking boots could feed a family of four for six months. Part of my briefing to John and his gang was to tell them to always be aware of the location of their boots before they went to bed. They looked at me like I was nuts. It gets worse: The income disparity between Nepal and the developed world is such that it triggers extreme acts of begging in order to get the attention of a rich-looking foreigner. Fathers would take their toddlers to the streets of Thamel, after having scalded the hair off one side of the child's head with boiling water. For dramatic effect, the father would pour red Merthiolate over the burns, and parade the suffering child in front of tourists. Mercifully, the police have cracked down on this practice, but you get the concept. Imagine if you were out of job and you heard that a filthy-rich Arab sheikh, or the equivalent, was coming to your neighbourhood and giving out thousands of dollars to children who looked needy. You would probably forcibly remove your kid from school, send him to where the sheikh was located and have him look needy in a hurry.

I didn't care. It was all the same for me. I was back in Kathmandu, and I felt I was once again home. The trek I would lead for John Brown and his group was exhilarating, but ultimately, it was just another means to an end. After a few weeks I would bid them goodbye and have Kathmandu and all of Nepal to myself, again. I realized that providence had stepped in to get me back to this point and I was filled with gratitude and optimism. There was a new outlook, a different spring in my step. Encouraged by Dr Larry's words months before, I was determined to keep my opinions to myself and just listen – listen to the needs, desires and passions of the Nepalese themselves. They were going to tell me how they wanted to shape the course of their own development. Projects, aid, assistance – whatever you want to call it – would now happen on an individual level, one person at a time if need be. Agendas and plans were finished for me. This new philosophy would launch me on an eight-year path that would be filled with the most creative, dangerous and possibly illegal creations that anyone would dare call "aid". All of it would come from taking a deep breath and just working on the problems that presented themselves, and from not trying to be a hero. But old habits die hard.

Chapter 11

The Big Sign Project

The Dolakha/Lamabagar corridor in north central Nepal was a muddled mess in 2002. Situated immediately to the east of the main highway to Tibet, it served as the nearest alternative crossing point to the border crossing at Kodari for undocumented Tibetans. Routinely, bribed local police constables from Barabise in the adjacent valley would jump over to the Dolakha side, and either apprehend or beat the hell out of any Tibetans they saw. The Chinese would pay a good fee for this service and give the cops a nice little red Chinese flag as a bonus. As word of this practice spread, Tibetans would often panic when they saw police in the area, and a big rock-throwing fight would ensue.

The police in the Dolakha valley were themselves not beyond reproach and were known to take a bribe or two. But for some reason, they generally followed the rules when it came to Tibetans and escorted them to holding centres in Dolakha city to await transportation to Kathmandu Immigration and, ultimately, the TRC. The problem was that these police knew that the average undocumented Tibetan making his way to Dolakha reflexively reached for a rock the minute he saw any blue uniform, so these cops were not always keen on performing this function.

Into this pressure cooker came the Maoist insurgency. Dolakha was considered to be a minor stronghold of the movement, and groups were beginning to form from every village in the valley. Since the government of Nepal was then, and remains today, almost willfully incompetent, Maoism offered a real and tangible alternative to ineffectual central governance. Mostly, however, the movement resulted in gangs of young men terrorising villagers and demanding food, money and obedience. It reminded me of a passage I had read in an article in the *Los Angeles Times* by PJ O'Rourke, and the sentiment was spot on: Revolutionary movements are fuelled and encouraged by the fact that bored young men would rather run around in jungles at night with guns and a nice hat than sit impoverished in their village and wait for something to happen. The Maoist movement was like that. It was about young people who were given an easy-to-understand, absolutist ideology, a sense of purpose, the opportunity to meet new friends and have some fun (!) – especially during episodes when they were forcing adults to follow their political rantings at gunpoint.

The Dolakha valley was never a dull place. All one had to do was pick up a newspaper in Kathmandu from, say, 2001 to 2004 and some item from Dolakha would be on page one, front and centre. Half of it involved Tibetans and the rest usually centred on the latest Maoist atrocity. We needed no advanced scouting teams or reports from Tibetan arrivals at the Reception Centre to know that there was a big problem in the area, and that Tibetan movements were part of the problem.

Those of us sitting in Kathmandu waiting for some Tibetan news were also bored and looking to run around in the jungle a bit. So a team was assembled, and off we went to the Dolakha valley. Our goal was to document everything we saw and survey residents on their interactions with Tibetans. We would go as high and as close to the Tibetan border as we could without arousing suspicion or Chinese weaponry. From the surveys and interviews, we would plan a course of action that would hopefully take a bit of the heat off the Tibetans who were moving through the area. As usual, we had no idea what we would find and no idea what we would do with it when we found it.

Ram Chandra was the lead guide: young, thin and with dark, exhausted eyes. He brought with him his cousin, Ramesh, who spoke no English but made up for it with the strength of a yak and a constant smile. The boys were two of Deepak's best trekking crew employees, and I felt a bit guilty for accepting their services during the peak months of the tourist season.

The road to Dolakha happened to be the exact same road that saw our group of 27 flight attendants pass through with their loyal guide Jim in tow a few years prior, but I was in no mood to repeat the journey on a bus, so we had Deepak charter a taxi for the trip. We stopped for the night about an hour outside of Dolakha in Mude. Our friend Mohan Khatri had a tranquil, isolated retreat called the Horseshoe Ranch, and we'd heard it had a sauna constructed by actual experts from actual Finland. We rolled through the gate and up a gentle grade to a low-roofed building nestled in a comfortable but not dense deciduous forest that was typical of the central Sindhupalchowk district where we were located and the foothills of the Himalayas.

Colonel Mohan Khatri was a man who commanded respect. He was in charge of maintaining equestrian capabilities for the king of Nepal, and was widely respected by his peers in the Nepal army. What little I remember of him brings back memories of a man with quiet confidence, not military swagger. One always wanted to hear his opinion, and always solicited his approval during polite conversation. After our visit the Maoists, looking for any symbol of the repressive Nepal regime, decided in their rural Maoist minds that Mohan Khatri represented everything that was corrupt in Nepal. They visited him at the Horseshoe one night, torches in hand, and, despite his pleading for understanding, overran and sacked the Horseshoe Lodge. By the end of the evening, Colonel Mohan Khatri was dead, beheaded by a series of khukuri knife blows to the neck. It was the beginning of mob rule in rural Nepal. The exhilarating momentum created by crowd anger was new to young, rural village men, and they were eager to maintain their newfound high-energy level. It took them away from their daily misery – that was all that mattered.

On this visit prior to his death, the colonel's plucky and business-savvy wife Krishna greeted us and showed us to our rooms.

The Horseshoe was originally designed so that Nepal army officers and designates could have a retreat space where they could maintain their conditioning and relax at the same time. The Finnish sauna was no rumour. A nice wooden room with all the expert input, design and accessories needed to heat rocks and douse them occasionally with water was in place and ready for use. There was also a series of log structures strewn throughout the complex that were designed to be used as a physical-training confidence course for military visitors seeking to enhance their blood flow ahead of a bout in the sauna.

For us, it was just a bed and breakfast. We were too tired from the journey to make much of a fuss over the aesthetics of the place. The three of us sat down in Krishna's nice central dining area and discussed our game plan.

"I don't know where to begin on this trip, guys. There's so much going on in this area, I think that it might be best if we just act like dumb tourists – you know, the usual strategy. We could just watch and make notes, agreed?" came my initial offering.

Ram Chandra would have none of it. "Jim *Dai*, listen. Tibetans come and they have to take care of themselves, right? Let's go where they camp and eat, and we can learn much more; we can ask villagers about these places," he said.

Simple, direct and to the point: the Nepali way. We had our strategy. We were ready to leave in the morning.

Dolakha is a functional, uninspiring crossroad. It seems no more than a junction between the Dolakha valley walking trails of local commerce and the Swiss-built road between Kathmandu and Jiri that shuttles a few thousand tourists a year to the Everest-bound trailhead on Jiri's outskirts. We walked for what seemed like an hour along nondescript roads, past centres of commerce and official buildings, before the trail got down to serious business and we began to wind around a narrow valley gorge that evolved into a real Himalayan trail. By this point, I had been seasoned by many walks through the Himalayas, but now the process seemed different. Each prior trip had always stood out in my mind as a means of gauging my performance – more specifically, as a prod to improve and measure up to past performances. This time, the Himalayas were telling me I was getting old.

I did not like the whole process of ageing. My hair was thinning, and I could no longer keep up with the nimble Nepalis on the trail and was walking well behind at a speed that suited me. I looked for something, anything, that would keep me in the game and allow this journey to continue. I was in the full-blown throes of the worst of human addictions: the need for wilderness solitude. Mine was of the purest and uncut Himalayan variety.

I drew some comfort from the imagery in my head of Daniel Day Lewis running through the woods at full speed during a scene from *The Last of the Mohicans.* I started to hum the little bagpipe theme from that scene, and soon all three of us were running as fast as thoughtful foot placement would allow. It seemed like an eternity had passed before we decided to stop. It felt good; I was beating Father Time for at least these few hours. I wanted to run more, and told Ram Chandra about it.

"*Dai,*" he said, "we are the *tin kukur jito hertza.*" (Rough translation: the three fast-moving dogs.)

The day ended in the little village of Piguti. We grabbed a few overpriced rooms near the town centre, had a bowl of instant noodles and turned in for a night of bug wrestling and aerial insect assault. There is a trick to hiking through the less-touristy areas of Nepal: Sleep is everything. If you don't sleep well, you don't walk well. I had somehow forgotten this simple axiom during the preparation phase of this trip, and was now stuck with neither a vermin-barrier cover sheet for the local mattresses nor a bug net for vermin of a flying nature. It was going to be a long night.

The next morning broke with reminders of my lack of preparation. Geometric, almost beautiful, linear patterns of bed-bug bites traced up my arms and onto portions of my upper torso. I displayed a few red welts of unknown origin, and had the creeping sensation that something had crawled into my ear during the night with the full intention of starting a thriving business. Regardless, scratching, I joined the boys after a light breakfast and we headed up the valley.

Bombed-out school buildings were displayed along the trail now. We were in Maoist territory, and my urge to run the trail was now replaced by a need to step cautiously. We were no more than half a day's walk from Piguti when we were met by a company of Maoists in full camouflage regalia marching down the trail towards our position. They didn't seem to be an aggressive bunch from a distance, and since there was no other way to proceed, we decided to pass through the middle of their ranks. They didn't flinch, turn, question or otherwise harass our manoeuvre, and aside from me accidentally hitting my forehead on the barrel of one of their ancient Enfield rifles, we made a rather boring passage.

"Hey, Ram, something was strange about that," I said.

"All *ketis, Dai,*" came his reply.

"You're full of it. That entire platoon of armed Maoists was made up of young girls. How young do they go?"

"Bairha," said Ram, Nepali for twelve.

Just as Ram suggested, we surveyed lodge owners and locals about their problems with the Tibetans, and where Tibetan campsites might be found. As we moved up the valley, we began to get a good picture of the territory from the stories that emerged:

"Tibetans just take and don't pay."

"I throw them out and they start a fight."

"They don't understand our language."

One frustrated lodge owner said, "Maybe if there were signs in their language, it would help." That was the answer. A few minutes before, we hadn't even known the question.

We would go back to Kathmandu and make signs that reflected the concerns of everyone in the valley. Bad communication was the big problem, and multilingual instructions with a few simple, yet key points would go a long way in calming down the tension in the area. We would return and post the signs at strategic locations in Dolakha, Singuti, Piguti and Lamabagar. Local problems, local solutions, just the way it should be, we thought. The three fast-moving dogs walked up the valley simply and got to the heart of the issue by simply listening – I was proud of this. It was a revelation to learn of the needs and ideas of locally impacted people. It was all about communication, and they thought signs placed along the trail would be the best way to solve their particular local problem.

We could have quit at that point and headed back to Kathmandu to begin our sign-building effort, but we kept walking towards the Tibetan border with enhanced curiosity as to what else this trip might reveal. On the northern edge of the most northern town in the Dolakha valley, Lamabagar, we stopped for a cold yet entirely hospitable stay at a small monastery. We resumed walking the next morning.

"Jim *Dai*, that is Tibet," Ram pointed out after we had travelled no more than 30 minutes north of our last evening's rest. A small convergence in one of the many rivers that flowed out of the Tibetan plateau had revealed a primitive, handmade bamboo-and-wood bridge.

"*Dai*, Tibetans make this bridge," said Ram without expression.

Strangely, there was no bamboo forest within miles of this place. Tibetans seemed to have gone to some special effort to haul these bamboo poles great distances to this little river crossing. But something wasn't right: Why would fleeing Tibetans take the time to construct such a structure? Surely the process of moving bridge materials across Tibet carried with it a considerable risk of detection, and it certainly wasn't a quick and nimble operation to arrive here and spend time constructing a fairly stable bridge. What was going on? Ram cleared the air:

"Jim *Dai*, I don't know everything, but Tibetans go both ways sometimes."

"So, Ram, what you're saying is that Tibetans risk their lives to cross into Nepal and go to India, and then do it all over again on their way back?"

I was incredulous. What I had learned about Tibetan migration through Nepal was all wrong. There was not the massive one-way exodus out of Tibet as I had been led to believe; this was a highway that ran both ways. I was to learn later that Tibetans would get to India, see the Dalai Lama, get his blessing, and then listen while His Holiness told them he had nothing permanent to offer and that they should go back to Tibet. In fact, many Tibetans had no intention of permanently fleeing Tibet, but took on the dangerous journey through Nepal as sort of a penitent pilgrimage simply to see the Dalai Lama once in their lives before returning. I was let down a bit – and a bit angry. The bulk of the "Free Tibet" Movement that I was now heavily involved with had based many of their arguments and positions on the tragedies caused by a forced exodus through Nepal. How could they overlook this two-way dynamic? To this day, multiple references can be found where the Tibetans' perilous journey into Nepal is explained – little or no explanations about going back.

My thoughts were occupied with the possible agendas behind Western Tibetan advocacy for the rest of the day as we began out descent out of the valley. I started to see the "Free Tibet" Movement as just like any other threat-based industry, where an image of constant crisis must be maintained in order to sustain an urgency to raise funds.

Nepalis are inveterate copycats. This skill can be realised at a high level when one lives in a country with virtually no intellectual property laws or patent and copyright enforcement. If one were to extrapolate, it would not be a stretch to argue that forgery and economic piracy may just be the engines that drive South Asian commerce. Poorly reproduced books, tapes, DVDs, sportswear – anything popular and Western can be found on display, without fear, in many a Kathmandu shop. Most tourists gleefully participate in this open black market. I loved to go to Shona's Sportswear in Thamel. A sharp, no-nonsense woman of Sherpa origin, Shona's specialty was the reversible fleece jacket with the phony North Face logo on the pocket. Not a North Face fan? Reverse the jacket and the pocket logo says Patagonia. It's shameless, unabashed fun most of the time – Sudesh hated it.

"I've got to lease all the tiny shops around my place or else someone will open another New Orleans Café right next to mine and think nothing of it – no kidding. They think the way everyone makes money is by calling their restaurant the New Orleans Café," he would say. It seemed like any venture that was prospering in Nepal, had a bit of name recognition and made a profit was ripe for artificial duplication – no kidding indeed.

"*Dai*, let me talk to these boys, OK?" Ram whispered as he quickened his step towards a group that was advancing toward us with what seemed to be intent.

"OK, Ram, but I don't understand...shit! Is that a pistol?"

It was. The young men were now in plain view; their thick shocks of pomade-slicked black hair and black leather jackets of an affordably artificial Chinese nature gave off an air of trouble, and they wasted no time in greeting us with nose-to-nose intimidation.

"Donation!" screamed what appeared to be their leader, as he began to wave an old revolver in the direction of my groin.

"CPN-UML Maoist donation, no receipt!" he continued with his small cache of English words. This, I thought, was a bit odd since Nepal's Maoist insurgency movement, for all its violence, had the strangely courteous practice of teaching its thugs to give a nice receipt after frightening tourists out of their vacation money. These guys were different, and a tense uncertainty filled the air for the next few minutes. The boys were not going to let us continue.

Eventually, some calming words passed between Ram and the lead thug, and I saw Ramesh pass a 100-rupee note to the boy, pat him on the back and send the group down the trail. Ram returned with a light, exhausted smile – like he'd been digging ditches all day.

"Fake Maoists, *Dai*. Gone now."

"Ram, how in the hell did you do that?" I was flabbergasted at the ease with which he had dispatched the trouble.

"We give a few rupees and say this is your last trek in Nepal – you have cancer."

The bus ride back to Kathmandu was bumpy and uncomfortable as usual, and I mused over the day's events – the construction and delivery of our signage, and the type of cancer Ram might have nominated for my condition. The fact was, Ram and Ramesh had saved the day, and this could only mean one thing: I was now officially responsible for their village drinking and carousing budget for the foreseeable future – they would see to it.

CHAPTER 12

CHANGING MONEY IN THE LAND OF THE GURKHAS

By 2002, I was no longer working at the clinic, but was still recognised by the guard at the gate and allowed passage. It was fun to walk around the grounds, reminisce and help treat some of the wounded again, and I always left with a full heart after each visit. The clinic was now housed in its own new building on the TRC compound and was far removed from its former location inside the main facility. This meant that I could no longer re-create the joy of walking through hordes of grabbing and giggling Tibetans as I made my way through the main hall and up the stairs to my former post. But grabbing and giggling were never in short supply at the Reception Centre, and I knew that a joke, a tiny hand or a cricket ball would eventually find me as long as I was somewhere on the grounds.

This new clinic was a no-nonsense upgrade, designed to move large amounts of people through its corridors quickly while keeping out all unnecessary people and distractions. Times were changing; the need to move Tibetans efficiently and securely through the TRC now took priority over the laughing and casual collegiality that defined the atmosphere during my period as a volunteer. The Chinese were now watching the facility more closely. And there were rumours afoot that the Tibetan Namgyal School, directly adjacent to the TRC, harboured strange hidden cameras that were aimed at the clinic.

The deliberate yet easy rhythm of the health workers was a familiar comfort to me as I looked for ways to make myself useful again. During these visits, it was increasingly interesting to hear a few staff members chatter on about Tibetans entering Nepal through the mysterious Gorkha valley. I had heard of this area, and was intrigued by the fact that while it was so very close to Kathmandu it managed to retain an odd remoteness. I found myself being led to distraction more and more by these accounts.

The Gorkha valley offered no modern conveniences to speak of and saw few, if any, foreign tourists. Yet it was steeped in rich history and legend, and was pivotal to the formation of the modern-day nation of Nepal. Without wading too deeply into a sea of footnotes, we can roughly approximate the Nepal we know today as a series of some 50 warlike and aggressive fiefdoms in the early 1700s, with no cohesive unifying themes other than those related to mutual plunder and destruction. In, quite literally, the geographic middle of all this was the region of Gorkha, which in 1743 saw the ascendency of the father of Nepal's royal Shah dynasty, Prithvi Narayan Shah, to the throne of the tiny Gorkha kingdom. Shah was a restless type, and through guile and takeover he managed to unify the disparate fiefdoms into something resembling today's modern Nepal. He even managed to make the Chinese a bit nervous through his northward expansion towards the Tibetan border, but seemed to reconsider just as he was nearing the Dragon's doorstep. The move proved to be a prescient foreshadowing of Nepal's future approach to its large and powerful neighbour. It was Prithvi Narayan Shah who first described Nepal as "a yam between two boulders", and the description could not be more insightful. To this day, Nepal does its best to leverage advantage and favour from both China and India, while trying not to be overwhelmed and crushed by the demands of either.

The fighting warriors of the Gorkha region were legendary for their terrain knowledge and ferocity. In 1814, the descendants of many of those warriors who fought at the behest of Prithvi Narayan Shah went to battle against a larger and better-armed invading force of British soldiers. Nothing less than the survival of the tiny new nation of Nepal was at stake, and incredibly the warriors from Gorkha fought the superior British forces to a stalemate. A deep mutual admiration between local warrior and British soldier emerged from this conflict, and the British not only offered up a series of treaties that stopped their advances and effectively preserved Nepal, but they began their long and productive history of commitment to the men of the Gorkha region. Since then, these "Gurkha" warriors have assisted British forces, and they are renowned worldwide for their loyalty, bravery and yes, that same ancient ferocity that served Prithvi Narayan Shah so well.

Their famous and terrifying war cry, *Ayo Gorkhali* (The Gurkhas are upon you), is something you just never want to hear coming towards you in a battle. A former Indian army chief of staff probably best summed up the mood of those who work with Gurkhas on a daily basis when he quipped: "If a man says he is not afraid of dying, he is either lying or he is a Gurkha."

Today, Western trekking tour outfitters simply refer to the area the "Manaslu Trek". More significant to my interests, Tibetans were entering Nepal through this valley and embarking on a relatively easy three- or four-day walk from the Tibetan border and down to a primitive bus pick-up point somewhere below Dhading, where transportation could be secured for the remaining five-hour journey to Kathmandu. To me, this represented an amazing improvement on the two to three weeks it took for Tibetans and their frozen feet to walk and ride from their entry point near the Nangpa La and Mount Everest, so I continued to listen with an increasing sense of intent whenever individuals at the clinic spoke of the Gorkha valley. Add to this the fact that the Everest route was now getting a bit too dangerous for Tibetans due to an increased Nepalese security presence, and it was clear that some alternative crossing plan had to be created.

I had heard that getting to the take-off point on the Chinese side of the Gorkha valley was no easy task, but it was not insurmountable – another few days by bus and another day of walking. But once over the passes near the Larkhe La, or the three trails near the more remote Tsum valley that drained into Nepal, the trail provided a reasonably unmolested experience for Tibetans who avoided trouble. Tibetans usually travel at night when they sneak into Nepal, and remain hidden and silent during daylight hours in the hope of avoiding corrupt Nepalese police seeking a quick Chinese bounty. From accounts, this did not seem necessary in Gorkha. This was undoubtedly in part due to the severely diminished number of police officers patrolling the region; which in itself was undoubtedly due to the fact that Gorkha was awash with Maoist insurgents, and the cops just weren't getting paid enough to patrol an area full of armed and violent teenagers who possessed a rather disconcerting tendency to return fire when fired upon.

Intrigued by the relative nearness of the Gorkha valley and its potential, I had my usual resurgent hallucination of looking like a hero, and began to think towards finding the means to make all fleeing Tibetans use this safer route that I alone could claim to have discovered. Predictably, not much convincing was needed to persuade Ram and Ramesh to join me for an assessment trip to the region, and we made our plans.

The "Three Speeding Dogs" were heading for the land of the Gurkhas.

Those times when I was running up and down the footpaths of the Himalayas with our little assessment team offered me my greatest joy, and I created every excuse I could to get us all out of Kathmandu for some fresh air and fieldwork. On the trail, the weight and pressure of the city melted into the repetitive, almost meditative daily walking and surveying routine. An encounter with villagers was cause for rejoicing. Stories of lives based on sweat and earth flowed after polite introductions and tea. Nights of wood smoke and mud floors gave way to morning departures and earnest, but hollow, promises to return. Fuelled with rice, noodles and chocolate – whatever the villager had, even if it was the last of what they had – we would set off towards the next town to the fading sounds of our newfound friends rising to greet their ancient toils of lowering implement to farm field, and of straining, hoisting and toting whatever their efforts produced.

Ram and Ramesh behaved like two unrestrained clowns most of the time, and could always be counted on to ask me for some extra money at the day's end for local whisky or gambling or whatever any given village offered for an evening. I was usually compliant. Ultimately, the two of them understood what we were trying to accomplish, and I admired how they built a sense of craft around both doing the tasks at hand and keeping me safe. They would climb off-trail to reach some high monastery to administer a survey and ask some obscure monk they deemed important questions, and return briar-covered and bloody-kneed with an indispensable piece of data. On one occasion, Ramesh did a credible job of acting drunk enough to distract a group of Chinese-sponsored vigilantes from an impending robbery long enough for us to duck into a local lodge. There was also that time in Dolakha when Ram thrust himself between me and a cluster of volatile Maoist-imposter thieves sporting for a conflict to tell them that: "The American is dying of cancer, he's no harm. Leave him alone." If I didn't owe my life to these two, in their estimation, I most certainly owed them a lot of money. And, as I feared, they kindly but regularly reminded me of that fact on most evenings along the trail. To get a sense of the bigger picture, Ram and Ramesh supplied to the world the bulk of our raw data about undocumented Tibetan movement in Nepal from 2000 to 2005. That, I believe, is beyond dispute. They went about their work with a carefree efficiency, and in total and dignified obscurity – again, the Nepali way.

For this Gorkha project, as a reward, I paid them a little extra money, and after much thought and beer, gave them some added pressure: I wouldn't be joining them. I was sending them out on their own for the first time. The assessment of the Gorkha region was going to be their project and theirs alone. They were to come up with the data, identify the problems and suggest a course of action. I had no idea how this would turn out, I just knew that I was starting to feel my mortality and I couldn't run through the Himalayas forever. I'll admit here that I had substantial doubts and felt considerable mistrust towards Ram and Ramesh when I sent them off. If there was ever a time when a distinction could be drawn between lazy Nepali fatalism and good Western techniques and work ethics, it would be now. At the very least, I could take some solace from the thought that Ram and Ramesh would get a good lesson from the experience, and perhaps pick up a few skills for the future during those few times that they weren't partying with local village girls. I let them know that I didn't expect much from their first trip, and basked in my contrived leadership persona as I placed them on the bus to Gorkha.

Humbled and ashamed were my feelings when they returned. After 20 days of traversing their way up the valley to the Tibetan border and back, the boys stumbled into Deepak's office in Kathmandu. Sporting an unmistakable Himalayan wilderness glow and looking a lot thinner, the two of them proceeded to shout over each other in an attempt to get all the details of their adventure out and available for my consumption as quickly as possible.

Ram and Ramesh had talked personally to dozens of shop owners and citizens as fellow countrymen, and asked them what they hated about interacting with the Tibetans they saw – Nepali to Nepali. Their results and suggestions addressed the problems directly, and were pragmatic, simple and brilliant. After hearing their refreshingly succinct accounts, the realisation hit me that I was no longer a vital or even necessary link in the process. These people in Nepal only needed a few of our Western resources and then they could conceive and execute their own programmes with better results than any top-down, "capacity-building" United Nations programme officer could ever hope to achieve. I began to wonder why any group or organisation feels they must impose their culturally incompatible ideas and techniques on an indigenous culture and claim it as "aid". The boys laid open the false assumption that rich cultures know something above and beyond poor cultures simply because they are rich. They showed us, through their findings, the power and the brilliance of creative thinking – free of paternalistic Western condescension and unrestrained by preconceived guidelines or methodologies.

Our groups had done many assessments of Tibetan crossing areas, so in Ram and Ramesh's report we were prepared for some of the usual suspects: the Tibetans didn't speak the language; the Tibetans were rude and fought with the shop owners; the Tibetans did whatever they pleased and paid no mind to local customs. We'd heard it all before. But this time, some new data emerged: It seemed that quite a lot of the difficulties that Nepalis had with transiting Tibetans in the area stemmed from the fact that these strange people carried money that was not recognised, and was certainly not going to be accepted. Tibetans carried Chinese yuan.

The boys went on to recount stories they'd heard of shop owners, confused by the strange bank notes, throwing Tibetans out of their places of business with a few choice words for good measure. Tibetans, being Tibetans, would start throwing rocks at the shop owners, and the downward and familiar spiral towards incarceration in a local jail would begin.

"Jim *Dai*, Chinese money is easy to change in Kathmandu, why not in the mountains?" was Ram's opinion. It was also his solution to the problem.

Within a few months, we sent out groups of boys, each of whom carried 7,500 Nepalese rupees, or about US $100, back to the Gorkha route that Ram and Ramesh had assessed. Their purpose was to use the rupees to buy back any Chinese currency that any shop owner may have accepted, and to educate any and all who traded with transiting Tibetans that Chinese yuan was acceptable and that the rate of exchange was about 8 yuan for each 75 Nepali rupees. We also told the boys to tell each shopkeeper they encountered that for the next year we would be sending people to buy their yuan from them and to keep them updated on the current yuan/rupee exchange rate.

How we sustained this effort in the months to come taught me a lesson on how wrong an individual's perception of their worth could be. There I was, the big white saviour of all souls impoverished and needy, waiting for my chance to bestow my Western wisdom and dollars on a big programme that would both affirm my cultural superiority and allow me to take my place among the pantheon of world-saving saints. Not a chance. Ram and Ramesh's idea was so simple and brilliant that I was shattered to the point of plunging into self-doubt once again. But they were right. I had to learn to shut my mouth and just do the work. I had to blend in. One thousand different individuals performing one thousand different acts of assistance was the idea. Avoiding full collapse, my lone face-saving contribution to the programme was to send messenger boys around to various trekking companies in Kathmandu, to ask if their Gorkha-bound trekking customers wouldn't mind exchanging some of their rupees for yuan while on the trail.

"Just ask a shop owner if they've got any of the funny money and offer to buy it at the current exchange rate. It makes a great conversation starter anyway, and will probably be fun. You lose a little with the exchange fees when you come back to Kathmandu, but it's all for a good cause. Oh, and pick up any info on Tibetans while you're at it."

Eventually, I allowed myself to feel proud of that programme. It focused like a laser on a significant local problem that involved Nepalis interacting with Tibetans. We eased the tension in those interactions by providing a simple currency-exchange mechanism, and we thought we were making a bit of a difference. I never pursued the idea of trying to shift the bulk of Tibetan transit to the Gorkha valley any further. It took Ram and Ramesh's efforts to make me refocus on the concepts I'd vowed to adopt: Drop your big ideas and just work on the problem that presents itself to you – and try a little humility while you're at it.

Chapter 13

Spying on Spies

There were a few bars in Thamel where the US Marines hung out when they got a few moments of free time. Most notably there was Tom and Jerry's – a third-floor bar with an old Thamel history and aesthetic. To get in, one had to navigate a dark corridor immediately off the wet, rickshaw-filled main street of Thamel, and wind around shuttered travel and T-shirt shops to a set of stairs. If Tom or Jerry were feeling particularly benevolent on that particular evening, there would be small candles at the base of the stairs to guide your way. After spiralling up a few flights, you would be greeted with the smell of a Kathmandu bathroom immediately to your left, but you would be undeterred and keep moving forward and into a room full of candles, dim lights, pool tables and flags of every nation and government organisation imaginable hanging from the ceiling. It had the type of atmosphere that made you want to curl up at one of the small wooden tables against the window, order a 650-millilitre Carlsberg and wait for intrigue.

It was a typical night during a typical bustling tourist season in mid-October, and around 11 p.m. Tom and Jerry's was doing its usual seasonal boom business and the house was full of the usual French trekkers, Jesuit school teachers, local gang boys looking for their white "visa girls", pimps, hash dealers, musicians doing shots of whisky between sets, volunteers, and Tibetans, Nepalis and Indians of every stripe, colour and motivation. It was hot and the place stunk. It was a magnificent human soup.

There were British Foreign Service types, odd loners and, above all, US Marines. As usual and way too predictable to be safe, the Marines that guarded the US embassy had taken seats at their traditional big table in the middle of the room. This was good. Not only did I like chatting up the Marines – they always seemed to be in a good mood – but I knew that they carried baggage with them. In Nepal, when the Marines went out on the town, at least to Tom and Jerry's, there would always be a couple of young guys hanging around, conspicuously avoiding each other and usually in plain view of the Marines. Welcome to the CIA training camp for new operatives: Tom and Jerry's, I fantasised.

I would watch these guys on occasion, and I began to make some generalisations. What kind of people should normally come to Nepal and go to Tom and Jerry's? What kind of things didn't seem to fit about these guys? For me, a few repeating themes started to surface. Nepal is a holiday destination. Hiking in the Himalayas is hard work, certainly. But generally, Western tourists are elated and talkative. A decided and pronounced lack of social skills or inhibition seemed to suggest something other than trekking as a motivation for being there, but that was stretching things and I could just as easily have been describing your average budget Israeli backpacker for that matter. But these people, these Marine "watchers", were different somehow. The thing that really stuck out was the sense of preconditioning I got from my interactions with them. There was never a word out of place or an unusual narrative. They were all just "in Nepal to check it out" or something to that effect. If I walked away from a conversation with them and didn't feel like I learned anything about them, it would arouse my suspicion. Humans make mistakes. They especially like to make mistakes when they are on holiday and in a bar. They like to let down their hair and make a few mistakes with other people. If one guards against this tendency too much, especially in a Kathmandu bar, it comes across as out of place. But the big test was the handshake. A big American iron grip that suggested these guys were in control of the situation always seemed to tip me off; even mountain climbers don't shake hands like that – too official. The combination of detached seriousness and physical strength gave me my archetype.

One night, I put this archetype to the test. A conversation with whoever would turn into a friendly arm-wrestling match. These generally created a minor spectacle and were always a lot of fun. I'd eventually wind up over at the table of one of my suspected "watchers" and ask for a contest.

"Hey, OK, you got me, but that was fun. I'm Jim – what's your name?"

He would mumble something and I'd ask again.

"Sorry, it's loud in here. Did you say John Langley?"

"You mean like Langley, Virginia?" one of them answered one night before he could catch himself.

"Well, no, and oops, I guess. You were just a little too quick on the release there, John. No, I don't mean Langley, Virginia, home of CIA headquarters, but you have a nice evening, OK?"

Another time I caught the attention of a heavy-set young Indian man standing at the bar.

"Hey, man, I saw you wrestling that guy. You want a beer? I just came up from Hyderabad for a tech show on the latest, cool (whatever). What do you do for fun in this town, man? Can we get some girls?"

First off, there was no tech show in Kathmandu. There were none scheduled and none planned. The only tech show the Nepalis would be interested in would be one where they learned how to keep the municipal power grid from shutting down for 12 hours per day. I'd go to that one.

Second, he was way over the top with his acting – a poor performance. He was irritating, so I gave him a handshake with the full intent of leaving. He wouldn't let go; damn strong for an Indian "tech" guy. So I bent his hand in a little bit of a Jiu Jitsu hold and he promptly slipped out. Fast and skilled.

"Hey, man, don't be trying that Jiu Jitsu shit on me! I'm just here to meet girls."

It had been a long night, so I just left him and went home.

On another visit, Raj, behind the bar, said, "Sorry about that Indian guy the other night. He comes here sometimes. He's with the RAW."

Well, that explained the grip and the slip. The RAW is roughly like an Indian version of the CIA. It seems Tom and Jerry's was on everyone's map.

Of course, playing Mr Big Spy-catcher can get scary every now and then. I was up at Tom and Jerry's, showing off for my buddy Chris Beall and pointing out prospective candidates, when a captivating Brazilian girl came to our table and sat down. She had a name that sounded like "Managua", the capital of Nicaragua, but I never quite got it straight – I'm not even sure she was from Brazil.

"What brings you to Nepal?" I asked as I offered my hand.

"Nothing really. I thinking maybe some trekking in mountains," she said as she grabbed my palm in a vise-like grip.

She, Chris and I talked merrily for what seemed like an hour, and then I starting feeling my oats a bit and felt like trying something risky.

"So, are you a shooter?" I asked. "I prefer a nice nine-millimetre semi, like a Glock. What about you?"

"Depends on what you use it for," was her harmless enough answer. "For me, the Glock is fine, but not with anything fancy like an extended clip. No need for more than the 17-round clip. Hard to hide and snags in the coat otherwise."

I retreated: "Oh."

"For me, if I use the Glock 17, I change to threaded barrel, 28 thread, left hand. The Lone Wolf is good, but it comes dirty and you have to scrub it. We make blueprint of the Evolution-9 suppressor and build our own, but we leave off the Nielson so it's no round cycling and no lost cartridges – one must always watch where one's brass falls, no?"

"Hey, Chris, look at the time! Jeez there, Mango, it was a lovely evening, but we've got to go."

I was fully confident that she would have a wonderful trek, and as Chris and I beat a hasty retreat, I was also confident that I would never find any of her spent cartridge casings, ever.

CHAPTER 14

GROUND ZERO AT 11,000 FEET

It was a typical autumn crossing season. It was a couple of typical seasons, actually. Over the span of three years, we made it a point to be up the Khumbu valley and based at Namche Bazaar during certain autumn months for the express purpose of grabbing bewildered and injured Tibetans coming off the pass from Tibet, and ensuring their safe transit to the Reception Centre in Kathmandu. No particular season stands out, truthfully, only a few particular accounts that I've compiled here.

Namche's residents were Sherpas: the legendary high-altitude Mount Everest experts, renowned for their courage, strength and loyalty. That typical rich Westerner who paid $50,000 to summit Mount Everest for the rights to brag about it at their next high-profile cocktail party probably failed to mentioned that they were "short-roped" or pulled up the last 1,000 metres or so to the summit of Everest by a Sherpa. Your average Sherpa, when they allow you to test their blood in a lab, has what is called a "high hematocrit" or, more specifically, an unusually high percentage of red blood cells. Simply put, this is good for Sherpas. It means that they can get more out of the decreased oxygen levels present at high altitudes than the rest of us can. Generations of adaptation to the harsh climbs of the Everest region have made them the unparalleled masters of their terrain and its altitude.

It was always amusing to me to be in the vicinity for the start of the Tenzing-Hillary Everest Marathon, the highest marathon race in the world. I happened to see the participants pass by one year when I was in Gorak Shep, a small settlement near Everest base camp. They were heading up to the Khumbu glacier at the head of Everest base camp for the start of the race. I witnessed self-possessed and too-skinny looking marathoners constantly checking the oversized watch on their wrist while sporting the latest Gore-Tex runners' base layer or whatever. They walked or jogged upwards based on the dictates of their watch, and sucked down sinister-looking glucose mixtures from plastic pouches.

The race typically began once each contestant had touched a foot to the Khumbu glacier – the Everest glacier – and waited for the starting signal. From the opening gun, marathon racers of every stripe and cunning would begin their race posturing and immediately settle into their running rhythm. The Sherpas walked. The race wound down from its start at the Everest base camp to Namche Bazaar, from 17,000 to around 11,000 feet on estimate – not for the faint hearted, and most assuredly not for the athletically arrogant.

Without fail, year in and year out a Sherpa would either win or take three out of the top four finishing spots in the race. It was their terrain, and their home-court advantage was like none other in the world. A race like the Tenzing-Hillary is not about conditioning or prowess, it's about patience and preservation, and the Sherpas had the formula wired. Most of them lived in or around Namche and spent their whole lives in the high Himalayas. This gave them somewhat of a local's advantage, to be sure. But for those of a more technical bent, medical studies have shown that physical exertion such as running at extreme altitudes requires tapping into energy reserves that are not recovered through sheer athleticism. Basically, you burn it at 17,000 feet and you don't get it back during a normal recovery period. Sherpas know this instinctively – hence the walking start. It wasn't until just below Lobuche, around the gravestone monuments to Sherpas that had died on Everest, that the Sherpas decided to start running. With plenty in reserve and generations of adaptability now on display, they easily passed the shocked and physically diminished Gore-Tex crowd and finished the race with energy to spare.

Sherpas, I have found, are not sentimental people. They do not seem especially intent on preserving the past. Back in the 1990s, the Sherpa Cooperative Hotel in Namche decided that in order to have a broader tourist business, they needed to have an attraction in their hotel bar. They managed to work an arrangement wherein a big Russian MI-17 helicopter airlifted a billiards table to the centre of town in three pieces. From there, a group of porters carried the massive slate components individually, in that same wicker *doko* basket that everyone in Nepal seems to use, the short distance to the hotel. The owners set up and levelled the construction and *voila*, the highest pool table in the world was upright and operational.

"It's a new way of life for us," a young Sherpa boy told me when I asked about the feat.

Namche was also the seat of the Tibetan underground back then, as upwards of 1,000 undocumented Tibetans passed through its horseshoe-shaped valley every year. Typically, Sherpas, feeling a strong sense of kinship, took care of their Tibetan brothers – whatever the cost. The word "Sherpa" is an evolved pronunciation of "Shar Bo" or "Shar Wa", which roughly means "eastern Tibet". God knows when, but Sherpas actually migrated from eastern Tibet to their place in Nepal and mountaineering history. Apparently, "Shar Bo" was the way these strange intruders from the north described themselves to indigenous Nepalis, and the name stuck. Sherpas *are* Tibetans. The few Sherpa language guides available in the one or two bookstores in Namche Bazaar reflect nothing more than basic dialectic differences between what is acknowledged to be the Sherpa language and the Khampa dialect of Tibet.

It was by sheer repetition and momentum that we always stayed at the View Lodge in downtown Namche. Ang Purba, the owner and former town mayor, had become a friend over the years. I trusted his local knowledge and treated it as holy writ. The View Lodge occupied the most central location in Namche Bazaar, and as such afforded all those who sat on its doorstep a walking intelligence catalogue. Chinese operatives, Tibetan border "guides", mountaineers, trekkers and charlatans all passed by its doors if they were in Namche. The Khumbu Lodge directly next door was famous for being the place where US President Jimmy Carter once bunked, but nothing compared to the View for its importance and positioning in Namche village life.

We rolled in one season with our usual "Ang Purba, tashe delek" greeting and were immediately quizzed about what we had done and seen since our last visit, and given a review of what we had talked about during our last stay. Nepalis never forget: Sherpas forget even less.

Like previous visits, we were intent on spending a few weeks making reconnaissance missions up the valley toward the Tibetan border, and escorting abandoned or ailing Tibetans to safety in Namche. This was always a speculative venture at best. We knew when the most likely Tibetan crossing activity might occur, but had no guarantee of actually confirming such activity, much less intercepting Tibetans in need. It was a gamble, but on one particular occasion we got lucky – so to speak.

It was called the Sagarmatha Club and it conducted its operations out of that pool-table hosting guesthouse, the Sherpa Cooperative, in downtown central Namche Bazaar. Monjo was the owner and overlord – he took a proprietary interest in a lot of things. Monjo would fill us with stories of pregnant Tibetan women being left on the Nangpa La (pass) by their guides because they were too slow, and six- and seven-year-old children grouping together and making the trek themselves, somehow without the help of such guides. These were remarkable stories of human migration and immense hardship as the altitude and the elements took their toll on each and all. Monjo and the Sagarmatha Club kept their eye on the Nangpa La trail and often conducted daring rescues of stranded and injured Tibetans strewn along its lengths from Namche to the Tibetan border.

One account involved a young Tibetan named Taga and his wife Chimi. Taga's leg circulation failed him on the crossing and his limbs began the steady progression towards frostbite. At some point after crossing the Nangpa La, he could no longer walk and Chimi took it upon herself to carry her husband on her back for what was probably a two-day journey to Namche. When they finally arrived, Monjo recalled the accounts of Sherpas asking Chimi why her shoulders were bleeding from the long walk.

"My husband's legs were so painful that he could not help but bite into my shoulders as I carried him. I didn't mind."

I later met Taga and Chimi in India. I had arranged to have our San Diego amputee monk friend Karma meet them and offer his perspective, as Taga had become an amputee as well – losing both of his legs below the knee to frostbite. Taga was smiling and animated while talking to Karma as he announced proudly that Chimi's shoulders had healed, and that their first child was resting comfortably in the next room.

Monjo was like a good casual acquaintance. He always knew my name when I arrived and always knew what I was up to. He gave me a Sagarmatha Club patch on this particular occasion, and I couldn't have been prouder. I admired Monjo and I admired the Sherpas in Namche. They believed in helping those in need and always seemed to be directed by a higher calling. In the face of police hostility, Maoist violence and Chinese pressure, they managed to assist, without fail, any Tibetans who made it over the Nangpa La and needed help.

On this one particular evening, we had an encounter with one of the "guides" who made his living shuttling Tibetans over the high mountain passes. He had left a few of his charges, frostbitten and bleeding, near the pass but accessible – just above the army post at Thame Teng. They were slowing down the group, and he couldn't be bothered to wait, so he just left them to fend for themselves.

"Guides" are noticeable on the spot. They generally have the appearance of former yak traders who may have wearied of Tibetans latching on to their yak caravans for safety as they crossed the Nangpa La, and decided there was a few yuan to be made by taking these people from Tibet and into Nepal. Rather perversely, their hair dangles with jewellery spirited from unwitting Tibetans; their coats are warm and full of Chinese currency; and their wrists bear witness to centuries of individual Tibetan family wealth with the turquoise and orange coral bracelets that were wrested as remittance for a safe passage to Nepal.

This guide was not keen to speak about what he had done. He told us vaguely where he'd left the Tibetans and that was all. He had his money and that was that. Fate had its own plans for the abandoned Tibetans as far as he was concerned. We had our own plans as well.

A few of the young Sherpa men from the village began to interrogate the guide with a decided ferocity. I was a few metres away at that point, but noticed that the guide's mood seemed to shift from aloof indifference to fearful indifference. Namche Bazaar was a safe haven for him as well, and the tone of the young Sherpa voices led me to believe that they were placing his room, alcohol and well-being in jeopardy for his abandoning those Tibetans up near Thame Teng. Gesticulations and shouting were followed by quiet acquiescence as the guide began to speak in more deliberate and more detailed language.

"Jim, we will be back late tonight with these Tibetans. You go to all the trekking shops and get all the bandages and medicine you can find, and bring them to the safe room at the Sherpa Cooperative. See you later."

With that, a handful of young men sped off into the evening and headed northward towards the Tibetan border. If they were lucky, it would take two to three hours to find the Tibetans, and another two hours to bring them back down to the makeshift clinic I was to set up at the Sherpa Cooperative Hotel.

It turned out that those left behind had made it, with at least some local help, to a certain Sundown Lodge. Apparently, the residents of the farmhouse where they were originally abandoned not only wanted nothing to do with Tibetans but knew the proper procedure for dealing with their presence, and promptly escorted them to this Sagarmatha Club-sympathetic trekkers' lodge deep in Thame village proper. It took our boys a while to figure this out, but they eventually found the pair – two girls – bandaged their feet as best they could and slowly walked/carried the girls to Namche. When they arrived, it was close to midnight.

Waiting just up the hill from Monjo's tiny "safe" room at the Cooperative, I heard the slipping sounds of weakly placed feet on stone, an impatient hinge swing and the crash of wooden door against rock wall. Making my way through pitch-black alleyways, whimpering echoes of cold exhausted voices greeted me through the darkness. The two pairs of eyes that strained towards the flame from my torch could not have been more than ten years old.

Resignation came from those eyes, resignation born of the knowledge that they would walk no further and that something painful and permanent had come into their lives, perhaps as a punishment they could not identify and could not understand.

Their blistered and torn feet could not bear the removal of shoes that had merged with dried body fluids and trail debris to form a false layer of skin. But the filthy remnants of their footwear had to be removed, and the children screamed in agony as blood flowed anew from freshly reopened wounds. No topical medications, no painkillers and no clean bandages could be given – none were available. So we struggled to staunch the bleeding with a few T-shirts and an old elastic knee brace. One particular area of damage kept shifting shape, making it almost impossible to pin down, control the flow and locate the source of the bleeding. We would have had better luck placing a bandage on a bowl of mashed potatoes.

In a few minutes, the air was filled with the acrid aroma of steaming Tibetan butter tea, which warmed and calmed the children. The blood loss had stopped. It was not readily apparent, but if these foot wounds represented the initial stages of frostbite, then the direct pressure we employed with our T-shirt-wrapped hands pushing against the ravaged flesh would ultimately have caused more harm than good. In the cruelest of ironies, we might have further destroyed delicate and damaged foot tissue in order to stop the tissue bleeding, and may have killed off any remaining chance for its full healing – we stopped the bleeding on a foot that may now have to be amputated because we used direct pressure to stop the bleeding.

With the children settled, I bid everyone a good night and shuffled back up the hill to my room. There was no thankful smile for the saving hero, no celebrations. Those kids were still in pain when I left and probably wouldn't sleep much that evening. Neither would I. It never left my mind from that night forward: the thought that I may just have stepped in shit once again. My best clear-headed efforts might ultimately result in ruining the lives of those two children. I had to stop the foot bleeding, right? Was there anything else I should have done? If I didn't have the skill level to know these answers, then what the hell was I doing out there anyway?

I didn't see those children after that night and I never learned their story. I didn't have to: We'd heard it before. A child walking with a group of adults falls behind the group due to excruciatingly painful feet and is left to fend for herself – it seldom ends well.

The children still had quite the journey to make to Kathmandu, and probably left the next morning before I woke up. It was now a race against time and infection to get them to the Reception Centre Clinic for proper treatment. The Sherpa community knew what to do – they'd done it hundreds of times before – and a precise mechanism began to unfold under Sherpa precision and Sherpa dedication.

First, the children had to be re-clothed to look like Sherpa children and/or budget trekkers. This was easy as Namche is a market town and plenty of cheap, Chinese-made, neon parkas are available. Add sunglasses and a hat, and the disguise was complete. If donation money was plentiful, the children could catch a helicopter to Kathmandu from nearby Syangboche; but this was a lean year and they would have to find a way to make it to Lukla, a two-day walk down the valley, where they would catch a less-expensive flight on an old de Havilland Twin Otter plane. Through a series of diversions and by stopping at safe-houses along the way, the children would travel day and night if necessary, and would expertly avoid the scrutiny of corrupt checkpoint officers through the efforts of their Sherpa escorts.

A phone at a nondescript lodge in Lukla would be picked up. Yes, two children, badly wounded, would be on the next Yeti Airlines flight to Kathmandu, the lodge owner would confirm. Turning, he would give the news to the Sherpa guardians.

"He will be waiting."

Our two rescued girls probably had their passage fare of around 800 yuan ($100) paid by a relative intent on providing them a better life by getting them out of Tibet, and who simply trusted fate beyond that.

In those years, family-sustaining jobs were in short supply Tibetans as scores of new and Communist Party-subsidised Han Chinese immigrants began to fill Lhasa and other major southern Tibetan towns looking for work and starting their own Tibetan-excluding businesses. From accounts I heard, Tibetan school children were denied access to quality education, and were forbidden to learn the Tibetan language or history when schooling could be found. Tibetan culture was being systematically assimilated, if not outright eliminated, at the hands of the Chinese government, and many Tibetans were seeking a better life by risking a hike into Nepal and the subsequent walk to India – the home of the exiled Dalai Lama.

Perhaps there were personal instances of cruelty and injustice that helped shape someone's decision to send these children over a 19,000-feet Himalayans pass in the care of a stranger, and the exact circumstances we may never know; but I can tell you a few things about the journey:

Tibetans seeking passage to Nepal need very few conversations before they are placed in front of the man or "guide" who will take them across the border. These guides typically assemble all potential and paying crossers at a gathering point, where they take their 800-yuan fee and load them on a bus bound for a location somewhere near Tingri in the Everest region of southern Tibet. When they disembark, the guide invariably tells his customers that heavy snow or an avalanche has obliterated the trail, and that he knows of an adjacent trail that is very difficult but the only hope of crossing for this group. He will need some extra money for the extra effort. Those without the extra demanded yuan are either left penniless at Tingri or are able to salvage their journey by forfeiting family jewellery and heirlooms to the guide. The trip then begins on foot over the same route that has been used for hundreds of years by yak traders, two-way pilgrims and fleeing Tibetans alike. As all of the guide's charges are first-time crossers, he knows that they have no idea that their path requires no special expertise or extra money; and if all goes well, his ruse will have worked once again and he will have pocketed a bit of a bonus.

In the foothills outside of the town of Tingri near Tibet's border with Nepal, the group of anxious and shivering Tibetans waits for nightfall. Ahead lies a series of ravines that will hopefully take them, undetected, past the notorious Chinese security encampment tower and prison facility. Will tonight be the night they pick the same ravine that the Chinese have picked for an impromptu patrol? It is a life or death gamble. Their guide whispers emphatically for quiet along the trail; they must not be seen or heard along this stretch, and will walk for almost one kilometre stooped down below one-metre high ravine walls to avoid detection. Out and above the ravine safely, the sounds of footfalls, rock tumbles and water splashes are all amplified tenfold in the light air and rock outcroppings of the open canyon faces that now define their route. There must be no talking, no giving away of position. Guards from the encampment can shoot a Tibetan in the back from 200 yards, and their deadly accuracy must not be provoked on this night.

There is no cover for the travellers, only darkness and cold. Their route meanders up the open and windy Tingri plain, where they would be in plain view, silhouetted black against snow-covered trails should they make this first day's journey during broad daylight. Only yak drivers seeking to ply their wares in Nepal go unmolested on this trail by day; but they should be avoided at all costs. Stories of Tibetans seeking a masqueraded passage with the caravans often conclude with robbery or cash-induced surrender to the Chinese at the hands of profiteering caravan leaders, and our guide is keenly aware of their particular brand of danger.

Some five hours ahead looms the ancient yak trail that crosses the ice crevasses of the Nangpa La pass at 19,000 feet. From there, with luck, the group can make it into Nepal and onward to India. Our two girls wonder if they will get to see the Dalai Lama, and they reach to grasp the hands of an old man in their group who seems, for now, avuncular and concerned. They have stopped for the moment and something appears to be wrong. The guide has noticed that the pace of the group is much too slow to make the "late camp" at the base of the Nangpa La in time for the requisite few hours of rest, and they all may have to begin the arduous climb with little or no stopping. If the pace of the group is too slow to maintain the proper crossing schedule at this point, guides have been known to turn around and flee – leaving the paid customers to fend for themselves.

But our guide persists. He has made a good living from these trips and is aware of the need to preserve his reputation. Still, he also knows that the schedule for crossing the pass is very precise and must be maintained in order for the group to have a chance. He's also failed to tell everyone about the new and aggressive People's Liberation Army (PLA) base that is located on a ridge just near the Nepal border, and his concerns begin to mount. But the weather is cooperating and he is of no particular mind to abandon his charges – the decision to proceed is made.

The key to success for any illegal Tibetan crossing of the Nangpa La is to make "late camp" at the base of the climb to the pass no later than roughly midnight. This gives the group a few crucial hours of rest before they begin their early-morning climb through the darkness, out of the Tingri plain and onward to the Nangpa La. The hazardous trudge through the snow demands no torches, no coughing and no talking. If the moon happens to be out and shining, travellers may view the sharp contrast of yak droppings against moonlit snow and count themselves lucky for the aid of trail markers – whatever the form. Following the droppings upward, it is important that the sunrise is well beaten by the time a group reaches the high ridge where the new PLA base is located. The odds are that no Chinese patrols will be out at such an early hour of the morning, and in all probability crossers can sneak through undetected if they move swiftly.

Our group is late. They didn't make camp in time for an adequate rest and the guide is unsympathetic to their pleas for rest – they must press on. The two children find it increasingly difficult to keep up with the adults: Their bodies do not handle the cold as well and their poorly clad feet are taking two steps for every one of the adults' in the deep snow. Their feet begin the agonising progression towards being frozen solid. Fatigue and pain merge into numbness as the group slips cleanly past the new Chinese base near the pass, and the sky lightens for another day. Relief arrives slowly. Sunshine and warmth are delayed as the Cho Oyu massif, directly over their left shoulder, obscures a clear dawn's welcome, and leaves them suspended in deep violet and grey hues. It is ten degrees below zero.

The climb to the Nangpa La pass is only realised when the nearly 50-metre long wall of prayer flags is visible to the immediate west of the ascending trail. Our children notice some of the older women in the group weeping and lighting fresh juniper sprigs as an incense offering at the wall. They have made it to the border of Nepal. A few of the men place *katas*, or frayed silk scarves, among the scores of flags, perhaps in spiritual thankfulness, most definitely as a marker of a struggle defeated. It has been a long night and early morning. The climb itself was tediously monotonous, sweeping and gradual, not particularly gruelling but extremely dangerous for our group due to the cold, exposure and lack of cover from anyone with hostile intent. Despite being chronically behind schedule and fearing discovery, our guide chose his ravines, trails and movement patterns wisely. He has managed to escort his group out of Tibet, past two security-force encampments and to the border of Nepal and freedom. But his work is not done. Not yet.

Surveying the descent into Nepal next to the frozen carcass of an unfortunate yak, the guide ponders. A few hours below the pass is the group's scheduled daytime hiding place: a roofless rock-walled enclosure that acts as a seasonal shelter for herdsmen seeking high pastures in the summer months. They should have made it to the shelter just as dawn broke, the guide thinks. Now they will have to risk a walk in the full morning light and rest in the shelter for a full day without knowing if some damn profiteering yak-dung farmer has given away their position. Another night on the ice will sap any remaining energy out of the group – that is out. They have to get down, regardless of the risk.

"It's your fault if we get caught," he barks at the children, as they finally make it to the shelter after an entire morning of walking exposed by daylight and in full view of any humans with, perhaps, a sense of opportunity and an eye for profit. "You're too slow and are endangering the rest of the group. If you don't feel ready to travel by this evening, we'll have to go without you."

He means it. There's a Nepalese army base another hour's walk down the valley, and precise and quick riverbed movements must be employed to get past undetected. If they are caught because of these children, the guide will lose all his money and newly acquired Tibetan jewellery to the soldiers, spend a few nights in a mouldy concrete cell and probably get beaten in the process; the Tibetans, much worse. By prior arrangement, the soldiers might forcibly return our group to the Chinese base at the top of the pass, where they most certainly would be beaten, tortured, imprisoned or all three.

Nightfall: The children's feet have worsened. They make a feeble attempt to walk but immediately collapse in pain. The decision is swift. Not bothering to look back, the guide sets off at a quick pace and shouts for the group to follow. In a moment they are gone. The two girls sit crying in pain on a trail in the Himalayas, alone, frightened and in total darkness.

Time passes. Death comes to many Tibetans along this trail. In the pitch-black, moonless Himalayan night, the children hold each other close at the sound of footsteps. Is it a dog? They heard from their old uncle many days before that the people in Nepal do not feed their dogs, and that they should always stick close to the group or the dogs would go to bed happy and full from a meal of young Tibetans. But the old man was gone, gone with the others. *Why did he leave us to these dogs?* they wonder.

Nearing now, the footsteps become quicker, more determined. From the darkness comes a rush of blankets, strong arms and calloused hands. The children scream in pain and terror.

Abruptly jerked from their puddle of tears, the children find themselves suddenly moving; not by their own power and not in the jaws of a famished Nepali dog, but moving through the blackness in the arms of humans – strange, peculiar-smelling humans. Soon, the silhouetted movement of black shadows emerges on the horizon. Thresholds are crossed, candles lit and the children are gently placed on yak-pelt blankets and woven rugs. Death will not come tonight.

True to form, I did not sleep well after our night of foot-reshaping. Stumbling down the stairs into the morning light of Namche, I was greeted by the sight of an eight-year-old Sherpa girl with an unusual cargo in the extra-large *doko* basket suspended from her head. A middle-ranking official with one of the big aid agencies had decided to take his wife and two small, pale and infinitely blond children on a trek out of Namche. Apparently fearing the onset of physical strain and footwear depletion, he hired a few Sherpa children to haul his kids along the trail in their baskets. These Sherpas – girls of roughly the same age and displacement as their blond charges – were to carry their precious alabaster loads of human entitlement up Himalayan trails for however many days Mr Dad had remaining of his holiday. And so as not to worry the reader here: the vactioning children were constantly supervised by a complement of toys that accompanied them in their peer-powered taxis.

CHAPTER 15

THE UN FINALLY DOES SOMETHING

We were nearing exhaustion from weeks of traversing the Khumbu valley looking for stray Tibetans and taking photos for the ICT when we first heard about a disturbing occurrence: Forcible repatriations were beginning again, but now at an accelerated rate.

Forcible repatriation occurs whenever someone is physically returned to their country of origin against their will, usually with no opportunity to claim asylum and no time to complain. If you are an undocumented Tibetan in Nepal, this is a particularly bad thing. Typically, Nepali policemen, under the incentive of a full and standing Chinese bribe, might be tempted into supplementing their income by capturing any loose Tibetans who happened to be wandering around the mountains, and turning them over to Chinese agents directly – without documentation, processing or identification. No questions asked, no records, cash on delivery. The Chinese would then haul their prizes back across the border and, so the stories went, either throw them into prison or lay them out, side by side and face up, on a gravel road and drive over their legs with a truck so they wouldn't run away again. Nice people.

The practice itself was not new, considering the remoteness and autonomous impunity afforded to those Nepali officers stationed, unsupervised, in the high Himalayas. But the new frequency and bold openness of these events suggested a more institutional thrust by the Chinese – and an enhanced zeal. No longer a remote and easily concealable activity confined to weak border policemen, these repatriations were now taking place in broad daylight, with Tibetans being snatched up by the handful, and along the Kodari highway: the main artery from Kathmandu to the Tibetan border and a major transportation route for Tibetans, both legal and illegal. It seemed that repatriations were moving from the odd reported isolated incident to wholesale open transfers – with the Tibetans themselves turning into a saleable commodity.

This kind of event could easily spiral downward to where Chinese border officers would take de facto control of all transportation corridors in northern Nepal for the purpose of completely controlling Tibetan movement and maintaining, as they like to say, "regional security". Nepal would be too weak to stop such advances.

We were stuck trying to figure out a solution. The United Nations High Commission for Refugees (UNHCR) wasn't about to do anything, and didn't seem to be aware of the problem, much less be in the process of issuing one of their weak and indecipherable statements, so they were neither a viable nor timely option for help. We had always considered any branch of the United Nations to be worthless in such matters, so this was not a particular cause for alarm as far as our group of independent trouble-makers was concerned. Aside from inspecting Tibetan refugees from time to time, the UNHCR didn't seem to exist on any demonstratively productive level in Nepal, and this was fine with our people, as it kept the UN out of our way for the most part. But now, their absence in the field gave us an idea: As it became clearer to us that the UN wouldn't be getting involved, and as such didn't seem to be using their logo and Letterhead much along the Kodari highway, we saw an opportunity.

We had never heard of anyone interacting with the UN out in the far Himalayas, so how would anyone know what they looked like? In Nepal, they didn't even wear those silly blue hats, so they could be anyone, right? Mental cogs began to turn. A plan was hatched that involved us travelling by car to every bribable police station and corrupt army check-post along the Kodari highway from Kathmandu to the Tibetan border, to see if we could scare the hell out of their repatriation plans by passing ourselves off as a group sanctioned by the UN. We would assemble a handful of fraudulent but official-looking documents to pass out, and coopt the UNHCR logo as a letterhead to make the whole thing look important. It was a brazen plan – probably illegal as well – and many potential problems stood out. One in particular: How would we be taken seriously? What kind of documents would we need to fake in order to pull this thing off?

"Well, *Dai*, something from the government always works," was the universal response from our Nepali field team, after little or no reflection.

They meant the Government of Nepal – a non-starter. We weren't about to march into some minister's office and ask for help in this. "You see, *babu*, we're going to save Tibetans by pretending to be the UN. Do you have any old forms lying around?" This approach would result in an epic failure. The average minister in Nepal not only couldn't care less about the fate of Tibetans beyond the tourist money they bring in, but more to the point, he probably just bought a new car from the money the Chinese gave him so he could more easily drive to India and visit his daughter, who was studying at a plush New Delhi private school that was prospering happily with the tuition it received from the Chinese on her behalf.

We settled on manufacturing a nice piece of stationery with a red border that reiterated an obscure and forgotten statement made in support of Tibetans by the Nepali foreign minister a few years prior. Never mind that this was a renegade proclamation from the pen of Madhu Rachman Acharya, the minister of record who would be ousted from office long before we were to use his words. And never mind that this was the only remotely pro-Tibetan statement to ever bear the imprimatur of the Government of Nepal – we were on to something, and momentum was starting to build.

Next, I found a copy of the UN's *Universal Declaration of Human Rights*, written in Nepali, on the internet. Again, never mind that Nepal was never a signatory or party to this declaration; the point was, it was written in Nepali and looked official.

For the final step, I had an old friend in the US who worked for the Defense Department send along a few UNHCR letterheads that, for whatever reason, happened to be in his possession. We would use these as a template to fashion a reasonable facsimile of a UNHCR royal edict, enunciation or whatever they call those mind-numbing papers they turn out, and with luck, the version created would successfully introduce our phony subcommittee of the UN and confidently display our own "UN-speak" statement.

This was not the era of Photoshop, sadly, and many of the computers in Kathmandu were running Windows 97. All we could do was cross our fingers, say a prayer to Lord Pashupati and hope our forgeries would be convincing through our best efforts on Windows Paint.

A credible UNHCR watermark was affixed, and we footnoted the effort with the address of some UN office in Geneva that conducted the standard benign UN business. Now, it came to composing the substance of our letter. It had to look official, carry an element of threat in its wording and create a fair amount of doubt in the minds of corrupt policemen as to the safety and impunity of their Tibetan repatriation side business. We determined that the letter would present us as an official subcommittee of the UN, and would take the tone of an agency that had just caught everyone in the act. We would call ourselves the "United International Independent Commission" of the UN, or the UIICUN (pronounced "We-con"), and the content of that letter read:

To: Immigration officials, border police and army personnel

From: The United International Independent Commission (UIIC)

It has come to our attention that policies adopted by His Majesty's Government of Nepal and the Office of the Foreign Minister of Nepal regarding the forcible return of Tibetans to Tibet have been violated.

According to the policies of Nepal and the International Community, you are to follow these rules immediately, and without question:

1. *Do not return captured Tibetans to Tibet. Contact the Tibetan Reception Centre or the UNHCR for Tibetan transportation to Kathmandu.*
2. *Do not release captured Tibetans into the hands of any police or immigration officials from other nations.*
3. *All captured Tibetans are to be kept safe from harm until transport arrives.*
4. *You are to act according to the policies of His Majesty's Government as outlined in the enclosed letter from Foreign Minister Acharya and articles 13 and 14 of the Universal Declaration of Human Rights at all times.*

We will be visiting your facility soon to ensure compliance.

UIIC Representative

By the early spring of 2004, the packet was finished. Fifty copies came off the printer, and a dozen staff members stood around our tiny office as the Foreign Minister's statement, the Nepali *Universal Declaration of Human Rights* and our contrived "UIIC" statement letter were folded in an official manner and placed into 50 high-quality white envelopes with a UNHCR logo emblazoned on the front.

That evening, a list of roughly 20 army posts and police checkpoints that dotted the Kodari highway from Kathmandu to Tibet was compiled by hasty consensus. Those Nepalis that sat with me around a candle-lit table staring down at the list rose in unison, raised their beers in a toast and clanged their bottles with mine as we vowed to meet again in prison should this thing go terribly wrong. This was breaking new ground. No one had ever wilfully impersonated the UN in Nepal for the purpose of stopping human rights violations. None of us were even quite sure of the punishment for such a thing if we were caught, but we had put so much time into this project and were now determined to try, regardless of the outcome. I can't say that this was a competent or even a wise effort. The only thing we knew with certainty was that we would not cross paths with the real UN trying to do the same thing.

It was time to make our delivery run. Ram Chandra had a young nephew who needed to earn a few extra rupees, and didn't mind a little excitement in the process. After a series of firm phone calls, the arrangements were made. The boy seemed the perfect courier candidate: young, poor and without a clue as to what he'd stumbled into. I never saw him and never knew his name, but the following dawn, Ram Chandra arranged to give him a taxi for the entire day and a few thousand rupees (around $30) as payment. His task was to deliver a single sealed envelope to the attending officer at every army and police facility along the Kodari highway, utter the simple introduction of "Document from the UN" and get the hell out. He was also given special instructions to take no chances at the notorious police station and jail at Barabise, where Chinese police were known to congregate and heavily influence the Nepali police constables stationed there. For that effort, he was to have his taxi at the ready, slide the package under the door and get out as quickly as possible.

Days later, Ram Chandra reported that the boy had struggled but finished his task up by Tatopani at the Tibetan border long after dark. It didn't go well. He was questioned at every stop. Just outside of Kathmandu at the Bhaktapur police checkpoint, the boy found himself face to face with a senior officer, who grabbed him, flung him to the floor and began screaming a series of indecipherable questions. The level of aggression increased to the point that, fearing for his safety, our boy saw his chance when the officer left the room, and he bolted from the guard shack and hid behind the wall of a motorcycle repair facility. Wild-eyed and hyperventilating with fear, he took off his shirt in an attempt to disguise himself as he sprinted through mud- and oil-covered alleyways, running for what he thought was about a kilometre before he stopped to catch his breath. Gathering his wits, he hung an old rag from his belt, coated his hands with oil from the floor of a nearby shop and pretended to be a local mechanic. The stench of grease and alley soil that he would now be forced to wear for the rest of the day accompanied him as he snaked his way gradually back towards the checkpoint, reacquired his taxi and headed to his next delivery assignment. Hey, 30 bucks is 30 bucks to a young man.

Oddly, the delivery to Barabise went off quietly.

The effort itself resulted in a dramatic and immediate improvement in the situation. We didn't hear of another instance of forced repatriation from this area for the next eight years.

On a personal note, I will always be grateful to the United Nations for the success of this programme, and I look forward to continuing the fraudulent utilisation of their credibility in the future.

Chapter 16

The Best and the Brightest

I was increasingly haunted by an image I had created in my head from John Kenneth Knaus's first book on the Central Intelligence Agency's (CIA) involvement with Tibet: *Orphans of the Cold War.* It concerned Ilya Tolstoy, grandson of the famous author, who was a commissioned military officer working in the Tibetan arena conducting somewhat covert missions for the Office of Strategic Services (OSS, the precursor of the modern CIA).

Tolstoy was a bit of a rebel and had a tendency to manufacture diplomatic gestures towards the Tibetans that were not backed by real initiatives. He strayed off message, and the OSS later deemed his missions to Tibet as having little or no value. Yet he was a fixer. He used his title and influence to arrange meetings; he took the pulse of the Tibetans' needs and political aspirations at the time; he made some of the first films and climatologic assessments of Tibet and provided volumes of raw data. The OSS was only impressed with the strategic aspects of Tolstoy's trips, in which he failed noticeably, but he was in the field understanding the situation to a degree that those in political power in the US had never seen before. And the Tibetans seemed to genuinely like and trust him – some failure.

We felt that we were a lot like Ilya Tolstoy. Our little group of troublemakers had no difficulty in reimagining ourselves into any position that served the need of the moment – often deriving ideas and solutions from whatever momentum presented itself to us at any given time. Like Tolstoy, we were effecting change from the ground level and measuring real progress, one contact, one project, one Tibetan at a time.

Unfortunately, Ilya Tolstoy has been dead for many years. All of us with individual approaches and a handful of personal funds making things happen on the ground on behalf of Tibetans and others, no matter how useful, will be dead one day too. The only things that will remain with any measure of initiative for the kinds of programmes we all ran will be the institutions – governments – and right now they just don't get it. They seem to be repulsed by the idea of understanding the realities of issues from the ground up. They like broad, policy-level strokes that never seem to address core local concerns. During this period, I came to believe that in order to see real change, efforts have to be sustainable beyond one person's achievements, and part of ongoing efforts backed by survivable policies. There has to be a *culture* in place that is ground-effective on the Tibet issue, not just a single motivated individual or two, and this culture must be consistently funded. Governments, particularly the one that runs the United States, value such standardisation of approach. The problem was how to convince the US of the need to adopt a standard culture of field prioritisation as a means of support for Tibet. Could we get them to deepen their feedback loop on issues and actually partner with local expertise? Until now, they had been lobbing long-distance money bombs at Dharamsala with little or no direct engagement at the field level. I decided to explore the idea further.

I'd like to say that speaking, working, fraternising and writing reports amongst the various agencies of the US government, both inside and out of Nepal was a rewarding and educational experience. I'd like to say that. More accurately, I'm compelled to say that my very first day of working with the US government was my very last day on earth with a full head of hair.

A great many individuals in governmental positions couldn't care less about speaking with any organisation about new and effective ideas surrounding Tibet; many were simply holding down a chair on a long career path. A rare few government officials showed genuine interest in what I had to say and did their best to direct me towards relevant resources. But they themselves were hamstrung by their own bureaucracy and inability to act on anything new. I encountered all of this during my years of experimenting with Washington bureaucracy.

There was Eric, who was a regional chair for an internationally concerned branch of the US Justice Department (DOJ). I approached him with an idea, developed by Nepal police personnel and our group, to strengthen border security capacities through international standardisation. Mind you, during the development phase of this project, we were careful to make sure a component of cross-border transit safety was included for Tibetan "pilgrims", and I was most certainly trying to squeeze my Tibetan issues into the cracks. But overall, this was a pragmatic and positive proposal that seemed to benefit all stakeholders. Eric liked what he understood of the programme, but was quick to remind me that he was in charge of all of South Asia for the Justice Department. Oh, and Africa too, by the way. And he'd had to literally beg to have a small $300,000 budget allocation for something he was doing in Sri Lanka. Sorry, Jim.

Being a government office – a big one at that (the Ronald Reagan Building) – I figured I'd be quickly forgotten along with my proposal, so I made sure Eric's staff had a few colourful rolls of Tibetan prayer flags to remember me by.

He kept referring to this branch of the DOJ called the INL, or International Narcotics and Law Enforcement section. They seemed to have the most direct pathway to the financing I needed to help out with the project I'd created. Some person named Vivien made the decisions, and apparently had created quite a bottleneck. Not much, if any, funding beyond token projects had found its way to Nepal from this branch. The few people I knew at the Justice desk in the American embassy in Kathmandu at the time were screaming mad about it.

There were congressional and bureaucratic budget battles like this going on constantly, and it made my pleadings seem very small and inappropriate. It was politics first and foremost, and the goalposts were constantly in motion. And even if one were to get through the "Vivien" gauntlet and find a willing and sympathetic ear, the official project submission process was long and cumbersome and had to be coordinated with existing Justice Department field contractors who had probably never set foot in Nepal. In essence, introducing a new programme to help any group in Nepal, or wherever, to the DOJ would require a year's worth of applications and submissions, which would only lead to a no-guarantee "yes" or "no" decision somewhere in the distant future; and this decision may or may not have anything to do with the merits of the programme.

The US military was no better.

Over the years, I'd developed some very close friendships with members of Nepal's various security forces. The Nepal army was an omnipresent quasi-political entity with pro-monarchy leadings; the municipal police force was a considerably less-disciplined group often influenced by its sense of opportunism; and then there was the Nepal Armed Paramilitary Force (APF). They were created to kill Maoists by Prime Minister GP Koirala around the year 2000, and they had bucked the trend of corruption and abuse, for the most part, that characterised other policing branches in Nepal. Their constables routinely took duty postings to guard UN facilities in such garden spots as South Sudan, Kosovo and the Charles Taylor version of Liberia. In essence, the APF was the face of Nepal in the international security community. A lot of the constables who were friends of mine through Deepak were now climbing the ranks. A few made deputy inspector general, just a few promotions behind the top APF leader, or the inspector general of police (IGP). Because the APF was a relatively new presence on Nepal's security-force scene, they were extremely eager to show their international-level talents, and were constantly looking for ways to improve their efficiency and status among Nepal's competitive security community. They were forward-looking and wanted programmes and funding for programmes from the US, and they were happy to welcome any advisors the US embassy sent their way.

I received an e-mail from a friend at the embassy, one of the last true Nepal experts left, who asked me to drop what I was doing in the US at the time, come out to Kathmandu and help with a proposal for the APF. A young officer from the US Pacific Command (PACOM) was working with the APF, and they wanted my suggestions and input. Some 30 hours of travel later, I met the young man.

He had spent a little time at the APF headquarters in Kathmandu, and briefed me on his progress. "Jim, I've convinced the APF to really buy into wiffle ball. I spent a few months 'socialising' the idea to the IGP, and he committed funds. Now we've got a small wiffle ball contingent at the APF that's learning the game quite effectively."

Wiffle ball: a baseball-type game, only with plastic balls and plastic bats.

This guy was teaching wiffle ball to people who had taken live weapon fire in Kosovo, or who may have been under a constant state of alert in Sudan. Somewhere way up the chain of command from this gentleman, the idea was conceived that to build relationships and trust with indigenous forces, the US had to teach them games. They would then be so overjoyed with the sound of plastic hitting plastic that they wouldn't notice the fact that we were collecting intelligence from them. So here he came, wiffle balls in hand, to build trust and "socialise" ideas with the APF. It was pathetic and insulting, and I needed to think of a way to curtail it or the US would risk looking like a laughing stock in the region. The Chinese, I was told, were already puzzled as to why the Americans were taking such an odd approach.

My embassy buddy had let me down, and I had just flown halfway around the world to work with an imbecile with no idea of what to do or why he was doing it in Nepal. This was going to turn out badly, I sensed. But hey, I was in Kathmandu again. I also thought of Ilya Tolstoy again, and decided to make the most of it. Bad choice.

The proposal the PACOM officer had me write involved setting up Little League-style playing teams for a wiffle ball league where "at risk" youths in southern Nepal could learn from the APF the fine points of the game while working harmoniously with the local municipal police. Dear God. At least I got him to change the damn sport to cricket, but the whole idea was a disaster from its inception. I won't even go into the fact that the APF and the municipal police forces hate each other with a vengeance.

"No, Jim, we gotta get these guys to work together here. I've socialised it and I know it's worth a try."

"You know," I said, "I appreciate that you've called me out here at the end of your time in Nepal to write your school assignment paper for you, but you're going to make everyone look bad with some of this stuff."

He would not be dissuaded from his task, so I told him I was adding a proposal to his packet to help raise the level of play a bit. I threw in that project I pitched to the DOJ: my border monitoring assessment programme that had some real substantive Tibetan initiatives tied to it. I was now working on it from the Nepal side with the APF and they were ready to go forward with it. He was happy. He got someone to do his homework for him and got a neat bonus as well.

With that, he was off again to APF headquarters to conduct a full-day seminar on how to use a bullhorn.

Long after this young captain had left Nepal, I met with his replacements: equally young and equally green about Nepal. I told them about their predecessor and how one of the general officers of the APF, who ran a training facility for the UN, came in uncomfortably close proximity to me after that episode and said:

"The APF is not here to train American children. If you want to continue to be welcomed at our headquarters, tell these army people to send us programmes we can use – and have them send men."

"Socialise that," I told the new guys.

Who actually serves in Nepal? What makes any foreign service or military person take a posting in Kathmandu? Without a doubt, those individuals who elect to serve their country through the foreign services are both dedicated and brave, but the pattern I've seen over the past two decades of such individuals coming and going suggests a subset composed of two types.

First, there are directors and staff who've just finished up their postings in difficult areas like Afghanistan and Iraq, and are looking for a little quiet time in Nepal. "Coasting postings" I call them. Former USAID Nepal director Kevin Rushing, who was charged with sitting on a roughly $200 million pile of money designated for Nepal, did just that – sit. We combed the internet and other sources for some clue as to why this USAID veteran, lauded and fresh from Iraq, would want to come to our little slice of heaven in Nepal. The most I was able to determine from his interviews was that he "wanted to see the Himalayas".

The other type is the "first poster" individual, who may be brand new to foreign service and has been stationed in Nepal to stretch their wings. Nepal as a training lab, if you will. This group mostly comprises young State Department guys and fresh-out-of-college types in whose visages resides a level of hope and optimism that betrays their newness to foreign service – and an endless supply of young military officers and operatives. Kind of like Club Med meets "A Semester Abroad".

It all led me to conclude: If you are in the US Foreign Service, you absolutely will not make a difference in the world if you are posted in Nepal. Period. But by all means, come visit the country when you need a break from Afghanistan.

The very mention of Tibet to these people is often returned with a blank stare or some reflexive reaching for a procedural guideline of some sort. Combine this with the fact that a posting in Nepal for foreign service workers is typically around two years, and you can be reasonably sure that there will be no talk of any solid policy on such a career-jeopardising topic as saving Tibetans. *Just ignore it and tell my replacement to handle it – or just ignore it.*

So, after much stress-induced hair loss, I've changed my mind. I have now come to believe that the Tolstoy model really does work for me. I don't care about sustaining efforts or programme legacies through governmental standards if they are sustained by bureaucratic, clueless baboons. Give me one Tolstoy on the scene every 40 years or so and that will be sustainable enough for me – it takes nearly that long to get a programme approved through government channels anyway.

That was it. I was done trying to impress anything or anyone from any multi-layered bureaucracy of any sort. They were a disengaged lot with narrow programmes that all seem based on keeping the tone and substance of any real progress to a minimum. I will confess that the lure of such institutions still pulls at me from time to time. What was still unclear to me was just how much the "institutional" approach was neutering the Western Tibet Movement, and how much I was to be haunted by the shift.

CHAPTER 17

THE "GENTLEMEN'S AGREEMENT"

It was mid-May in 2014 and I was wincing over something I'd just read. It was personal to me and I continued to wonder why I must be singled out to endure this same ridiculous exercise once again. Didn't these people ever learn? I'd winced this way before – too many times – always over the same issue.

On this day, the ever vigilant and opportunistic Human Rights Watch had just come down hard on the Government of Nepal in one of their screeds for failing to enforce an idea known as the "Gentlemen's Agreement", which, according to its current interpretation, is supposed to guarantee the safe passage of undocumented Tibetans through Nepal and onward to India by the Nepalese government. It's a well-meaning concept and it tries to define the delicate nature of Tibetan migration as something performed with a wink and a nod, while adding a sense of identity to something that has always been unspoken, assumed and close to the ground. It has been misused, misinterpreted and misunderstood for years by humanitarian organisations and politicians alike, who have shouted the term from the treetops as if it describes the very nature of Nepal's relationship to Tibetans and to the US. It is also a mocking testament to my own hubris and failure, and it prods the same confession every time I read it. There is no hiding – it's like a photo someone takes of you drunk at a party, while covered in something foul, that keeps surfacing on the internet. The confession always comes: "I defined the 'Gentlemen's Agreement' and am partially to blame for the damage it has done." I seldom feel better after saying that, and perhaps that is a good thing – I don't need a shallow catharsis, and the sting has its own uses. I'm reminded of a young man's eagerness to please and establish his credibility at the feet of those who portend wisdom on the Tibet issue from Washington; of good intentions gone sour; and of broken promises and betrayal by those you trust.

It started back in late 2000. I had just read that the United Nations High Commission for Refugees (UNHCR) was outraged by the fact that the Nepal government, due mostly to the 17th Karmapa's escape from China, had closed down the avenues for Tibetan border migration through Nepal. The UNHCR feigned high disappointment at this and protested that they were unable to do their Tibetan-monitoring-and-fact-finding function. This was complete bullshit, and I wrote John Ackerly an e-mail saying as much. The UNHCR was nowhere near the Tibetan border on the Nepal side, and sure as hell wasn't conducting any fact-finding missions on behalf of Tibetans. We all knew that. A few years later, I created a phony UN commission that conducted phony UN business because we all knew that. The last thing anyone anywhere near the Tibetan border expected to see was any group calling itself a UN anything – that's how we pulled off our little masquerade, and that's why these new UNHCR protestations were bullshit. This was a classic UN back-door credibility ploy: Scream bloody murder about a lack of access that you had no intention of using in the first place.

In the e-mail, I mentioned for the first time that there must be some sort of informal arrangement between Nepal border security forces and the Tibetans that allowed for a brief look-away as the Tibetans crossed into Nepal. The reasoning for this, and perhaps the reasoning since 1959, was that these Tibetans were not some illegal gatecrashers bent on subverting the cultural equilibrium of Nepal, but rather pilgrims on their way to India to see the Dalai Lama. Unbeknownst to me, this was the first time such a dynamic had been brought to light for the West, much less transferred to the Tibet lobby in Washington.

Some weeks passed, and I remember talking again to John about this arrangement during an informal conversation: "It only works because we keep it quiet," I said. "It's something like a gentlemen's agreement."

The term stuck – too well. To my surprise and fury, John published the ICT's first *Dangerous Crossings* pamphlet a few months later, which prominently displayed a section that took an air of proprietary authority in diagramming a "Schematic of a 'Gentlemen's Agreement'", complete with balloon captions and arrows. A few months later, the Tibet Justice Center presented its own deeper-reaching history based on the now-catchy "Gentlemen's Agreement" coinage, and the cat was officially out of the bag. The wonderful and efficient arrangement that quietly and tacitly allowed for the movement of Tibetans through Nepal and onward to India was now heading down the road towards high publicity and political manipulation. Tibetans who were used to getting through Nepal with relative ease were about to get a rude awakening, and whatever was going to happen was going to be my fault because I shot my mouth off to the Tibet lobby in Washington and they would soon be building their brand with my mistake.

I was furious and contacted John to voice my opinion.

"Goddamit, John. You just can't let the world know about this arrangement. The Chinese will freak and the Nepalis will clamp down on all Tibetan movements. The key to this thing is that it remains under the publicity radar and doesn't embarrass the Chinese. We can move Tibetans through Nepal and the Nepalese will cooperate as long as the whole process isn't brought to the surface and used to drive home some political point. Basically, we're screwed if this thing goes public."

My only hope at that point was that no one with any influence over the Tibet issue would take such exposure to heart, and that the idea would fade into obscurity. For a few years it looked like I was going to get a break. The ICT's *Dangerous Crossing* publication was too small in scope to raise much of a stink to anyone important, and I was feeling good about the prospect that we could continue to keep the "Gentlemen's Agreement" quiet, and that Tibetans would continue to move through Nepal relatively unmolested – relatively.

Unfortunately, people who care about such things were paying attention. The Chinese were paying attention. By the time we performed our little UN dress-up masquerade that broke the wave of forced Tibetan repatriations in 2003, the "Gentlemen's Agreement" had well established itself in the lexicon of Tibet activism and, perhaps, Chinese Communist Party (CCP) infamy. Clues to the future were everywhere. The Chinese were everywhere as well – angry as hell and moving with near impunity through Sindhupalchowk, Dolakha and the upper regions of the Kodari highway. We never could solve the riddle of why the Chinese were now so bent on grabbing Tibetans in Nepal. They had always known about the practice of letting Tibetans quietly move through the tiny Himalayan country, and aside from a few arrests and flashes of anger for the party faithful, the CCP was reasonably content to allow this arrangement to continue. It finally dawned on me that we condescending and imperialist running dog Americans were making a bit of noise on the subject with all this "Gentlemen's Agreement" talk, and China had egg on its face. It was time for the CCP to do what it had always done in the face of Western criticism: double down and push back. We witnessed perhaps the first wave of this in 2003. The emphasis on the "Gentlemen's Agreement" and the steady stream of comments by the ICT, Nepal-bound US congressmen and State Department officials alike were about to make it much worse.

In 2010, Mary Beth Markey, then director of the ICT, communicated with Kate Saunders, communications director of the ICT, and the decision was made to "push the Gentlemen's Agreement like the Magna Carta". In July of 2010, an ICT press release reflected this new focus:

> Nepal has violated the well-established "Gentlemen's Agreement" with the U.N. High Commissioner for Refugees (UNHCR) and contravened its obligations under international law by forcibly returning three Tibetan refugees to Chinese border police in early June. This is the first confirmed case of the re-foulment of Tibetan refugees from Nepal since May 2003. Two of the Tibetans who were returned, a young woman and a monk, are now in prison in Tibet.
>
> The "Gentlemen's Agreement" between the Government of Nepal and the UNHCR provides for the safe transit of Tibetan refugees through Nepalese territory and onward to India, and was put in practice after 1989 when Nepal stopped providing refugee status to new arrivals from Tibet.

From press releases such as these, the actual substance of a de facto condition whereby apprehended Tibetans were turned over to the UNHCR for status determination morphed into a manufactured condition whereby Nepal was supposed to guarantee safe passage of Tibetans onwards to India. This was a dangerous extrapolation created out of thin air, and it fired a boiling cauldron of tension in Nepal. It was a cauldron that many visiting US officials were only too happy to stir in the coming months:

February 13–14th, 2011: Under Secretary Maria Otero visited Nepal. Embassy staff were blindsided by the first official mention of the "Gentlemen's Agreement" and the apparent scolding given to Nepal for its lack of adherence to its "provisions". Secretary Otero was accompanied by Todd Stein, government relations director of the ICT.

February 13th: Nepal police forcibly shut down Tibetan elections for a local welfare group, seizing ballot boxes. This was a first for the group, who had held many unmolested election events in the past.

March 10th: In Kathmandu, the usually peaceful demonstration commemorating the Tibetan uprising of 1959 was met with a brutal police crackdown.

June 5th: Deputy Assistant Secretary of State Kelly Clements visited Nepal and continued to push the "Gentlemen's Agreement".

June 21: Twelve Tibetans were arrested during a peaceful protest meant to support Tibetan protestors in Tibet.

October was a particularly heated month, with Chinese ambassador to Nepal Yang Houlan stating on the 16th: "We have authentic information that our oldest and nearest friend Nepal is turning into a playground for anti-China activities. Some international and domestic forces are coordinating their activities against China."

A few days later, US Congressman Jim Sensenbrenner arrived in Nepal and chided Nepal's prime minister for again not enforcing the "Gentlemen's Agreement".

The US officials' visits had played a part in the increased crackdown on the Tibetan community in Nepal. And China very clearly viewed these visits as meddling. By November 1st, 2011, I was getting fed up with the endless stream of State Department underlings and back-bench US congressmen showing up in Nepal and summarily scolding the Nepalese for their treatment of Tibetans. In these cases, it was evident – perhaps only to me at that time – that the official visitors were quoting from rhetoric supplied by the Washington-based Tibet lobby, and were causing more harm than good. It was also clear that China was demonstrating a cause-and-effect relationship by wasting no time in retaliating whenever these bloviating Western officials stepped in to raise trouble in their backyard. Often through pressure on the Nepali police, China was sending calculated responses to each and every American official who felt the need to speak on Tibet while in Nepal.

Aside from prodding the Nepal police into cracking down on Tibetans, the commerce-killing closure of the Tibet/Nepal border was another frequently employed means of accomplishing this pressure, and the Chinese implemented the tactic again in November of 2011. There was some concern from China that Tibetan protests would erupt, but the base reasoning was that this was a control gesture orchestrated for its retaliatory effect. More directly, according to one Nepali university professor, the motivation for the move was simple: "China fears the entry of Western and Tibetan leaders."

Overall, the entire episode was a ham-handed Western take on the dynamics of a people and a region. The "Gentlemen's Agreement" was becoming the sort of politically expedient soundbite that politicians use to appear knowledgeable and to mask their overall ignorance on a subject. Still, by 2011 the entire Western-based Tibet Movement bet heavily on the idea that the key to saving Tibetans as they moved through Nepal was to shed light on this new "Magna Carta" they had manufactured for themselves.

What created this cauldron? First, Nepal was an easy target. The tiny country was low-hanging fruit for those looking to make a point about the Tibet issue. Washington politicians could freely scream their indignation in Nepal's direction without fear of political retribution – screaming at China would be out of the question. More directly, a weakness was exposed that showed a decided inability on the part of the US to not only articulate a clear Tibet policy in Nepal but also control the narrative of visiting officials coming through Kathmandu.

After the onslaught of US officials had done its damage, the realisation came that corrections were in order. In September of 2011, US Representative Steve Chabot took his turn visiting Nepal as well, but this time there was a big difference. During his press conferences, he was accompanied by US Ambassador Scott DeLisi, from whose office it was apparent Mr Chabot had received a thorough briefing. As reported by the *Kathmandu Post*, Chabot's tone was decidedly different:

> "I am impressed by what the Government of Nepal has been doing about the Tibetan refugees," he told a press conference in Kathmandu. U.S. embassy officials in Kathmandu had no immediate response, but a spokesperson noted, possibly referring to the September 30 press conference, that the U.S. Ambassador DeLisi had publicly recognised "all that Nepal has done for the Tibetans in Nepal who seek safe passage to India."

Shepherded by DeLisi, Chabot remained diplomatic, but DeLisi and the US embassy had already been wounded by previous visiting US dignitaries, and it was clear that they were not prepared to reign in the entire flood of visits from the "Gentlemen's Agreement" crowd who were acting without restraint and were making their comments from an agenda that was contrary to the opinions expressed through the US embassy.

But something deeper was emerging. By my perception, the methods of helping Tibetans seemed to be going over to the new way of thinking – the "dark side", as I began to call it – full of attention-grabbing stunts and crude, undefined bludgeoning of the issue. My view of the ICT began to change as well.

At that point, I had given about ten years of my life to supplying data to the organised Western "Free Tibet" Movement, and my disappointment with this apparently new direction was palpable. I fired off a comment to the ICT:

> The "Gentlemen's Agreement" implies very strongly that the government of Nepal is in some sort of collusion with the international community to assure the safety of transient Tibetans. They are not. No agreement exists. What does exist is a centuries-old cultural tradition of Tibetans migrating to and from Nepal. For this, the Nepal government looks the other way when the refugees make their move. It is only under pressure from the [CCP] that Nepal acts adversely towards the Tibetans.
>
> A gentlemen's agreement mocks a "One China" policy by appearing to give official sanction to activities that are viewed as being against that policy. It is seen as overt, suspect and politically embarrassing to the [CCP]. It directly challenges Chinese authority on the matter.
>
> Look, our goal is to save Tibetans. The way we do this is to take attention away from their movements, not flaunt some rebellious agreement that will only serve to provoke and anger the Chinese towards a more restrictive posture.
>
> [Mary Beth Markey] is not gaining a political foot-hold with this, she is lighting a fuse.

The Nepalis, to their credit, politely ignored or were just plain befuddled by the "Gentlemen's Agreement", and were good hosts. The bottom line was, no one in with any connection to the issue in Nepal knew what they were talking about, and the US embassy initially had no supporting documentation or counter-arguments from which to form a diplomatic frame of reference. In essence, the "Gentlemen's Agreement" was a rogue concept supplied by the Washington-based Tibet lobby, and no one knew what to do with it. The only observable ground effect was a deterioration in the conditions within the Tibetan communities of Kathmandu.

I screamed my head off to ICT over what I thought was their uninformed meddling in US diplomacy and their jeopardising of US/Nepal relations. In an October 18th, 2011, e-mail to Mary Beth Markey, I left no doubt as to whom I felt was responsible for this entire disastrous gambit:

> The "Gentlemen's Agreement" approach belongs to ICT. It has since 2000. ICT was pushing the concept hard prior to these recent State visits. No one else prioritises this approach. ICT owns it, and is responsible for its effects.

It did not seem to matter. When responses from the Tibet lobby centred around the mechanism of "That's very interesting and we'll get back to you on it, Jim", I knew that my long years of supplying data to the ICT and others were coming to an end – they would no longer be a reliable partner.

Then, without warning, out of the Beltway came the comments of US Congressman Frank Wolf. Here was a gentleman who legitimately and passionately sought to help Tibet and Tibetans. He had visited Tibet in 1997, and the journey must have lit a fire of sorts in his mind. Unfortunately, Frank Wolf did not, in 2011, possess one ounce of relevant foresight, research or background that might have prevented him from what he was about to say on November 3rd of that year. Frustrated by Nepal's seemingly aloof stance towards Tibetans, Wolf found his voice on the issue and made threats against Nepal's future receipt of aid funds if Nepal didn't improve its treatment of Tibetans to his standards.

"We're not just going to cut them, we're going to zero them out. If they're not willing to do it, then they don't share our values, and if they don't share our values, we do not want to share our dollars," Wolf bellowed.

Wolf's comments were pure ICT-speak. Kate Saunders would offer denials by saying, "For the record, ICT had nothing to do with the Wolf statement," but the damage was done in Kathmandu. Nepalis were incensed. Who were these American congressmen telling them what to do and threatening to cut off their funds? Wolf's statement continued to backfire as pundits and bloggers alike began to draw immediate comparisons with China's "unconditional" foreign aid generosity. Complicit with the Wolf statement or not, the ICT was building its brand by telling Congress how to address the Tibet issue, and the result was an uninformed and barely controlled mess of scolding and admonishments that threatened Nepal's view of the US and caused real Tibetans to be persecuted in Nepal in real time. US mitigation efforts were meek in comparison to onslaughts such as Wolf's.

The "Gentlemen's Agreement" juggernaut was out of control and seemingly unstoppable.

As usual, the fact that I had no clear remedy for the situation did not inhibit my diving headlong into the fiasco, but at least I felt revived – my anger brought me back – and I did manage to come up with an idea. I would use my contacts in the Nepal media and directly counter the assertions that were coming out of Washington. I knew by their statements that congressmen and State Department officials were virtually clueless on the intricacies of Tibet politics as they pertained to Nepal, and I wanted to try to throw some sanity into the mix. I fired my opening salvos through both the *Himalayan Times* on November 20th, 2011, in an article entitled by the editors "Pressing Nepal on Tibet Uncalled For", and in a personal interview for the *Annapurna Post* given to Nepal's legendary journalist Guna Raj Luitel. A big, combative game had begun. In the interview with Luitel, I tried to shed some light on the field of play:

> Tibetan lobby groups are wrong. Nepal has done a fair job handling the issue. Threats, such as the one issued by Wolf, are uncalled for. Handling the situation is already a tough task for Nepal. The Nepali government [has] been reiterating its "one China" policy time and again. If [Western Groups] push harder, it will make Nepal's job at the border more difficult. Nepal is doing its best, given the circumstances. Nepal can do more and should do more, but we understand they're under pressure. Wolf's comment on Nepal is extremely excessive.

At that time in 2011, Ambassador Scott DeLisi and I seemed to be on the same page with regard to this issue. We had met a few times prior to this period – most notably and benignly at the annual ambassador's Thanksgiving programme at his residence – and he was always cordial to me for some reason. "Jim, how are you and good to see you again" was his standard form of greeting, and his delivery implied that he had more data about our operations – and about me – than he would reveal. The day after my publication in the *Himalayan Times*, Ambassador DeLisi published his thoughts in the *Kathmandu Post*:

> My government has long valued the fact that successive governments in Nepal have protected vulnerable groups such as the Bhutanese and Tibetan refugees and respected internationally-recognised norms regarding their rights. I am troubled, however, that today we find some who seek to make Nepal's respect for refugee protection and human rights an issue of political debate, and there are others who seek to portray

> Nepal's hospitality toward Tibetan refugees as "pro" one country or "anti" another. In my view, it is neither.
>
> Instead, I would argue that if anything, Nepal's generosity toward its long-staying Tibetan population and the hundreds more who cross its borders each year is "pro-Nepal." Why? Because it offers one of the strongest, clearest and most consistent examples of the values of this nation and its people. Despite its own almost overwhelming development challenges, Nepal's time-tested commitment to protecting the rights of the most vulnerable stands as a testament to the inherent decency and depth of compassion that define its citizens.

For the record, this was not a coordinated effort – and yet it somehow was. Scott DeLisi and I shared the same opinion on the Tibet issue. We both felt Nepal was doing the best it could under the circumstances, and that the US does not play favourites but supports all refugees equally.

We met informally a few times after that, and I couldn't resist implying a solidarity that did not exist.

"Well done, sir. It looks like we took back control of the Tibetan narrative, didn't we?" I said, mostly to impress the embassy girls standing nearby at this particular function.

"Ha, well. OK, Jim," came from his mouth, and I knew that I'd opined a bit forwardly.

The debate continued in Kathmandu, however, and I felt another article was in order. On December 6th, I made it clear, again in the *Himalayan Times*, that Nepal deserved an apology for all of this:

> It has been a difficult time for Nepal. Over the past year, Nepal has had to endure a rash of criticism over its handling of Tibetans. We have seen a parade of U.S. State Department officials and Congressmen scold Nepal for failing to enforce some "Gentlemen's Agreement" that cannot be enforced; watched as Tibetan Support Groups (TSGs) embellished events in Nepal for their own purposes; and suffered through Congressman Frank Wolf's threat to punish Nepal by cutting off all foreign aid.
>
> Nepal deserves better.
>
> How did we get to this point? Put simply, some in the U.S. believe Nepal must guarantee the safe passage of Tibetans traveling from Tibet through Nepal, and onward to India. China believes this to be an "anti-China" activity and throws its usual tantrum every time any Westerner brings up the issue. Unfortunately, this tantrum extends to pressuring Nepal

> into clamping down on anything that even remotely resembles free speech or cultural expression among its Tibetan communities. Tibet groups and politicians then seek to maintain their relevance or political high ground by condemning Nepal as cruel and inhumane. Whomever screams the loudest gets the most attention.

By December 12th, Ambassador DeLisi released the fourth and final opinion. It was a stance that he had held all along, and the same position that he applied to the issue when he accompanied Congressman Steve Chabot on his Nepal visit a few months prior. Now, he was trying to tie off a controversy that had become unmanageable with a clear statement of the US position. It was an unwanted damage control job that was necessitated by an unclear US policy on Tibet:

> I don't want to speak for Congressman Frank Wolf.
>
> Personally, I believe that Nepal has actually done a very good job of addressing a difficult problem. But fundamentally for us, again the issue is quite simply a matter of how do you deal with the needs and protect the rights of one of the most vulnerable populations. This is not an issue that has been articulated by the administration. In fact, we have been very clear in our appreciation for the constructive role that Nepal has played in respecting refugee rights in general.

All of the articles seemed to work as intended. From the end of 2011 forward, no visiting staff delegation member from either the US Congress or the State Department mentioned the "Gentlemen's Agreement" with any kind of force. In April of 2012, when Under Secretary of State for Political Affairs Wendy Sherman arrived and fielded questions on the "Gentlemen's Agreement", Scott DeLisi was by her side and ready. During the press conference, Secretary Sherman mentioned on several occasions how pleased she was with Nepal's treatment of Tibetan refugees. She did let the term "Gentlemen's Agreement" slip from her lips and the Nepal press pounced:

> **Press:** Did you talk about refugee law and Gentlemen's Agreement because we have refugees from different places like Bhutan, Tibet and many more countries? And did you discuss refugee law, which has been applied in Nepal?

Both Sherman and DeLisi appeared to lose their footing for a second, but DeLisi, perhaps sensing the start of another round of "Gentlemen's Agreement" roulette, moved in and grabbed the response before Sherman could speak:

> "I don't consider that we are dealing differently with any of these refugee populations. Our goal is the same in every case. Refugee populations are among the most vulnerable anywhere in the world. Our goal and our commitment is to protect their rights and to ensure that they are allowed to live lives with fundamental dignity and where their rights are protected, and we work to do that in many different ways."

I don't believe we will ever again see a visiting US official in Kathmandu being left alone with a microphone or a room full of journalists.

*

So, on that day in 2014 when the "Gentlemen's Agreement" resurfaced, I reflected on the seeming futility of my efforts in 2011 to curtail a very bad strategy. Would this ridiculous soundbite ever die? And would I ever cease feeling responsible for its creation?

Maria Otero's tenure as official advocate for Tibet was noteworthy in that it accomplished nothing noteworthy for Tibet. It can be argued that her visit to Nepal, combined with USAID funding for Tibetan refugees in India, actually moved the Tibetan struggle into a counterproductive reversal. The entire episode surrounding her visit to Nepal and her very possible intermingling with the Tibet lobby left a bad taste in my mouth. I knew it was coming and had suspected it for quite some time, but watching a now struggling Western-based Tibet Movement work its cynical strategy in Nepal, while a seemingly clueless parade of government officials were content to ape that strategy without so much as a morsel of inclination towards researching the validity of their spoken words, forced me to admit what I had been reluctant to admit previously: The Movement to "Free Tibet", as I had come to know it, was dead. It had been taken over by those looking to manipulate the issue for their own purposes. It had become something that was not to be solved but sustained.

The death throes of West-based Tibet advocacy have been as hard to watch as they have been numerous. The recent history of Western efforts has defined success by processes initiated rather than problems resolved. These processes, as we will see, have given us nothing more than displays of sound and fury.

CHAPTER 18

RISE AND FALL

They all waited. It would be any day now. US State Department spokesperson Victoria Nuland had just made an announcement that the US was going to provide a major statement on Tibet and the tragic, recurrent horror of Tibetan self-immolation. Could this finally be the moment when the world's lone superpower stood up to the Chinese and made human rights a non-negotiable priority? Were the Tibetans about to get a renewed and firm commitment from the United States? There was palpable excitement among those in Washington who monitor Tibet issues that perhaps the corner was about to be turned after decades of dithering and non-binding US involvement, and that real substantive progress was nearing. Tibetan pundits took to Twitter and floated the idea of a "coalition" that might finally force China to listen. Adding to this excitement was the rumour that the European Union would soon follow with a statement of its own.

Finally, Maria Otero, the US State Department's under secretary for civilian security, democracy and human rights, and US special coordinator for Tibetan issues, launched her much anticipated statement. It was December 2012.

> The United States is deeply concerned and saddened by the continuing violence in Tibetan areas of China and the increasing frequency of self-immolations by Tibetans. Chinese authorities have responded to these tragic incidents with measures that tighten already strict controls on freedoms of religion, expression, assembly and association of Tibetans. Official rhetoric that denigrates the Tibetan language, the Dalai Lama, and those who have self-immolated has further exacerbated tensions.

> Senior U.S. officials have directly raised the issue of Tibetan self-immolations with their Chinese government counterparts. The U.S. government has consistently urged the Chinese government to address policies in Tibetan areas that have created tensions. These policies include increasingly severe government controls on Tibetan Buddhist religious practice and monastic institutions; education practices that undermine the preservation of Tibetan language; intensive surveillance, arbitrary detentions and disappearances of Tibetans, including youth and Tibetan intellectual and cultural leaders; escalating restrictions on news, media and communications; and the use of force against Tibetans seeking peacefully to exercise their universal human rights.
>
> We call on the Chinese government to permit Tibetans to express their grievances freely, publicly, peacefully, and without fear of retribution. We hope that the tragic acts of self-immolation end. We call on China's leaders to allow journalists, diplomats and other observers unrestricted access to China's Tibetan areas. We call on the Chinese government to engage in dialogue with the Dalai Lama or his representatives without preconditions.

The European Union's Catherine Ashton followed some days later with a statement of her own:

> The EU is profoundly saddened by the increasing number of Tibetans committing self-immolation, many of them young people.
>
> We are concerned by the restrictions on expressions of Tibetan identity, which appear to be giving rise to a surge of discontent in the region. While respecting China's territorial integrity, the EU calls upon the Chinese authorities to address the deep-rooted causes of the frustration of the Tibetan people and ensure that their civil, political, economic, social and cultural rights are respected, including their right to enjoy their own culture, to practice their own religion and to use their own language.
>
> The EU fully supports the statement made by the U.N. high commissioner for human rights, Ms. Navi Pillay on 2 November 2012. The EU calls upon the Chinese authorities to respect the rights of Tibetans to peaceful assembly and expression, to act with restraint, and to release all individuals detained for taking part in peaceful demonstrations.
>
> We also urge Chinese authorities to allow free access to all Tibetan autonomous areas for diplomats as well as for international journalists.
>
> Recognising their intense sense of despair, the EU calls on Tibetans to

> refrain from resorting to extreme forms of protest such as self-immolation, and on their community and religious leaders to use their influence to help stop this tragic loss of life.
>
> Finally, the EU encourages all concerned parties to resume a meaningful dialogue.

That was it. That was the big news. In all due respect to the legacies of Joel McCleary, John Ackerly and Blake Kerr, Lodi Gyari, Richard Gere and Adam Yauch; the Dalai Lama's Nobel Peace Prize; "Free Tibet" banners fluttering from the Golden Gate bridge; hunger strikers in Dharamsala and elsewhere; Martin Scorsese's *Kundun*; Brad Pitt's *Seven Years in Tibet*; celebrity-speckled public-service announcements; nuns shot in the back while entering Nepal; and yes, to more than 150 individual Tibetans who chose to light themselves on fire – this could not have been what they were hoping would be the result of their efforts and sacrifices over the last three decades.

They punted once again. The US, European Union and, for the record, eventually Canada all took a safe and benign road. Those same pro-Tibet pundits immediately went to work by saying how "strong" the statements were, but at the end of the day, the big governments of the world offered nothing new for the Tibetans. They "called on" China to start talking to Tibetans again, expressed "concern", and threw in the obligatory assertion of Western values – the same rhetoric they've used for 20 years.

It was a further, and perhaps the penultimate, example of how the Western Tibet Movement had failed. After years of gorging on the attention, "Free Tibet" had grown inert and repetitive. "Internationalism" of the Tibet Movement had distilled itself down to lobbying the governments of the world to somehow use their voices to shame China into easing up on the Tibetans, with the full knowledge that these governments have been and continue to be spineless in standing up to China on human rights-related issues. Furthermore, countries like South Africa and England were fresh on the heels of either denying the Dalai Lama visiting rights or forbidding their members of parliament to speak with him. So these statements by world governments in support of Tibet not only carried no weight and were not binding, but they seemed hypocritical – I'm sure China was shaking in its boots.

Significantly, it was not the effect of some great coalition of governments uniting to help Tibet that resulted in the statements above. The sad fact is that it took the extreme acts of Tibetan self-immolators to compel the governments of the world to issue even these most feeble of declarations on behalf of Tibet. Photographs of Tibetans running down the street on fire and perhaps moments from death forced the hands of those governments that consider themselves democratic and compelled them to make at least some sort of acknowledgement – the accumulating mass of dying Tibetans was becoming too great to ignore.

Tibetans wanted the attention of the world and they got it, but the world just gave them another passing glance.

I was not entirely surprised by either the tone or the content of the statements. They represented the latest chapter in the arc of a movement that began with great hope, witnessed initial success and prosperity, and then marginalised itself under the weight of its own complacency. These were not the statements of governments that were substantively engaged in the issue; these were governments giving lip-service to a cause that was no longer of significant interest to the West – and was on its death bed.

I and a few others lived through all of the changes in the Tibet Movement and the arc of its existence. Sharing this perspective was one of the prime motivators for me to write this book. Perhaps the things that I know and have seen are a default benefit from my two decades of service to Tibetans. But in all honesty, it's a salvage operation for me. I don't want the past 20 years of my life to dissolve into obscurity or be dissected into small lessons to be cherry-picked by a new generation seeking to cover the same ground and reinvent the wheel on Tibet activism. I want to do what people like me should have been doing all along; I want to leave a foundation – such as it is. It's time to talk frankly about the "Free Tibet" Movement: what went wrong, what continues to go wrong and what we need to do to fix it.

For me, modern Tibet activism was born in Lhasa in October of 1987 when a couple of adventurers, John Ackerly and Blake Kerr, ventured into the ancient city and found themselves in the midst of bloody rioting in a Tibetan community chafing under Chinese oppression. There were other groups dealing with the issue at the time, but John and Blake woke everyone up to the problem. Through the efforts of Joel McCleary, US Senator Dianne Feinstein and a host of qualified others, the first organised attempt at solving the Tibet issue was conceived. The International Campaign for Tibet (ICT) was born, and its first president was to be John Ackerly. It announced through its very name that Tibetan desires to "internationalise" their struggle would be taken to heart – and that's what the ICT did.

From John Ackerly's vision, the ICT grew into a force for raising awareness of the plight of Tibetans.

Early campaigns involved supporting local, regional and international Tibet Support Groups (TSGs) by giving them information and literature for their various meetings and functions, creating public-service announcements filmed by celebrities, and actively working to assist Tibetans in need in hotspots like Nepal – that's where I came in. Our group maintained a vigorous schedule of monitoring and rescuing, where possible, Tibetans crossing the border from Tibet into Nepal.

The ICT maintained a cluttered but busy office on an obscure floor at 1511 K. Street in Washington. Ideas and programmes would flow from that office at a speed dictated by intense personal conviction. Great introductory campaigns like the *Why Are We Silent?* video and the *Dangerous Crossing* pamphlet came out of this period, and accurately introduced many individuals, groups and members of Congress to the ground realities of Tibetans trying to make their way through Nepal towards India. The effort was inclusive, expansive and open to all.

It was working. Richard Gere lent his considerable celebrity to the Tibet cause and was quite involved with ICT proceedings. He was the face of the "raising awareness" years of the Tibet Movement and the ICT was the most effective mechanism for delivering that awareness. Fieldwork was laser-focused on fact-finding and developing programmes that helped Tibetans where there was the most immediate need. Partnerships were forming, partnerships that saw Westerners working equally with Tibetans to find ground-based, real-time solutions.

Then something happened: maybe not a particular thing, but an evolving series of things. Most symbolically, the ICT moved into a dedicated building on Jefferson Street in Washington.

My first words to John were, "Are you nuts? Let's forget the huge costs for now. A dedicated facility with its own big front door means that everyone walking through that door who's not a deliveryman has something to do with Tibet or the Tibet Movement, right? If I wanted to know who had business with the ICT, all I'd have to do is sit in a car and watch the door!"

This was no joke. The Chinese were as paranoid about Tibet back then as they are now. Recently, John had been banned from travel to China because of his work. So had Brad Pitt.

"Well, we had the place swept for bugging devices before we moved in," he replied.

This was not the same thing, I told him. In my view, you might as well give the Chinese a list of everyone who supports Tibet and save them hours of spying. It's nice to move up in the world, sure, but I felt that giving up the security of being an anonymous tenant in a big office tower for a shiny building of one's own was monumentally short-sighted.

I was also speaking with John about his thoughts on the future of the movement during this period, and he related his feelings that, as an exiled group in India, Tibetans were pretty well supported. The significance of that statement and its relevance to this book would not be apparent to me for another decade, but at the time it was true to an extent: People were throwing money at Tibetans and they were receiving lots of attention – but very little direction. I told John there was still plenty of work to do in the field as Tibetans were continuing to endure a tremendous amount of suffering, both in Tibet and Nepal, and we had not yet established any kind of a foundation of support that gave Tibetans hope for the future. Couldn't we just hold off buying the new office furniture for a while?

But I knew after my conversation with John that I was pleading against the momentum and future direction of the Tibet Movement itself. My words made no difference. The ICT was successful now, too successful to work in an activist capacity. They had bills to pay and appearances to maintain if they were to have continued access to the halls of power in Washington. Running around screaming and waving "Free Tibet" banners – or supporting groups that did – might alienate potential donors and get one labelled as a "maverick" organisation on Capitol Hill.

Shortly after, John Ackerly gave up the directorship of the ICT to Mary Beth Markey. There would now be no impediments. The main thrust of Western-based Tibet advocacy would now be fully defined by lobbying and legislative priorities.

The Tibet Movement was at a crossroads in the early years of the 2000s. Attention and money was flowing towards the Tibet issue and decisions had to be made. We needed to take the time to develop the expertise to build sustainable programmes for Tibetans, and use Tibet's new and considerable popularity to form more partnerships that focused on ground-based initiatives – that's what we needed to do. Instead, we entrenched, made good paying jobs for ourselves and focused on trying to persuade the governments of the world to do our work for us.

We did not lay a foundation for future generations of Tibet activists. In subsequent years, new people with a passion for the issue would arrive and begin simply repeating the same arguments...the same condemnations of China we had been using since 1987. We gave the new generation of Tibet advocates no shoulders to stand on, and it has resulted in the complete stagnation of the movement.

The philosophical death knell of modern Western Tibet activism has been long in the making, but it seemed to solidify in a discussion thread conducted about an online article in May 2012 by Joshua Keating on Foreignpolicy.com: "Does the West Still Want to Free Tibet?" Todd Stein, then government relations director for the ICT, responded to the article's assertion that the Tibet Movement was sputtering by offering that it had in fact become "institutionalised", and that this was somehow a good thing. It was a "leave it to Washington, we can handle it" assertion, and was also a default roadmap that told a rudderless popular Tibet Movement to get out of the way. This was most decidedly NOT a good thing.

Institutionalisation invites categorisation, which invites prioritisation. Tibet issues could now be shelved between, say, farm subsidies and education reform on any given congressional agenda. Institutionalisation had given our politicians the choice on when and how they would act on Tibet – the activist edge was gone.

In the early days of the Free Tibet Movement, great strides were made in introducing the cause of Tibet to the Western world through activism. Activism succeeds because it is "active", and the main tool for this activity is the element of annoyance. Activism works best when the targets of the activists are made uncomfortable enough that they finally relent.

Madeleine Albright, then secretary of state for the United States, knew this. Tibet activists were an unknown and uncontrolled commodity in the 1990s. Her area of interest was in Eastern European affairs at that time, and she was afraid the newly emergent and pesky Tibet issue and its banner-wavers would usurp her priorities. By 1997, she had initiated the sequence of events that would install Greg Craig, a high-powered Washington attorney, in the position of the first special coordinator for Tibetan affairs office. In retrospect, it had the effect of throwing an emerging Tibet activist community off track by giving them the appearance of having a champion in Washington. Greg Craig didn't see it that way.

Craig was a go-getter who actually wanted to get things done on behalf of Tibet. Unfortunately, his title gave him little or no influence. Albright had balked at the idea of naming Craig as a "special envoy" for Tibetan issues, as she thought it might offend the Chinese and throw a wrench into her policy of engagement with China. But no matter, the main benefit of the special coordinator's post to those in positions of power in Washington was that it took the annoyingly persistent Tibet out of the mainstream political debate and shunted it firmly to the political and diplomatic sideline – where it remains to this day. It was a brilliant move. Tibet activists, who were evolving into a loud, influential and persistent wildcard by this time, would now focus their energies on impressing – hat in hand – the new special coordinator. And members of Congress could now refer all queries about Tibet to this duly nominated and named special coordinator, and thus give the impression of progress and seriousness of purpose on the issue while eliminating the need to speak intelligently about Tibet.

Washington hubris would reason that all groups and individuals concerned should now be satisfied with the knowledge that Tibet had been recognised with its own office in the US government – regardless of whether or not that office actually accomplished anything for Tibet. It was a promotion to nowhere.

Greg Craig saw opportunities. Working tirelessly, he kept the Tibet issue in front of President Clinton as well as his contacts in the Chinese Foreign Office, and he believed his efforts had opened new pathways. He believed that the Chinese, through Jiang Zemin's proactive interest in discussing Tibet, were ready for a more substantive dialogue on the issue. The timing and the players were aligned perfectly. Jiang was receptive and President Clinton was more than ready, having brought up the subject of Tibet to his Chinese counterpart on more than a few occasions. Tibet was on the verge of getting a fair hearing from the highest levels of Chinese leadership, and Greg Craig was the man responsible for moving everyone to that point.

But Craig was too good for his own good. Events would prove that Craig's desire to legitimately work the Tibet issue may not have been what was intended by his superiors. In 1998, Greg Craig was abruptly taken from his position and put in charge of conducting Bill Clinton's impeachment defence. He was no longer to work for Tibet. Those prone to sexist extrapolations might posit that Monica Lewinsky did more to sabotage substantive progress on the Tibet issue than anyone before she and her tumultuous 15 minutes of fame had commanded the attention of the

American public. My feeling was that any reasonably competent Washington lawyer could have defended President Clinton during the political theatre of his impeachment proceedings. Why was an extremely effective advocate for Tibet abruptly yanked out of a job to do so?

"No, that last section is wrong, Jim. Don't make this into a conspiracy," said Greg Craig as I read the above sentence to him in March of 2016.

It had taken a few weeks to wrangle through the rescheduling and delicate slotting required to get to this point, but there I was in an office that overlooked the north lawn of the White House, speaking to Greg Craig, counsel to presidents Bill Clinton and Barack Obama, and first special coordinator for Tibetan affairs under Secretary of State Madeleine Albright.

"I like to look out and keep track of the vehicles coming and going from the White House," the amiable and joyfully accessible 71-year-old super-attorney chuckled.

We sat down for a chat around a small coffee table in his office at the law offices of Skadden, Arps, Slate, Meagher and Flom on a blustery Washington DC morning. The man who once directed a small army of attorneys from his White House command centre seemed content in his current surroundings. Behind his desk were photos of Craig with the Dalai Lama, Nelson Mandela and a few others I couldn't make out from my chair.

A recent shoulder surgery was still painful and his arm was bound in a sling, but the smiling, snow-white haired Craig wasted no time in reaching out to me with his good left hand, and warm introductions were exchanged.

"So what was it then, Greg, if not a conspiracy? Secretary Albright had balked at giving you the title of 'special envoy' and all the diplomatic cachet that implied. They all *had* to know you were making progress on Tibet. Did they just not care?" I leaned in as best as I could.

"I wasn't aware of all that 'special envoy' talk...that was before my time. It may have played a part, and I see how you might think that."

Raising his hand above his head, Craig explained: "No, this was not just a sideshow. The impeachment hearings were way up *here*, way above the Tibetan issue, and I was the only attorney who was close enough to the Clintons [to represent them properly]."

He was confident in his relationship with Secretary Albright and felt that he had not been just a moving part in some scheme to sabotage real progress on Tibet. Still, he had no trouble with my other assertions and the cumulative effect of their reading did seem to give him pause. He laughed heartily at my comment on Monica Lewinsky and held firm in his opposition to my theory on Madeleine Albright.

"What you have to realise, Jim, and what the world doesn't know, is that Madeleine Albright really wanted to solve the Tibet issue. She mentioned it repeatedly to Jiang Zemin on four occasions, I believe."

He went on to mention that his and Secretary Albright's work on the Tibet issue and their ability to synchronise Chinese interest in the topic may have represented the best and most singular opportunity to make progress on Tibet. It was a very small window. Unfortunately, whether planned, calculated or just poorly timed, removing Craig as special coordinator undoubtedly helped to close that window.

"We should have kept the dialogue going. Not through State Department channels but at the White House," Craig told me.

It was a lost opportunity and he knew it – we both knew it. What has always bothered me is that no one fought for, or even considered reopening, that rare window of opportunity that Greg Craig had created. That window remains closed even today.

Having a special coordinator for Tibetan affairs at the State Department serves the purpose of letting the US government take control of the Tibet argument and tone down the rhetoric from Tibet support groups. Greg Craig was doing his job, but he didn't read between the lines on his job description; he didn't feel the need to tone down anything.

In the years since Greg Craig was pulled from the special coordinator's position, various individuals have assumed the post: some with a genuine desire to advance the Tibet issue, some with perhaps no more than a sense of duty to fulfil their job description. Since 2012, the portfolio exists as one of many buried under the appointed position of under secretary of state for civilian security, democracy and human rights. It is a portfolio that has never held as much potential for Tibet as it did under Greg Craig.

Tibet advocacy in the US has now been so well institutionalised that it exists only as a small fraction of a State Department under secretary's yearly agenda. Mission accomplished. Institutionalisation succeeded in taking Tibet activism out of the hands of activists.

*

The penultimate achievement of the Tibet Movement, and their crowning example of institutionalisation, would be the Tibet Policy Act. For a number of years, and unbeknownst to many with a concern for Tibet, senator Dianne Feinstein and her husband Richard Blum had been working behind the scenes to take advantage of their personally friendly relationship with Premier Jiang Zemin in the hope of creating some positive momentum for Tibet. It was during that small window of time when the West had a realistic chance of working out a Tibet solution with the Chinese. Beijing, mostly Jiang, was leaning towards the pliable. Eventually, a more hard-lined stance emerged from Beijing and the efforts of Feinstein and her husband came to nothing. The senator had flirted with the idea of introducing legislation that addressed Tibetan concerns directly and offered the steps needed to adequately address key issues, but she was perhaps reticent to go forward until all efforts with Jiang had run their course. Now, there was no need for further delay.

Despite strong objections from Beijing, her Tibet Policy Act (TPA) emerged under Section 611 of United States House Resolution 1646-50: The Foreign Relations Authorization Act, Fiscal Year 2003. Not since the time when congressional staffers had worked pro-Tibet language into various bits of legislation had there been such a direct addressing Tibet in a US law. In truth, for all its pro-Tibet language, the meat of the TPA merely solidified into law many of the ideas and concepts that had already been given a test drive. What new ideas it brought to the table were floating in an ether of wishful thinking. Highlights of the act include:

1. Ensuring that Tibetan language training was available to US Foreign Service officers.
2. Making a reasonable effort to establish a US consulate in Lhasa.
3. The official, legal establishment and recognition of the office of special coordinator for Tibetan affairs.
4. The usual scolding of China for its attacks on religious freedoms.
5. The usual call to continue throwing humanitarian aid at Tibetans.

The entire TPA can be found online. Read it – take a good look at it. I think it attempted to articulate a rudimentary US policy stance on Tibet, but did so in a manner that suggested fatigue and a desire to move past the issue. It is also reads with a vague tone of exasperation.

Moreover, the TPA seemed like the US Government's attempt to tie off with a nice bow their involvement in Tibet. The new items proposed were either cursory or implausible, and unlikely to take effect – parting shots at best. It was as if the act was one last final acknowledgement of what already existed and what was hoped for in an unfulfilled wish list for the Tibetan struggle. To date, the United States has yet to (and is unlikely to) introduce such strong Tibet-supportive language again in any piece of legislation. Senator Feinstein's bill pulled the blinds, turned off the lights and locked the door on direct US advocacy for Tibet. Some final instructions were left for the caretaker – in this case the special coordinator's office – but on the whole, we were done.

*

Kerry Dumbaugh is one of my heroes. She's one of the first, highly credible researchers to suggest that the workings of the Tibet "lobby" in Washington as well as the legislative efforts of the US on behalf of Tibet be questioned for their efficacy. In a report from her desk at the Congressional Research Center in 2008 entitled *Tibet: Problems, Prospects, and U.S. Policy*, Dumbaugh was, perhaps, the first to dare offer the idea that "many fear there is little hope that Beijing will make significant changes in its Tibet policy, despite even the urgent advice of China's friends". She saved her harshest criticisms for another report in which, relaying the input of her sources, she took down the Tibetan Policy Act that seems stalled, save for State Department language training in Tibetan and some reporting provisions. She took aim at the special coordinator for Tibetan affairs office as well:

> According to these observers, while the TPA theoretically imposes obligations on a number of U.S. government agencies concerning Tibet, it establishes unclear lines of communication and no mechanism for the Special Coordinator either to facilitate interagency coordination or to task other U.S. government agencies.

The report was also of the opinion that the narrow scope of work the TPA assigned to the special coordinator – encouraging dialogue between the Dalai Lama and Beijing – is counterproductive, both to US interests and to the welfare of Tibetans. According to this observer, the special coordinator's brief suggests that the only answer to Tibet's problems lies in the formal dialogue process – a focus that ignores many of the real, deep-seated grievances of the Tibetans living in Tibet.

She goes on to say that the TPA's ineffectiveness has a lot to do with Beijing not wanting to play ball on the issue. And this underscores the political brilliance of the TPA: It could demand anything, no matter how bold and ridiculous, like a US consulate in Lhasa, with the full knowledge that everything would be brushed aside by the Chinese – dead from the start. This would give lip-service to any pro-Tibet group and cost the United States zero, politically.

The "Free Tibet" Movement was sputtering badly by 2007–2008. Still, the chance to address the questions and concerns raised by people like Dumbaugh, as well as a very Buddhist opportunity for much needed self-reflection in the Tibet Movement, slipped by. Not only were no adjustments made, but the mistakes, as we will see, continued to mount.

*

The Western world was beginning to look around and take note of the fact that we were not freeing Tibet as promised. In a television interview with George Stroumboulopoulous, the then leader of the Students for a Free Tibet, Lhadon Tethong, offered no answer. George was tough and asked many of the questions we were all asking privately. My heart went out to Lhadon Tethong. Here was a young Tibetan woman who, like many of us, was compelled to do something – anything – to help Tibet. But "raising awareness" campaigns, concerts and small-scale demonstrations can only do so much.

> **GS:** I saw you at a Tibet freedom concert...and that was ten years ago. And we're here today. Is this an East Timor thing...are we waiting for decades and decades?
>
> **LT:** We never know. That's the beauty of history and world events...it's about what I think is the right thing to do in the moment...

There was frustration and a bit of impatience in George's questions; there was a calm, non-substantive "let's just keep the faith" aura around Lhadon Tethong's answers.

Had our priorities been better realised, Lhadon should have been doing things like recruiting people for fieldwork that might have been starting its second decade of cooperation with Tibetans on self-determination issues, or, perhaps, managing a private investment fund that directly benefitted Tibetan entrepreneurs. She deserved what she got from George Stroumboulopoulous – but she also deserves much better.

*

Someone I look up to after the long months of research I have done for this book is Joel McCleary. If you remember, Joel McCleary was almost singularly responsible for the Dalai Lama's first visit to the United States back in 1979. A Harvard graduate, he served as a White House aide under President Jimmy Carter and as treasurer for the Democratic National Committee. He also submitted a 165-page list of problems and options that the US needed to address before it decided to plunge into Tibet advocacy. After reading Ken Knaus's *Beyond Shangri-la* and the snippets of that report Knaus exposed, it was clear to me that McCleary was a level-headed pragmatist who should have been given a greater voice. I wanted to hear that voice for myself. I wanted to ask McCleary about that report and its bombshell revelations, like:

> The objective is to win administration neutrality. The administration can never openly support the Tibet cause. The most that you can hope for is that they will not oppose congressional action or, if Congress does pass legislation favourable to Tibet, they will not impede its implementation.

Even more, his report would go on to outline practical suggestions on dealing with the Tibetan diaspora's shortcomings on strategy, organisational structure and overall philosophical goals. From what little I was able to glean from Knaus's summations, McCleary knew that for Tibet to be free, individuals and politicians working diligently from the ground up would offer the only effective means towards that end. He seemed to have no patience for wishful thinking and blind hope, and admonished those mulling over their Tibet approach to "stop dreaming about internal problems causing the [People's Republic of China] to crumble and get to the negotiating table".

Joel was a hard guy to pin down. I had been trying to strike up an e-mail dialogue with him since early 2014 and had only achieved limited success. There was always a sense of melancholy and heartache in the few responses I was able to get out of him; a sense that perhaps a wound or two may still be hovering around his Tibet years. "Happy to talk," he responded in February of 2014. "Not sure what I can add. Have spent much time and energy on the Tibetan issue over the years and have to declare my thinking and advice have not been right or effective – so I am a humbled conversationalist."

I wanted to ask him about his recommendations on Tibet; I wanted a copy of that report. Joel informed me it was not to be:

> The report was never written for public consumption. Actually, some other memos were first leaked (to Knaus) and then the cat was out of the bag. But for obvious reasons, he did not want the entire report to be in the public domain because of the use to which it would be put by some interested countries.

It was starting to make a bit of sense. McCleary's report was real and incisive, and it burned the ears of early Tibet Movement organisers who may have been thinking more about elevating the image of Tibet in a public relations-oriented campaign, or perhaps romanticising the Tibetan struggle in a different way. They wanted public exposure for their efforts, not McCleary's policy and programme red meat. Perhaps that was the reason for his melancholy. He foresaw how the current version of the "Free Tibet" Movement would wind up from his 1979 perspective, and had to sit by sadly and watch it unfold before his eyes. Empty statements that "called on China" from powerless government officials with no discernable positive effect for Tibet was one of the things he saw, and he told me so in an e-mail in March of 2014: "Doubt seriously [with some basis for my thought] that China takes 'Western pressure' seriously because it never has been serious, nor could be."

I finally met Joel McCleary at the Café Leopold, Georgetown, Washington DC, on March 1st, 2016 – just a few hours after my meeting with Greg Craig. There were the usual missed phone calls and e-mails, and I was still wondering if we were going to get a chance to meet when he nimbly shot into the chair opposite my position at the café – Joel McCleary was 30 minutes late.

"Hi, Jim. So tell me about this book you're writing."

Diving right into the subject saved about 15 minutes of introductions and small talk – Joel's directness was much appreciated in that regard, since I had a plane to catch. I did my part by deflecting the initial question and going right after the atmospherics surrounding the release of his 165-page road map for an emerging Tibet Movement.

"I was pushed to the sidelines after submitting that report, Jim."

There seemed to be some regret behind what he was saying and I asked him about it.

"What happened? What did you leave on the table back then?"

He told me that no one knew exactly what they were about to unleash with this new Tibet thing, and there was no sense of where it might lead.

I got the feeling that Joel's report was the first serious look at all the aspects of Tibet support – and everyone else at the table was scared shitless by it.

"In retrospect, I should have pushed harder for the recommendations in that report," he said.

"Joel, for God's sake, if they would have just listened to your recommendations, we would have saved 30 years of 'Free Tibet' bullshit that went nowhere. Don't you agree?"

"Jim, I obviously can't answer that and won't answer that."

He also, pointedly, did not refute it.

There was a bit of an awkward silence at that point and I was choking on my sandwich when Joel looked up with what appeared to be an activist's twinkle in his eye and came to conversational life. An intellectually curious man, he had plenty of questions for me.

"So, Jim, what do you think of Modi?" (Modi was the Indian prime minister.)

I thought he was duplicitous but basically doing what any Indian politician would do, which was commit to nothing and hedge all bets.

"So, do *you* trust anyone in the Tibet Movement anymore?"

I said I still had a lot of respect for John Ackerly, but basically the only one I trusted was sitting across from me at the table.

"What did Greg Craig have to say?"

I told him how no one knew about Madeleine Albright's fire for the Tibet cause, and how close everyone came during those years to getting something done.

"Something you can use in your book is that the Chinese are extremely clever in reacting to our moves on Tibet," he said.

He went on to describe that he felt those Tibetan leaders who possessed the greatest knowledge of Tibetan history, Tibetan Buddhism and Tibetan culture were of the greatest value as "targets" to the Chinese. I was beginning to glaze over as I listened to the depth and breadth of this man's knowledge and his clean logic, but I did manage to assimilate one key takeaway from the exchange: No gesture, programme, deed or word from either the West or the Tibetans themselves is ignored by the Chinese. And almost every measure anyone takes on behalf of Tibet is weighed for its equivalent countermeasure.

A more significant takeaway for me was that Joel McCleary seemed to be at peace. If there was any lingering anger at those who refused to listen to his wisdom on Tibet, it had long faded. Joel McCleary has moved on. He is a fascinating individual; I look forward to talking to him again – perhaps when I've moved on as well.

*

The US once made an attempt to help Tibet. It was back in 1959 when the CIA did all sorts of things to feed their Cold War fever and piss off China. They trained Tibetan paratroopers, supplied arms and kept a bit of pressure on the Dalai Lama to speak up against Chinese Communism. It failed miserably. The lesson that was observable through this exercise was that Tibet gets attention and is useful only as a pawn for whatever larger US–China agenda can be helped along by its mentioning. Greg Craig pushed hard against this lesson by giving the Tibet issue its own inherent value. At the very least, his good efforts were ignored. At worst, those efforts may have played a part in his removal as special coordinator for Tibetan affairs. For Joel McCleary, his pragmatic recommendations were too substantive and results-oriented, and would have perhaps diminished the scope of a new movement that had its own ideas on how it wanted to envision the Tibetan struggle.

Today, the Tibet pawn has all but disappeared as a political weapon. Perhaps this is why those who are concerned about Tibet have had to exert immense effort to extract the most benign statements or perfunctory utterances from members of the US Congress. Tibet does not directly relate to the national interests of any Western nation to the point that they are willing to potentially jeopardise their relationship with China. "It's just not on a fast track to anywhere, this 'Tibet' thing," a congressional aid buddy told me. This is the truth. Tibet is also a non-issue when one gets down to the field level. The US embassy in Kathmandu has a "refugee coordinator" on site to be sure, but they cannot bring themselves to make any official Tibet-specific commitments. Our little group introduced Nepal border monitoring programmes through US agencies where the first words in the first meeting were: "I hope you realise that the Tibetan border is a non-starter with this; what are your plans for the south?" It is a sticky subject on the diplomatic front and the current approach is a non-approach – from everyone, not just the US. The best way to play the Tibet pawn these days is to not play it.

The elephant in the room here is that Tibet gets no traction in the political realm because we don't want to jeopardise any "potential" that might exist with China. It's our greed, really. We in the West salivate over how much money we can make by opening up Chinese markets. Tibet gets in the way of all this. Economics drive our lack of a coherent Tibet policy. China knows that as long as they can lead us around by our wallets, we'll never make Tibet a condition of anything. If we are truthful with ourselves, we know that this has informed the Tibet conversation for almost two decades.

It is like a dance. Typically, the West, in response to whatever current pressure and hand-wringing from whatever group or event that compels them to a "Tibet moment", decides to make a statement. The statement is usually diplomatic mush and always non-binding – no direct punitive actions against China are ever authorised. Then it is filed away, banished to the archives of public record obscurity. Duty done, the brave Western governmental officials shake hands with each other, perhaps have a reception, and go tackle the real issue of how to increase trade with China. Our pawn is thus artfully deployed as a bluff – a mere housekeeping measure.

The failure of the Western Tibet Movement represents a confluence of events that can be described as "derailments" in that courses of action were changed for the worse and ideals came off the rails. I've counted three major derailments here. First, the establishment of the special coordinator for Tibetan affairs was a willful and effective means of taking charge of the Tibetan narrative by the US government and of derailing the effects of activism. After that, the acceptance of institutionalisation as a means of dealing with the issue by the TSGs was premised on the misguided belief that the Western governments of the world could bring increased effectiveness to the Tibetan struggle simply through the laws and edicts they passed in Tibet's favour. A vibrant activist community's voice, achievements and future direction were derailed by imperiousness and a desire for exclusivity. Finally, a clear realisation now exists that the cause of Tibet will always take a back seat to economic concerns in the West. We continue to demonstrate that the lives of Tibetans are not worth their cost in economic development: a moral derailment of the first order.

CHAPTER 19

TIBETAN FIRE DRILL

The most recent few years have taken me out of the Himalayan foothills that I love and have forced me to spend more time in Kathmandu. Our little NGO, Himalayan Aid, still scrambles for funding, but we manage to get a school toilet or two built here and there, and occasionally we get one of our interns up to the border regions for a photo assessment in the old areas as well. Some loud anchorwoman from CNN felt the need to drag a camera crew up to Kodari a few years ago and start a shouting match with Nepali border security about Tibetans. I wonder who the local Chinese operatives will smack around for that little blunder – I hope it's one of the Barabise cops.

I do find myself still going to Washington to try to get some traction on new Tibet project ideas and some of our programmes, but it goes weird and I still get those "How did you get this far into the building?" looks from an entrenched bureaucrat or two. I was in a congressional office building in 2013, looking forward to just such treatment, when I noticed small groups of people roaming the hallways with little Tibetan flags and clipboards in their hands. Reaching out, I managed to get just enough feedback to realise that various Tibetan groups were conducting their annual "Tibet Lobby Day".

Apparently, the ICT hosts an annual gathering of Tibet supporters, who visit various congressional offices during a two-day period in mid-winter and get very little done other than having their pictures taken with congressional staffers. Sometimes real blood is drawn and someone gets a photo with an actual representative of Congress. Curious, I looked up the event on the internet and found that this sort of thing has been going on for a few years. There were pictures taken with all kinds of dignitaries, including Al Franken, who I can't say has ever stuck his neck out for Tibet – not to say that he won't someday. Mostly, it seemed like a big conditioning exercise for the "institutional" approach to Tibet. The ICT was even hosting "training" sessions, presumably on how to handle oneself in such august company and environs. Lots of excitement from the 30 or so individuals who attended the event, and I read that one breathless supporter chirped, "I got to meet a congressman."

The event continues, year after year, and has generated no significant changes for Tibet. And what if it had? Would one more letter, proclamation or congressional decree make a bit of difference? "Tibet Lobby Day" is all one needs to know about the state of the Tibet "lobby" today: It's an ineffective series of meaningless gestures. In January of 2016, I looked up the event once again to see if it had grown more focused and relevant. A Facebook exchange from January 13th caught my eye:

> **Q:** What are we asking our representatives to do for Tibet?
>
> **ICT:** We're working on that right now. Depending on what legislation comes up, we might be asking them to support different things. We should have more specifics soon!

I managed to sneak into the Tibet Lobby Day planning reception in February of 2016 to see if they'd come up with any more "specifics". It turned out they had: three pieces of legislation. The Global Magnitsky Human Rights Accountability Act (H.R. 624), the Tibetan Refugee Assistance Act of 2015 (H.R. 2679) and the Reciprocal Access to Tibet Act (H.R. 1112, described briefly later) were outlined and given to participants as talking points with their congressional representatives. The first act is non-specific to Tibet, and the other two are listed by GovTrack.com as having only a two per cent and a zero per cent chance, respectively, of being enacted.

*

The unique part of having been involved in the Tibet Movement for so long is that now I have a broad overview of the arc created over the past 20 years or so. The worst of it is that I can mentally document when the movement was at its peak and directly compare it to the ineffective mess I see now. It's not an unfamiliar arc in America. It's not an unfamiliar pattern. In America and the West, there seems to be a finite time for good causes –

a limited shelf life. Tragedies and sympathy-inducing scenarios all degenerate into farce if they are not resolved quickly enough for our limited attention spans. The space shuttle *Challenger* explosion spawned a series of crude jokes after weeks of inundating coverage and repetitive film footage saturated our brains. We can't help it: As an issue fades from our personal sense of relevance, it travels from being an object of concern to a joke. Tibet was now heading down such a path and was threatening to become the eye-rolling "Save the Whales" drone that convulsed all of us during the 1970s. Groupon's callous "Save the Money" commercial, which aired in the US during the Super Bowl of 2011, confirmed my suspicions:

> **Timothy Hutton:** "The people of Tibet are in trouble. Their very culture is in jeopardy. But they still whip up an amazing fish curry...and since 200 of us bought at Groupon.com, we're each getting $30 worth of Tibetan food for just $15 at [the] Himalayan Restaurant in Chicago."

The backlash was immediate. But instead of being a teachable moment – viewed by millions worldwide – the controversy was short-lived and not expanded upon for Tibetan benefit. "Free Tibet" had dropped the ball again.

*

The bulk of the Tibet support groups continue to grasp for any traction they can find. Students for a Free Tibet spent time and energy parodying the popular "Gangnam Style" video of 2012. They gave it a Tibetan repression theme and had someone dancing around wearing an oversized caricature head that was supposed to represent Chinese Premier Xi Jinping. The ICT continues to focus on its institutional approach and holds events like "teaching" seminars on the effects of the US elections on Tibet policy, hosts book-release discussions and generally performs a lot of self-validating busy work. Apparently, the more than 150 desperate Tibetans who ended their lives in fiery demonstrations of self-immolation failed to get the memo on these activities. Perhaps those they left behind can take some solace in the fact that the ICT monitors and maintains an accurate and updated body count every time Tibetan self-immolation occurs.

Tibet groups are looking for anyone or anything that might unify and reinvigorate their movement. A classic example of this is the Avaast.org petition of November 2013.

The brief story is that Avaaz.org, an online petitioning organisation, coordinated a petition to challenge China's impending election to the US

Human Rights Council. Interested individuals were to go to the Avaaz.org website, make a donation, and thus be part of the ever-growing petition to "get China to back off from its hard-line policy to be sure of getting the 97 votes it needs". The language of the petition was presumptive, and assumed China would bow to mass pressure. Many individuals saw through the campaign to the data-mining purposes beneath. The occasionally sane folks at TibetTruth.com made the correct assessment in their post 'Why We Won't Be Signing AVAAZ Petition on Tibet':

> ...the action by AVAAZ, though valuable in terms of shining light on Tibet, is naïve beyond any measurable scale in that it's based upon the belief that China's blood-soaked tyranny can be encouraged to moderate what is described as a "hard line policy." A phrase that itself falls very short of the genocidal assault waged for over six decades against Tibet and its people. But hey, we need to appeal to a fluffy majority who subscribes to the existence of the tooth-fairy, so the wording needs to be positive, hopeful and promising change.

Nevertheless, the wheels were in motion and Avaaz was leading the way. The Students for a Free Tibet broke out the old universal Chinese premier caricature head again and planned a rally in New York City to correspond with the day of the big vote that promised: "giant Tibetan skeleton puppets representing the victims of China's human rights abuses in Tibet will haunt a massive Xi Jinping caricature as Tibetans and their supporters carry colourful banners and flags..." The credible Tibet Justice Center bought into Avaaz's "send China a strong message" theme, and became part of the loose "Tibet Coalition" that also included the Students for a Free Tibet and the International Tibet Network. Five of the leading Tibetan Support Groups in India joined in as well. Even ICT, perhaps smelling an opportunity, jumped on board and wasted no time in adopting the naive mass-appeal language of Avaaz on their Facebook page posting of November 8th, 2013:

> We are 93% of the way there! Please sign and share this link to help us reach the goal of one million signatures on the Tibet petition, which says China should not be on the UN Human Rights Council unless they make dramatic improvements in the situation in Tibet. Thank you!

China made it onto the UN Human Rights Council in 2013, as predicted. The fact that so much effort was spent to send this type of inert message to China prior to the vote is regrettable. Plus, the petitioning organisation, Avaaz, may have had no intention of forwarding the cause of those misguided supporters. Avaaz and/or the representatives of the various TSGs were supposed to deliver the petition to 193 UN missions in New York and to foreign ministries in various parts of the world prior to the vote. It is unclear whether or not anyone followed through with this, or if they did, whether there exists any record of any responses from the 193 missions. What suggest a lack of rigour is that, as of October, 2016, the same Avaaz petition was still collecting signatures for the same issue on the same website and is still using the same pre-UN vote language, well over two years after China gained its seat on the UN Human Rights Council from that vote.

Avaaz is a for-profit "clicktivism" organisation that harvests fees and names through the gaining of support for petitions aimed at legitimate causes. In a telling article from the Guardian.com entitled 'Inside Avaaz – Can Online Activism Really Change the World?', Avaaz founder Ricken Patel comes across as a guy who seems more interested in the technological tweaks that would compel the maximum amount of people to sign his petitions than someone who actually wants to solve any given human rights issue. But who knows, maybe throwing millions of signatures on a petition and parading around in huge Chinese premier-heads is the best we can hope for today.

Still, none of this reaches Tibet itself, and that's why this type of "clicktivism" or "slacktivism" or whatever you want to call it is wrong on many levels. Suppose the Avaaz petition had worked. Then what? The UN Human Rights Council is shamed into voting down China's seat? So what? Celebrate this little victory quickly, petitioners, as you are about to be slapped in the face by the fact that it just doesn't matter.

First, when has the UN Human Rights Council ever effectively advocated for Tibet or, more importantly, against anything China does? Better yet, conduct your own internet search of the "achievements" of this UN Council. Results will show that "convening special sessions", "supporting resolutions", "renewing mandates" and establishing "special rapporteurs" is their standard fare. These are not the type of achievements Tibet has time for. The UN Human Rights Council is worthless to the cause of Tibet. They are a paper advocate with skills that go no further than observation and reporting.

Second, what makes one presume that any message sent through any denial or objection to any kind of UN seat has any effect on China whatsoever? China has its own agenda. At the end of the day, the Chinese really couldn't care less about what seat they have or do not have on some

UN Council. China keeps its own counsel, and any punitive actions against China on the world stage will be seen as insulting and, oh yes, they are likely to trigger some form of retaliation. For Tibet, successfully petitioning against a China seat at the UN table might actually result in an increase in Tibetan persecution inside Tibet.

The most glaring problem with the entire unfortunate Avaaz.org episode is in the way most remaining and leading Tibet organisations jumped towards it and embraced it fully. They had not seen any sort of mass rallying point like this in years, and they were willing to follow anyone or anything that promised a glimmer of hope for new momentum in Tibet activism.

*

I truly believe that the field programmes we initiated years ago represented the progressive spear-tip of the Tibet Movement. Today, however, any spear-tips for anything are the property of social media, and social media is demonstrating new ways to confound and disorganise the Tibet Movement. Twitter, most notably, has become a sounding board for opinions on Tibet. Factions and tribes form around intolerance and narrow viewpoints. Twitter accounts like @tibetans, @BhoRangzen and virtually any account that uses a Tibetan flag – be it static, waving, illustrated or otherwise – vie to preach their own narrow opinions on Tibet, and woe betide anyone who dares question their positions. I've observed their responses and their thin-skinned diatribes, and have decided to name them the "Tibetan Thought Police". Questions about acceptance, self-reflection and cooperation within the Tibet Movement and diaspora are met with an eerily familiar shrill rebuttal that usually carries some or all of the following: "___(@your name here)___has been spreading lies and untruths...boycott this imperialist running dog..." The spear-tip of the Tibet Movement has devolved and dissolved into tribal identification clusters and bickering factions, if Twitter be the gauge. So divisive is the discussion on Twitter that it could be cited as a brilliant piece of Chinese anti-Tibet cyber-espionage, but I've yet to see any Chinese hacking be so successful in its divisiveness.

Facebook fares no better. Apparently, after Facebook founder Mark Zuckerberg's visit to China in 2014, Tibetan self-immolation videos were banned in what some believed to be an appeasement gesture. Facebook defended their removal manoeuvre, saying they don't have the proper "tools" to warn people about "graphic" videos. So they removed those videos. The absolute last person you want to piss off about all of this is Tsering Woeser:

author, poet and one of the few authentic Tibetan activists making her outrage heard today. She let go on Facebook's duplicity:

> Western democracies have recently resolved to strike ISIS, and the public support for this is largely the result of the Jihadist videos of beheading hostages that have been disseminated online. Facebook defended its inclusion of these beheading videos which it claims to not show the graphic moment of beheading. But I, for one, saw the video of the beheading moment on Facebook. I even saw footage of the executioners putting the severed head on the torso of the dead. Even with a video without the moment of beheading, does it not "involve violence" and is it therefore not "graphic?"

*

Definitive proof that a movement has turned sour is in the way it evolves towards desperation: the need to stay relevant by throwing any idea out into the public realm to see if it resonates. It's akin to those movies where an adventurer throws a dart at a map of the world and says, "Let's go there!"

A major and ill-informed dart was thrown in 2013. It came in the form of lawsuits brought before Spain's National Court under the principle of universal jurisdiction. For those not familiar, universal jurisdiction is the idea that allows virtually any court to cross international borders and issue arrest warrants for those it deems in violation of universal norms regarding human rights, torture and various other big-time international no-no's. The actions were brought by a Tibetan support group called the Comite de Apoyo al Tibet, but right from the start the ICT had its hands all over it. In the most absurd theatre of farce, the Spanish court's ideal outcome would be to have former Chinese President Hu Jintao and other Chinese officials extradited and brought to Spain to stand trial for persecuting Tibetans.

International jurisdiction is a disaster. Henry Kissinger hates the concept. It breaks down judicial structures, nullifies the legal due process of nations and, as Dr Kissinger points out, guts the idea of national reconciliation. Basically, national wounds cannot heal properly if some other country arrests your criminal for the same charge. The stunt has been attempted on African strongman Paul Kagame as well as George Bush without success.

Never mind that no extradition treaty exists between China and Spain, and never mind the consequences of such a manoeuvre. Spain, Europe's economic basket case, was going after China over Tibet. Fortunately, it was a short-lived and sparsely publicised tactic that did nothing but incite China into threatening Spain. More importantly, it showed that Tibet activism was regressing towards tabloidism with this carnival side show. Spain backed down under Chinese pressure, but I received an email from the ICT in which they tried to spin their way out of the farce by proclaiming that the whole thing drew attention to something about "offshore" Chinese investments – whatever that meant.

*

Remarkably and stunningly, in 2014 the ICT published a statement saying that the situation in Tibet was now worse than ever. After reading this, I fell out of my chair. I can't say that I knew quite how to interpret what I had just read – I was possessed of two minds as I tried to take it all in. For a group like the ICT, that had been at the helm of steering Western Tibet advocacy for the last 25 years, this sounded like a de facto admission of failure. To state that the objective of one's existence and fundraising efforts has not only not been fulfilled but has taken a turn for the worse on your watch has to be disheartening indeed. To date, and to the ICT's credit, it is the closest any Western group has come to any form of self-reflection on what went wrong. My other take was more cynical. The report gave the impression that rather than being involved in solving the problem directly, the ICT was stating its new role as chronicler and reactive reporter of all things Tibet as business as usual. "Hey, we just monitor and report. We were always on the sidelines, so don't blame us," was the sense.

*

Today we see none of the harder-edged pro-Tibet legislative language that was the hallmark and acme of the Tibet Movement in the 1990s and early 2000s. The Western governments of the world are, for the most part, squarely in China's pocket, and would not dream of upsetting their trade relationships with the Big Dragon by causing offence over something a trivial as human rights in Tibet. We in the West cannot even summon the courage to meet with HH the Dalai Lama on official terms because of that fear.

US Presidents Clinton, George W. Bush and Obama all took turns avoiding a direct and official meeting with the Dalai Lama, although Obama has done the best job through a series of informal or "spiritual" meetings. Whoever comes next into the US presidency will likely have the same hands-off approach, and will adhere to the dismissive doctrine of "China and the Dalai Lama need to talk" as a default US Tibet policy. But don't just stick it to the Americans – the Yanks are not now, and were never, alone in their contemporary national-scale meekness on Tibet. Many Western countries and dignitaries are equally complicit. Most of this takes the form of cowering to China over economic ties, and this cowering takes the form of snubbing the Dalai Lama in various forms.

The Dalai Lama, speaking from Prague in 2013 and appearing weary of the pattern, mentioned that he did not mind the fact that the Czech Republic's last two presidents, Miloš Zeman and Václav Klaus, refused to meet with him. Weary or not, the pattern continued.

In 2014, South Africa denied a visa to the Dalai Lama and he was unable to attend a World Summit of Nobel Peace Laureates being held in Cape Town.

In that same year, Norway allowed the Dalai Lama entry into the country, but basically treated him like a leper, and government officials refused to meet with him. Norwegians called President Olemic Thommessen "cowardly" for his refusal to see the Dalai Lama personally.

In Britain, David Cameron's 2012 meeting with the Dalai Lama caused such a backlash with the Chinese that it took a few years for Britain to regain the Dragon's good graces. A September 2015 talk between the Dalai Lama and British parliamentarians was scheduled to be hosted by Speaker of the House John Bercow, and while representatives from both the UK and the Dalai Lama were quick and loud in pointing out that no official meeting with the prime minister was requested, the meeting was cancelled due to "unforeseen circumstances".

In a grand display of unification around the idea of economic primacy and subservience to China, Denmark, Korea, Canada ("not meeting but not snubbing"), Australia, Taiwan, Russia and Pope Francis have all taken turns rejecting a meeting with His Holiness. Thailand rejected a visa for his sister, so the prognosis is not good for a future Dalai Lama seminar in Bangkok.

*

Sometime in June of 2014, US Congressman Jim McGovern introduced the Reciprocal Access to Tibet Act. It was designed to deny Chinese officials who work in Tibet access to America if they don't open Tibet for American access. Dart-throwing was now moving down the road to what could rightly be characterised as "playgroundism": You won't let me in, so I won't let you in. Understand that such bills are unlikely to get a fair hearing on Capitol

Hill – this one, as of March 2015, remains stuck pending committee consideration – much less the full, supportive weight of a paralysed and polarised US Congress. But we're not just dealing with congressional ineptitude here. The Chinese take this stuff seriously and probably have a quid-pro-quo response poised and ready should this bill become law.

It gets better. Later that same month, Frank Wolf, our old friend, managed to squeak an amendment to the 2015 appropriations bill past the committee. It stipulates that the street in front of the Chinese embassy will be changed from International Avenue to Liu Xiaobo Street, after the Chinese dissident. Wolf and others went on to ape the usual "send a clear and powerful message" mantra that usually accompanies this sort of thing. Playgroundism is generated when deep thought initiatives give way to the "anything is good" mentality and childish, binary choices. That's the clear and powerful message I get.

*

An entire new volume can be filled with the follies and foibles of governments and Tibet groups alike, and maybe that should come next. But I can only go so far with the finger-pointing here, since I'm equally guilty of the same types of incompetence I rail against above. It's been almost ten years since our days of dirty field projects and there has been plenty of time to let things settle and to re-check our work. I'm not entirely pleased.

In 2012, we sent one of our interns up to the Dolakha valley in an attempt to locate any remnants from our sign project and to assess what the current situation in the area held for transiting Tibetans. It had been many years since we had placed our helpful signs. For the first few years after the completion of the project, we were getting stories from the Reception Centre that Tibetans had seen the signs, understood them and been so overwhelmed by the communication that they would bow and prostrate themselves in front of every sign encountered as they made their way down the valley. Now, things were most decidedly different. An unusual transformation had taken place.

The Chinese were everywhere, building hydroelectric substations and dams up and down the length of the valley. The beautifully meandering river-gorge trail that led up through Siguti and Piguti over a two-day walk was now a bus-ready road full of dust and roadside merchants. Chinese construction labour camps fashioned out of corrugated metal dotted the trail. Heavy construction dump-trucks and bulldozers threw up a dust film that coated the livelihoods of simple village merchants. The foot trail that Ram, Ramesh and I took while whistling the theme from *The Last of the Mohicans* was obliterated, and only Chinese dam-building hardware and subsistence-level roadside vending remained. The life was being sucked out of the Dolakha valley by large-scale construction and newly built, homogenising ribbons of transport. Plus, the report I received from our intern included photos of an area undergoing not only a deep commercial and social transformation but also an intense level of Chinese scrutiny.

The Chinese were supplying many of the labourers for this project. They had artfully secured various positions from the main general contractor in Norway, and seemed to be using their position for purposes outside of whatever agreements they had negotiated with the Norwegians.

"Jim, we went into a tea house and were followed by these big Chinese guys who didn't smile and didn't order anything. They just watched us. They didn't look like dam workers either," our intern reported.

The locals were now afraid to talk about anything that had to do with Tibetans. The few that were forthcoming said that only one small avenue remained at a secluded crossing point, and that the Chinese were posting cameras along all the other known crossing routes.

"Well, jeez," I said, "did you get any pictures of those Chinese border cameras?"

He didn't. What's the world coming to when you can't get an intern to risk being shot by the Chinese for a decent photo anymore? These kids today...

The most interesting part of our intern's report centred on the idea that the effort seemed totally unnecessary. Nepal was constructing a new paved road through an inhospitable gorge that ran parallel and superfluous to the main Kodari highway – just one valley to the west. There also seemed to be no apparent infrastructure for moving hydroelectric power to either China or through Nepal. It was being billed as the great "Upper Tamakoshi" water project and was expected to be completed sometime in 2013, but from the photos I had seen, the project seemed like another typical Nepali big-dam boondoggle – of which there are many.

Since 2007, this project has been plagued by the usual and almost immediate incompetence of the Nepali government. Eventually, enough was enough. The main contractor Statkraft, out of Norway, decided to give up on the project, and in 2016 cited "bureaucratic hurdles, geo-political instability and [a] fragile political situation" as the reasons. I'm not sure that this abandonment will diminish the Chinese presence in the Dolakha/ Lamabagar valley in the least.

There is political genius in such projects. Due to Nepal's bureaucratic ineptitude on all things, especially big hydro projects, the Chinese, who insinuated themselves into this project, can do things at whatever pace they see fit and keep an eye on the valley for as long as they choose. This is in keeping with their demonstrated, if not stated, policy of: "We couldn't care less about helping Nepal. We just want to harass Tibetans and piss off India." I have never seen any Chinese activity in Nepal that did not adhere, directly or indirectly, to this philosophy. In this valley, cameras and hundreds of Chinese observers harass the Tibetans, and anything that seeks to regulate the flow of water southward through Nepal pisses off the Indians.

None of the posted signs from our old project remained.

My sense of screwing up kicked in and I began to wonder if our signs had drawn unwanted attention to the Dolakha valley. After all, nothing like that had ever been tried in Nepal and the effort looked reasonably official. The Chinese have flipped out over less, certainly, but were we the cause of the mass, infiltrative Chinese presence on this project? Nepal didn't need another big dam project, it just needed to cut the corruption crap and finish the projects that were already in progress in other parts of the country. The Chinese certainly did not care about Nepal's water needs, but they had consistently demonstrated that they would spare no expense in clamping down on areas known for experiencing undocumented Tibetan foot traffic. Did we tip them off with our signs?

*

Ground Zero up at Namche Bazaar is no longer the hotbed of activity it once was. The Sagarmatha Club, if it even exists at this point, has a diminished agenda and Tibetans just do not cross through the area anymore.

I did hear an interesting rumour not too long ago from a Sherpa friend who was up in Namche in 2011. He encountered a very nervous and officious-looking Chinese man who asked a few of the community members about their thoughts on China digging a tunnel from the Chinese border to Namche Bazaar. The outsized arrogance and scale of the plan authenticated it as Chinese, in my mind, so I leaned my head in for a closer listen.

Apparently, China wanted to tunnel through miles of high Himalayan rock in order to be able to move quickly and intercept "unauthorised" travellers who happened to make it to Namche.

*

I'd like to offer apologies all around for the doom and gloom. At some point, the reader might suggest I carry a bias against all Western pro-Tibet effort; that I have an axe to grind against all Tibet support groups and the Washington-based Tibet lobby. To an extent I do, in as much as I'd like to force a bit of self-reflection and regrouping, but that's it. We need a Western effort, it just needs to step back from its current approach and ask a few questions. What have we done right? We have thrown millions of dollars at every Tibetan who can possibly benefit, and yet the level of despair among Tibetans is at an all-time high. The Dalai Lama has met with and accumulated many powerful friends and allies around the world, and has influenced many legislative efforts and governmental statements on behalf of Tibet; but what, ultimately, has he achieved by this? The Chinese haven't budged and seem only too happy to wait for our next half-hearted scolding so they can hit it out of the park with yet another calculatingly shrill rebuttal. Can we label one thing that we in the West have done that has been of essential benefit to the cause of Tibet? Tibet support groups are hopelessly ineffective. "Raising awareness" doesn't count and only goes so far. The Western governmental ethos of "institutionalising" the Tibet issue is just a code for controlling and sidelining the debate at the highest levels. What then?

I believe firmly that the key to recovering any momentum for the Tibet struggle is to realise that all changes, all ideas and all programmes designed to further the Tibet cause must originate from the Tibetans themselves. It was a mistake to think that a Western approach to an Asian problem would offer the best outcome for Tibet. The West blew it, and now it is time to move on. The Tibetans themselves are beginning to sense this. Already the realisation of a new Tibetan struggle based on localised ideas, pragmatism and regional priorities is taking shape, but Tibet will still need the support of a friendly world power in order to bring these new ideas to fruition. Still, there is good news and there is hope: "Free Tibet 2.0" has begun, and that powerful friend is India.

CHAPTER 20

THE SNOW LION RISES

If one were to ask those who originated the West's Tibet Movement back in the late 1980s – Joel McCleary, John Ackerly, Jeffrey Hopkins, Dianne Feinstein, Richard Blum and all the others – if the current situation in Tibet mirrors the hopes and goals they all had when they started, what would their answer be? Ask them if their ideal outcome from their 1987 perspective included a worsening of conditions inside Tibet and more than 150 anguished Tibetans lighting themselves on fire by 2015. Ask them if an almost relentless focus on legislative initiatives for Tibet by Western governments has yielded one note of concession from China. If we could ask the late Adam Yauch if the tens of thousands of people who attended his Beastie Boys concerts in support of Tibet made one bit of difference to one Tibetan in Tibet, what would he say? Ask all of them how the simple "raising awareness" campaigns of the Tibet Movement helped channel one bit of change or prevented one Tibetan from dying in flames. If anyone can look you in the eye and say that the last 25 years of our efforts to free Tibet have been anything more than a tragic waste of time, they are either delusional or protecting a paycheck earned by one of the entrenched institutions that claim to support the Tibet cause. Today, China is stripping away large, heaping chunks of Tibetan freedoms and religious autonomy at an accelerated rate. The full assimilation of Tibetan culture into "Greater China" is proceeding at an unprecedented pace. Tibetans are killing themselves. The Western Tibet Movement continues to hold the equivalent of a bake sale in response.

Our overarching "white man's burden" sense of responsibility dictates that we Westerners insert ourselves into every human rights discussion in every corner of the world. And while we may mean well, our know-it-all approach is oftentimes so culturally and practically incompatible with ground realities that we wind up doing more harm than good with our interventions. That little lie our parents told us about our place in the world continues to hold sway, and we believe that our Western values trump all others; so we continue to lob long-distance and half-conceived darts of assistance at issues that are realistically beyond our capacity to improve. Our approach to helping Tibet is overblown and ill-suited to the daily struggles of Asian people. It is time for us to get out of the way.

Western ineffectiveness carries with it the momentum of half a century's effort at foreign "aid". As Tate Watkins states in an article for *The Christian Science Monitor*, this aid has a life of its own:

> The problem with this idea is that systematic foreign aid creates opportunities for corruption, cultures of dependency, and disincentives to develop. The aid faucet misaligns incentives between donors and recipients, making it extremely difficult to turn off the flow.

This is uniquely dangerous when the aid is aimed directly and publicly at Tibet. As I've mentioned, Tibet lobbyists in Washington take great pride in announcing the "institutionalisation" of the Tibetan struggle. This means that Tibet will continue to get at least a perfunctory morsel of attention and funding from the governments of the world, and the remaining full-time Tibet support groups will keep up their same drumbeat of condemnation and awareness-raising to satisfy the needs of their donor bases, keep their names in contention for whatever scraps of funding they can obtain and keep the lights burning in their entrenched offices.

It would be nice to simply ignore this dynamic and let it evaporate into obscurity and disinterest, or perhaps be entertained by letting people like William Easterly or Dambisa Moyo write about it. Unfortunately, every dollar that is earmarked and delivered by a Western government for anything Tibetan brings with it the risk of some form of Chinese retaliation. Every gesture the West makes, no matter how small, has real consequences. Be it police brutality towards Tibetans in Nepal, or the detention of Tibetan protestors prior to a Chinese dignitary's India visit, China likes to "send a clear message" of its own: If you try to make a public show of your support for Tibet, we'll make twice the public show of how much we control the Tibetan presence in our sphere of influence.

The Chinese can't wait for our next word on Tibet. They love using the Tibet issue as a means of establishing a sense of equivalency against what they perceive to be Western hegemonic encroachment. The rabidity of their rebuttals tells us this. They are tired of the West dictating the definition of world order, and they use the Tibet issue as a means of asserting their belief that it's their turn to bring their perspective to the forefront. The big point is that China wants to invent its own reality and its own world stage from this moment forward. There is no head-to-head, confrontational approach or fundraising event that will change this dynamic.

If we care at all about Tibet, it's time we stopped playing into China's rhetorical hands. We need to begin the process of walking back from the mess we've made of Tibet advocacy. We can start with a few easy things:

First, stop scolding China. It doesn't work. In fact, it has the opposite effect. Every time I read some commentary on Tibet by the expert of the moment, I tend to stop reading and cringe when, inevitably, I get to the phrase "China needs to..." or "we call on China to..." because I know it will be followed by that predictable, almost gleefully angry rebuttal from China. If we realistically want China to feel the pressure on Tibet, it must feel the pressure from the Chinese citizens themselves, at the town and village level throughout China. A village revolt in Wukan back in December of 2011 displayed the rage Chinese villagers felt over corruption from village leaders. Higher ranking provincial officials had to step into the fray and call the village grievances legitimate or risk having events spin out of control. Now, this kind of pressure may never be used directly on behalf of Tibetans by ethnic Chinese, but it should be encouraged as a first step in giving all groups and citizens in China the feel of taking control over their respective communities, and it is a big step towards self-determination for all. Work for change from inside China and stop throwing political darts from the other side of the world is the message here.

Next, it is arrogant and foolish to think that Tibet and Tibetan culture can somehow be saved simply by lobbying the US, or any Western, government towards some action or policy aim. US Tibet policy has been nothing more than an exercise in rearranging political furniture, and the world has been given no real reason to believe it would ever progress beyond that, so leave US lawmakers alone. Let them do what they want, as long as they avoid causing harm like we've described in Nepal – maybe something will come of it – but by no means make their approval, actions or statements on Tibet represent the spearhead of Tibet activism.

The next thing we should do is deprioritise "raising awareness" about Tibet as a form of effective activism. After more than 20 years of banner-waving and leafleting, it is safe to say that awareness has officially been raised. If we want to help Tibet, it's long past the time that we move on to "Free Tibet 2.0" and start prioritising concrete programmes and ideas. Constantly and repetitively feeling the need to raise awareness saps the momentum out of any movement, and eventually becomes code for not knowing what to do next.

Lastly, but not finally, stop throwing money and programmes at Tibetans. It does not help and creates a sense of dependency. Tibetans are not pets and they are not on this earth for our Western philanthropic amusement. Tibetans can create their own programmes and their own future, we just have to let them. I asked a friend some ten years ago what it is that the Tibetans want. This friend knew the old Dharamsala activist crew of Jamyang Norbu, Pema Bhum and a few others; he told me emphatically and with certainty: "Cut off the money!"

It is presumptuous to pretend to speak for those individuals in Tibet who have chosen to end their lives by setting themselves on fire, but the sense of desperation in their actions is undeniable. Desperation is enhanced by a complete lack of pathways for self-determination. Statelessness combined with the lack of identity born of living in a constant state of dependency on foreign handouts cannot possibly give Tibetans confidence in the future. Shift the movement and the money entirely to Tibetan control and stop throwing chunks of money at Tibetans which only reflects our Western ideas and priorities and may or may not do any good. Currently, the US chunk is around $6 million. Our job in the West should be to support whatever the Tibetans feel is necessary and to offer our opinions and assistance as needed. Return to doing what we do best in the West. For most of us, that means fundraising. And we shouldn't fundraise for what *we* want to do, we should fundraise for what the Tibetans tell us is necessary. Cut off the money? Not entirely. Stop imposing our will on the Tibetans with our money? Yes.

The West is too far from Tibet. The distance makes us ineffective and misguided. Yet our arrogance leads us to derive strategies and conjure solutions that our hegemonic delusions tell us we must forward. The distance shouldn't matter, we say. The processes that unfold based on our concerns for Tibet that lead towards the development of our type of democratic progress should be enough, we believe. In truth, this belief is dead from the start. The perceived weight and influence of our best intentions and governmental proclamations on Tibet are not shared by China. The Chinese know we are too fearful of upsetting any trade relationships to do anything substantive on Tibet, and so the West wilfully approaches China from a position of weakness on the issue. The Chinese have never once responded positively to any of our pleadings, scoldings or admonitions on Tibet and they never will – they know they don't have to. The West has lost the moral high ground on Tibet.

*

It's mid-2014, and India had just given its roughly 150,000 resident Tibetans (there are only about 5,500 in the US) the opportunity to register and vote in Indian elections. It is a magnanimous gesture on the part of the Indian government. The Tibetans respond poorly. Only a fraction actually signs up to vote. The problem is that there is a perception in the Tibetan community that voting in an Indian election would cause them to give up their Tibetan citizenship and thus neutralise their struggle. Tibetans mostly reject the Indian overture, but do so graciously. They have lived for more than 50 years with security and a degree of autonomy under their Indian sponsors, and upsetting this balance with ingratitude would not be a wise thing.

Why would a national government do this for Tibetans? Are they not afraid of China? Everyone else seems to be, so what gives? India is not the West. The relationship that India has with Tibetans spans centuries. The Dalai Lama calls India the great "guru" of all Tibetans and the Tibetans themselves are *"chelas"*, or servants of the guru. Theirs is a cultural kinship that transcends any apprehensions over losing mere economic opportunities with China.

Historical ties between India and Tibet run deep. The Buddhism that Tibetans practise originated from Indian Hindu Prince Siddhartha, who became the Buddha. In Nepal, Buddhists and Hindus coexist peacefully and often share the same temples for their various rituals. Look closely and you find that many aspects of ancient Tibetan history seem to find their genesis in some connection to India. A piece I found on the internet called "Cultural Relations between India and Tibet" drives home this point:

> In 127 BC, the inhabitants of Yarlung valley elevated Nyatri Tsenpo as the first king of Tibet. The legend tells us that he was a sort of God-like being who descended from the sky using a kind of "sky-rope". Nyatri, continues the legend, was originally from India; he was the son of a royal family related to the Buddha's family. Before reaching Tibet, he had been wandering between India and Tibet, and finally came down in Yarlung Valley where he met some herdsmen grazing their yaks. The Tibetans believed that he had come from heaven. Twelve chieftains took him on their shoulders and made him the first king of Tibet. His enthronement marks the beginning of the Yarlung Dynasty of Tibet. The Tibetan royal calendar still dates from that year.

Documentation of the India/Tibet relationship is wide and extensive, and the literature on the subject is vast. But it is no better illustrated than through the most current of events. Indian politicians have seen the value of this relationship and have been increasingly vocal in their support of Tibet in recent years. As an example of one of many such events, a "Solidarity with Tibet" rally was held in Hyderabad in January of 2014. Indian government officials stood shoulder to shoulder with Tibetans, and the two distinct peoples pledged everything but their undying love for each other. Indian Congressional General Secretary G. Narjan was one of many who expressed his (perhaps strategic) feelings toward Tibet when he announced that "we will fully support your non-violent struggle, and we will be with you always". This was not US Senator Bob Dole of 1991 grandstanding to make sure he got his sharp comments heard by China; this had the sound of a partnership that was forming. It was also a fearlessly unilateral statement that could not care less about China's reaction.

On May 15th of that same year, India put muscle on its pro-Tibet rhetoric. The Ministry of Home Affairs officially extended welfare services, land allocations for markets and educational programmes for children to all Tibetans living in India, saying in clear terms that Tibetans "are as entitled to all the development schemes of the Government of India as any Indian citizen". India was taking the lead. There was no hollow urge to "call on China" to do anything. India was demonstrating that it would do whatever could be done to assist the Tibetans in its charge.

All of this has enabled a new Tibetan confidence and allowed the Central Tibetan Administration in Dharamsala to spread its wings a bit. Shortly after the Indian government's generous offer was announced, Lobsang Sangay, the political leader of the Tibetan government in exile, offered his own direction for the Tibetan people. He hit the "reset" button on the Dalai Lama's middle way approach by stating that the Tibetans themselves would now begin a global campaign for autonomy using the middle way philosophy. In a few words, the middle way signifies a non-polar political means of compromise that allows Tibetans the freedom of existence and self-determination without denying Chinese sovereignty – there's quite a lot more to it than that, but this can do for now. Sangay's announcement was nothing less than a complete expression of reproach to decades of failed Western efforts, in my view, and I could not have been more pleased. In the weeks following his announcement, I published an article in the *Tibetan Post* that expressed my feelings:

> Tibetans may have wearied from the plodding calculations of Western-based efforts that seem to find their struggle more useful as a political pawn than as a compelling human rights issue. The recent announcement by the CTA is not only a call for Tibetans to take more control of their own fate, but a none too subtle message to the West that enough is enough, you have had your chance, we will control the narrative from here forward and India will give us their wise counsel and the freedom to do so.

India is not far from Tibet in many ways. India harbours more Tibetans than any other nation in the world, and shares cultural and religious similarities with Tibet. Indians are immediately, proximally and strategically close to all things Tibetan. Indians also seem to have a better understanding of how best to deal with China, and they have no fear of Chinese retaliation – for now. India has been in Tibet's corner and has physically acted on behalf of Tibetans since the time of Nehru. In short, India has a vested interest in Tibetans, and India is the only major international force that can adequately champion the cause of Tibet.

India is also not stupid. Indians know that supporting a people that the Chinese vehemently dislike offers them an oddly favourable position when dealing with China – a position of strength, which the United States and the West can never attain. As much as India's support infuriates them, the Chinese appear to show a grudging respect for India's display of spine on the subject. This is the dynamic of regional politics. Unlike the Western world, the object of Chinese ire is not half a world away and easily cowed by economic priorities. India is a powerful and proximal neighbour. Any shrill screaming and retaliation by China against India invites the very real possibility of regional consequences beginning along the various volatile borders China shares with India. China shows more of a degree of care when dealing with India over Tibet.

Tibetans serve a purpose and the Indians understand how best to exploit their presence for political gain. Unless China is willing to invade northern India over the issue of Tibet, the Indians can see nothing but benefit from their attention to Tibetans. The timing could not be better for India to take the reins from a stalled Western Tibet Movement that stumbles repeatedly in its efforts and is devoid of any substantive thinking on the matter. Championing Tibet and Tibetans can benefit India in the following ways:

1. India can show world leadership on an issue that has vexed the West, and create a human rights "win".
2. As mentioned, India can showcase a strong presence in its negotiations with China by the mere presence of the Tibet card in its negotiating deck.
3. This card, conversely, represents a no-harm pressure valve that can be released when a bit of Chinese appeasement is required. Witness the locking up (and immediate release) of Tibetan demonstrators prior to Chinese Premier Hu Jintao's visit to Delhi in March 2012. India can dangle hollow Tibetan containment gestures at the Chinese as leverage on any issue.
4. India gains major favour with the West by taking the Tibet issue off its hands. India can push this idea of being the West's human rights and democracy surrogate in the region, and offer a clear contrast with China, to the point that, all things being relatively equal, Western businesses can be perceived as either pro-human rights or anti-human rights depending on their choice of investment: India or China.
5. The seeds of pro-India sentiment can be planted deep inside China through the correspondences of the Tibetan diaspora in India and Tibetans living inside Tibet and China at large.
6. As the world's largest democracy and emergent superpower, India can show its capacity for tolerance and willingness to help those in need and immigrants who wind up on its shores – the "new America", if you will.
7. Of most immediate importance, there is a very real possibility of China cooling down its repressive treatment of Tibetans once the US is out of the picture. Tibetans get smacked around almost predictably after some pontificating US or Euro

> condemnation of China's handling of their situation. It never has a positive effect. The Chinese immediately tell the world that it's a new day, and categorically condemn the meddling in their "internal affairs". To show they are serious, the Tibetan persecution increases. It is deliberate, purposefully timed and meant to show a sense of proportionality aimed squarely at telling the West to mind its own business. India is unlikely to scold China in such a manner. It will lance the ribs of China with its proactive, Tibet-forward actions. India is capable of realising an intolerable scenario for China: the idea that Chinese Communist Party's attempts at self-validation through public expressions on Tibet are being ignored. Ultimately, China will not be able to create the type of political equivalency it craves – ideological impasse and stalemate with the US – if India does all the heavy lifting on Tibet.

It's a big list of potential benefits, certainly, and a lot of hot air on my part. But what does India need to do right now to move closer towards the role of Tibet's primary advocate? What are some of the preliminary steps that are needed or already in their beginning phases that can lead to the types of benefits listed above?

Most importantly, India needs to continue the reach-out effort. Tibetans can be stubborn, especially the newer generation that has perhaps never seen Tibet. They tend to want to fling themselves into conflict rather than think things through more pragmatically. India needs to continue the new spirit of welcome that began in 2014 when Indian-born Tibetans were offered the vote. While it was rejected by most Tibetans, India still seemed to see the need for such gestures. Undeterred after the rebuff, India opened up a wide array of social services and educational benefits to Tibetans in 2014. It was not a giveaway like the US State Department's $2 million dollar "shut up and stay in the refugee camps" bribe, announced smilingly by Special Coordinator for Tibetan Affairs Maria Otero in 2012; rather, it had the feel and language of Tibetans being offered a seat at the table of India: a chance to make it on their own.

Next, India needs to do what India does best: play all positions at once. Don't stand on some phoney ideological high-ground, scream at the Chinese and basically paint a big target on your chest like the Yanks. Further the cause of Tibetans by providing cover for their efforts. Appease China by arresting a protester from time to time; enrage China by offering social services to Tibetans. This is balance, New Delhi style, and can be managed so as to forward the aims of India's Tibetans and minimise the international embarrassment and challenge that causes China to retaliate.

Third, take care of your young Tibetan men and women. This generation was born in India without ever having seen Tibet and they've got flashes of anger that surface from time to time. Appease their sense of "rangzen" by offering a substitute: Give them Ladakh. Okay, yes, it sounds nuts, but hear me out. Ladakh is full of Tibetans already. It is feasible to offer a few silent, unpublicised incentives for Tibetan-Indians to set up shop in Ladakh. Start with a unique Tibetan autonomy in the region. Stimulate with financial incentives and perhaps "Indian cultural heritage"-oriented subsidies. India: Continue with the spirit of your previous gestures and offer actual property ownership options, and legitimate and legal business registrations and permitting. Offer infrastructure projects and deep support to maintain this area, as well as incentives for Ladakh-specific enlistment in the Indian military, and you will create a loyal buffer state within a state. Already, the fine Tibetan-made film *Little Tibet* explores aspects of this option from a Tibetan perspective. Perhaps it's time for India to take a serious look at this option as well.

For those thinking the Ladakh approach extreme, my excuse is that we should not be afraid to put all ideas, good and bad, on the table for rigorous discussion. A larger point is that many young, Indian-born Tibetans are itching for a fight. If offering opportunities in Ladakh, or wherever, can give Tibetan youths living in India a positive view of their future and a sense of self-determination, then, these options must be explored. If the Tibetan struggle is allowed to turn violent, India's support will wane and the international community will lump the Tibetans in with every other rock-throwing, dissatisfied group; they will be relegated to the status of being the Palestinians of Asia. Non-violence is unique and it distinguishes the Tibetan struggle from all others. It gets the world's attention and it charms the hell out of Indians who think Gandhi invented the concept. Tibetans: Don't lose this edge.

The most basic of summations here is that the international campaign to "Save Tibet", "Free Tibet" or whatever term your bumper sticker prefers has failed under the weight of its own hubris. Internationalism has shown a ponderous and ineffective approach to an issue that needs more nimble actions that are best dealt with on a regional level. Only India has the ability to move quickly and identify areas of most immediate concern and benefit to Tibetans. Only India has a strategic self-interest in doing so.

CHAPTER 21

HOMECOMING

It wasn't the same. I really wasn't expecting it to be, but I didn't expect this – this feeling. I'd been hitting the town for about an hour by now and I was unable to come to terms with the atmosphere: weary faces that no longer looked at me with hope – resigned to exasperation and unwanted permanence.

It had been fifteen years since I took on my first journey to this place. It was a long bus ride from the Majnu Katilla section of Delhi back then, crammed into a seat next to an impossibly tall Khampa Tibetan – his long black hair in red braids thrashing across my reading material. He took pity on my condition and barked compliance from a fruit vendor who happened by our window during a scheduled stop. I remember sharing an orange and exchanging a few smiles with this descendant of an ancient Tibetan warrior clan, and being on that bus for 15 hours or so – that's about it.

This day, I'd landed by plane. To get to where I was standing meant a 45-minute taxi ride up winding mountain roads and through a large Indian army encampment. I was perched on the uppermost finger of a mountain ridge above the Kangra valley in Himachal Pradesh, northern India, in a location that served as the home-in-exile of the Dalai Lama, his government and numerous Tibetans who had somehow found the will and the resources to join him there since the early 1960s. The West call this mountaintop refuge Dharamshala out of convenience, but the real Tibetan presence was further up the hill, in McLeod Ganj.

The settlement was given to the Tibetans by India as a base of location on humanitarian grounds, but the land and opportunities remained finite and there had been very little room for physical expansion since. Tibetans were stuck here and they knew it. When I came those many years ago, there was no sense of a dead end, however. The US and the world were on Tibet's side, and myself and other Westerners were treated with a kind of deferential reverence. Eyes lit up when I tried to speak a bit of U-Tsang Tibetan back then. It was a source of pride for the residents of McLeod Ganj that a foreigner should even attempt the intricacies of spoken Tibetan, and it was taken as an indicator that Tibetan language and culture would survive at the hands of these rich white people.

Now, in September of 2014, I was not sure what I'd gotten myself into. A few words of Tibetan to a shop owner elicited an impatient response in English. Too many Westerners trying their hand at the language over too many years had left Tibetans frustrated by their lingering role as humanitarian novelty. The good will was fading and the fun and games with Westerners were in retreat. They'd played along with our condescending giddiness long enough to realise that the West really had no intention of delivering the goods. White people like me would never free Tibet; the residents of McLeod Ganj knew it and they were starting to let the tourist traffic know it as well.

I noticed that for the first time the local vendors were beginning to sell T-shirts with simply "Tibet" stamped on the front. The "Free Tibet" shirts now had to share the billing. Both shared the dust from the endless applications of cement and stone block being applied to the streets. No one was complaining. A new road, any paved road, was an improvement on the mud and gravel tracks that were being replaced.

One still saw the occasional "dharma" seekers. They'd made their pilgrimage from their Western nests and come to answer some compulsion. Meditation, yoga, and arts and crafts at the Norbu Linka Institute brought the wide-eyed and hopeful, all looking to cut off their own proprietary piece of the Tibet story.

My old hangout, the Shangri-la Hotel, was still in existence, but this trip I'd become fond of having breakfast at the Snow Lion café a few doors to the north. These mornings were treasured and they gave me a few moments with my journal and the opportunity for a bit of reflection. As Tenzin, my meticulous waiter, brought two pieces of buttered white toast and a French press full of coffee along with the stern admonition to "wait three minutes", the morning began to take some shape in my notebook. I had memories of a similar scene, years ago. Travellers bragging about how "hard it was to get here" and where they've been and where they're going – all at full volume so that no one in the room would miss a word. Today I noticed a group doing the same thing, only without the verbal display and never without the umbilicus of their electronic devices of choice.

I had no business being in McLeod Ganj 15 years ago. I came on a whim during one of my vaccine smuggling trips to Delhi. It was Losar – the Tibetan new year – and all activity had ceased among those with whom I was dealing, so I said "what the hell" and headed for Dharamshala, hoping to see something. I remember meeting up with Karma, our San Diego monk, and Taga, the double amputee, and doing quite a bit of solitary reading and tea-drinking.

Now I was there for a reason, a good one. In Kathmandu I'd just hosted Ernesto Sirolli, a lecturer who was riding high after his humorous and prescient TED talk about entrepreneurship went viral with more than two million views. We had just finished a series of his lectures that left me exhausted. I had poor Ernesto shuttling all over Kathmandu, meeting entrepreneur groups, Tibetans, business leaders and social entrepreneurs. I liked his programme. He decided a long time ago that the best way to help people is to "shut up and listen" to their ideas and stop being the bossy Westerner with the white man's burden. Coincidentally, I also happened to be in contact with a Tibetan student who was studying entrepreneurship among the Tibetan diaspora and I wondered if Ernesto's ideas would be a good fit for Tibetans in India – it seemed they were.

Through a series of e-mails and conversations, I wound up being invited to present my Tibetan-hybridised version of Ernesto's ideas to the Tibetan government in exile – the Central Tibetan Administration (CTA). This was what I was looking for. Not some condescending Western solution that was miraculously conceived a world away, but a chance to incorporate some Western thinking in a discussion that helped add to Tibetan conceived ideas and programmes. It was the "Free Tibet 2.0" that I had envisioned, and now I was about to help start the show.

Pema, the coordinator for the Tibetan Business Consortium in Delhi, was given the assignment to find me somewhere on the north side of McLeod Ganj. She was a relative of Lobsang Sangay, the current *sikyong*, or prime minister, of the Tibetan government in exile, and she was also tasked with keeping tabs on my location and helping with my scheduling. I had no idea where or when I'd run into her, or what she looked like other than an image I had seen on her LinkedIn profile. We had exchanged e-mails over the last few weeks and she seemed serious in her work and in her communications. I stepped out into the street and looked around. I expected to meet a businesswoman who was all business.

"Ha! Jim-la, there you are," came a cry from halfway across the main bus square.

We exchanged smiles and brief hellos before she plunged back into her iPhone business with urgency. Witty and bright, Pema was a young, fashion-conscious Tibetan woman with a busy schedule to which I seemed a hasty addition.

"Anyway, good to meet you, and this is Dorje."

She gave a no-look elbow flip in the general direction of her ascetically clad companion, the first transsexual or transgendered transvestite (thick maroon robes prohibited my comprehensive reading of Dorje's gender identification choice) Tibetan monk I'd encountered. This had to be a first for Tibet, and I chuckled at the thought of how a rigidly structured and conservative monastic community was dealing with this cutting-edge manifestation of modern zeitgeist.

Pema looked up from her phone. "I've told him to quit the monastery. They don't know how to deal with him and he embarrasses the other monks. Anyway, you're scheduled for a meeting at the Ministry of Finance tomorrow. Want to go get a coffee?"

We made a curious threesome: a modern Tibetan woman, a non-gender-specific monk and an aging white activist, as we sat in a nearby restaurant owned by Pema's friend. I can't begin to tell you how widely the conversation ranged, but I will say that I thoroughly enjoyed myself. At one point, Lobsang Sangay himself called Pema to check in and, thoughtfully, ask how well the new road construction efforts were progressing. I was quite a bit impressed by this. Time passed quickly and the conversation continued on at a brisk pace until I tried a long-shot question just to see the effect:

"Guys, I have an old friend I haven't seen for years. He's a monk at Sherab-Ling Gompa. Karma is his name and he's an amputee – lost one leg above the knee."

"Ooh! I think I know this guy, ooh," sang Dorje as he riffled through the files of photos on his phone. Taking the device from Dorje, I saw a familiar face: It took me a moment to see past almost two decades' worth of aging, but yes, unmistakably, it was my old friend Karma. Instantly, memories of San Diego and my very first years in the Tibet Movement came rushing back: the demonstrations, fitting Karma for a new leg, the meetings at San Diego Friends of Tibet, the distribution of Tibetan public-service announcement film clips to cinemas – good memories, all of them.

But as I looked into the face that stared back at me from Dorje's phone I saw something else. It was the same expression I'd seen on many a street vendor here in McLeod Ganj: bewildered disappointment. Life had let Karma down and he could not conceal his heartache for any photo; the cruelty of it all had taken its toll.

"I need to go to him right away," I barked.

"Jim dear, this photo is old and I don't know where he is anymore. I know he's not at the monastery," Dorje replied, seeking to temper my urgency.

I still wanted to see Karma, but in that moment I felt strangely relieved and compelled to recoil from pursuing the matter further. Maybe Karma didn't want to see *me*. In truth, all I really wanted was some closure and would that have been fair? We helped fit Karma for a state-of-the art prosthetic leg back in the late 1990s. After we were all done congratulating ourselves, we let poor Karma go his way, and I was now unprepared to hear an update of what he may or may not need from the West at this stage in his life. I refused to buy into the idea that any form of aid implies ownership of the problem forever. I knew from my work with Himalayan Aid in Nepal that charitable gestures often result in subsequent and infinite requests for more giving, and my vision of Karma as a stoic and noble monk dealing with his lot in life could not bear the possibility of a dialogue along those lines. I let the episode go, but the larger implications of what had just happened stuck with me. I was pulling back from my 20 years of service and folly on behalf of the Tibetan people. But it was impossible for me to admit this to myself outright: My actions were speaking for me.

*

"Oh my, here comes the undertaker," said Tsering Dhondup, the *paljor kalon*, or finance minister, of the Tibetan Administration. Tsering was a gentle and friendly man with bright, inquisitive eyes and touches of greying hair around his temples – I liked him immediately. I was in his office to meet his new entrepreneurship development team and to tell him what I knew.

Directly on my heels came a serious-looking American gentleman who walked in and sat next to me. He seemed reluctant to continue a conversation beyond our cursory handshakes and greetings. His name was Randy.

Randy worked for one of those American Tibetan support organisations that acted as a quasi monitoring and administration unit for USAID, which, when it came to Tibet issues, was more than quasi in bed with the US State Department. He raised more than a few "institutional alert" hairs on the back of my neck, so I laid down some defensive cover: a variation of the old "dumb tourist" routine that had rescued me from many a jam in the past. This version required me to keep the conversation going with a rapid-fire litany of everything ranging from my accomplishments for Tibet, to general political philosophy, to Nepali politics, to the proper way to turn a French omelette. The goal was to have Randy view me as a bit loony and not to be taken seriously, so that whenever he reported what he needed to report to whoever, I would come out looking like a wildcard and be given a wide, unencumbered and dismissive seal of indifference from the US Government or any concerned agents thereof. The most effective cover is to do a bad job of faking your own importance – I'm good at that.

I was all too happy to introduce my hybrid entrepreneurship concepts and the *paljor kalon* was eager to show me what his staff had concocted, so for the next hour we cheerily exchanged ideas and polite barbs over some of the worst instant Nescafé coffee I'd encountered in all my years of Asia travel. As our time together came to a close, we promised to keep in touch like a couple of old fraternity brothers, and Tsering assured and promised me that we would continue to work together on this programme for the foreseeable future. I promised on the graves of my ancestors that I would bring him a decent coffee machine next time.

"By the way, Jim-la, would you like to meet the *sikyong*?" Tsering said rather off-handedly.

Lobsang Sangay, a tall, Harvard-educated Tibetan, was now the political leader of the Tibetan people. The Dalai Lama had grown weary of the strain of politics, and had stepped back and given Lobsang's *sikyong* portfolio the power to act and speak politically on behalf of all Tibetans living in exile.

In reality, the *sikyong*'s job was a delicate balancing act: He must represent the views of Tibetans as a whole while dancing with the desires of the West,

China, India and the numerous and wedge-driving political factions that seemed to be springing up daily in the Tibetan community. I knew nothing about the man. The last thing I remembered reading about him was an interview he gave to the *New York Times* in which the reporter marvelled at how passionate and knowledgeable a baseball fan Lobsang was. His heart, soul and loyalties were with the Boston Red Sox and this allegiance was made abundantly clear through this article.

Now I was to meet him, face to face. It was not a shock. I was working at the highest levels of the CTA and I knew there was a good chance I was to be presented, eventually, at his office. So, taking a gamble, I had prepared something on the odd chance I'd run into him on this trip.

"Jim! Good to finally meet you!" The tall-framed Tibetan rose from his chair and his hand clasped mine. Lobsang Sangay's English was perfect, and aside from his traditional Tibetan dress, he looked as though he had just stepped out of a corner office at Goldman Sachs.

"Please, have a seat. Tell me what's going on."

"Well, no," I replied coyly. "I'm afraid I can't really speak with you just now."

Instantly, Sangay turned to the *paljor kalon* who had accompanied me to the meeting and raised a quizzical "What is this?" kind of eyebrow.

I continued: "I read your article in the *New York Times*, *Sikyong*, and I can't in good conscience continue this conversation knowing that you are a Boston fan and that you've just alienated all baseball fans on the entire West Coast of America. Nope. Not gonna do it."

I love awkward ice-breakers like this, and I had Lobsang right where I wanted him.

"You are just going to have to put on this hat before we continue."

I pulled from my bag an official Major League Baseball cap from the World Champion San Francisco Giants. Lobsang somberly placed it on his head and all three of us at the meeting began to laugh heartily – my little gamble had worked.

"Actually, Jim, this is great," chortled Lobsang-la. "I sometimes go walking in the mountains and I don't like to be recognised. No one would ever dream I'd wear a hat like this, so I'll take it with me on my next walk. The disguise is perfect."

From then on we discussed openly and without inhibition. I laid out my ideas on the need for Tibetan self-determination, and Lobsang briefly outlined his 5/50 idea to return all Tibetans to Tibet in either five or fifty years, and he said that we should actively plan along both tracks.

"So, Lobsang-la, what's up with this Randy guy?" I threw out.

"Ah, Randy and I were school friends," he said. I was unclear if this meant they were school mates at Harvard or some other institution, but I was starting to make connections now.

I went on to describe most of the adventures I've documented in this book, and found myself in my usual froth of self-righteousness about Tibet and on the verge of jumping on a table in full evangelical fury when Lobsang interrupted to speak with the *paljor kalon.*

"He has such a passion, doesn't he?" I heard him say. Then, to me: "Jim-la, I'm going to arrange a meeting with the entire CTA staff for tomorrow and I want you to present everything you've told me here. Can you do it?"

"Let me get this straight: You want me to give a speech, cold, on decades of Tibet activism in Nepal with no preparation and in front of an entire professional staff of maybe 80 or 100 people who not only have a better understanding of the issue than I do but will probably be visibly angry at a few things I'm going to say? Sure, what's not to love about that?"

I had to do it, there was no question. After I gave my assent, we rose from our seats and headed for the door.

"Jim, let's exchange e-mail addresses so we can keep in touch," Lobsang said. We shook hands one more time, and I was beginning to make my way out of the building when Lobsang Sangay shouted something to me from his door: "Welcome home, Jim."

The remaining hours of the day were spent in a coffee house cramming together an old PowerPoint presentation I'd given to the ICT in 2003 that gave a map of all our operations in Nepal. I would document each programme, point to the map a lot and just improvise. Not a great way to present oneself to an entire administration, but it would have to do.

Long after dark I made my way back to my room, plugged in my laptop and was cheered to find an e-mail from my new friend Lobsang Sangay. I opened it eagerly:

"Giants suck."

The next morning broke early for me and I was awake and staring at the ceiling long before the sun came up. It was one of those overwrought, anxiety-driven mornings steeped in existentialism, regret and doubt, and by the time the Snow Lion opened up at seven a.m. I had been waiting outside the door for more than a few minutes, eager to get inside and change my mental scenery. Parked at my usual table, I stared for what seemed like an eternity at nothing in particular on the opposite wall until I was snapped back to the real world by the crash of my breakfast order on the table.

"Three minutes," said Tenzin, and with that I began to find my bearings.

In my notebook I had brought along an old copy of the *International New York Times* crossword puzzle I'd brought from Kathmandu and I began to make a half-hearted attempt at fiddling with the clues. It was one of those killer editions where even a good puzzle player might make one complete pass through all the clues without writing down a single answer. There's really nothing I can do with these kinds of puzzles other than to start, as always, with clues that imply a plural answer and write the letter "s" in the last square. It's a simple, educated leap of faith that usually leads to the completion of a few other answers I may not have seen the first time. But this morning being what it was, my mind began to wander towards a story I'd heard about a young Tibetan activist, Lingtsa Tsetan Dorje, who in June of 2013 could handle the frustration no longer and walked into Tibet to wage a "peaceful struggle" and to see what he could accomplish for Tibet on his own. He knew that once he crossed over, once he committed to do this, his options for survival would be bleak, but he was out of ideas. He told Radio Free Asia that "the right place for us to struggle is inside Tibet". He could think of no other options and he couldn't solve the puzzle, so he made his decision and took his best gamble. He started with his own version of the letter "s".

It was what had been on my mind all morning. As good as our little entrepreneurship programme was for the Tibetans, did I just get involved in it to be a big shot? Was this programme the most effective and immediate ground-level use of my time? I'd met the *sikyong* and now I was addressing an entire government body. For whom was I doing this? More importantly, after the reality slap brought on by seeing Karma's photograph the day before, being a big-shot saviour for Tibet had lost its lustre, its meaning. I no longer saw merit in any of it. There needed to be a million Lingtsa Tsetan Dorjes all doing their small and laser-focused bit for Tibet if there was to be any real impact. I knew this now.

The sweet air of the mountains greeted me as I left the Snow Lion that morning. The CTA had arranged to have a car pick me up and transport me to their offices just a few minutes down the mountain. I was invited to have my favorite *tingmo* dumplings with some of my new friends from the *paljor kalon*'s office at the staff mess, and from there I would be taken into a great lecture hall and begin my presentation. I enjoy the company of Tibetans in general, even angry ones, but at that moment I was feeling a bit uncomfortable wondering why Jigme, one of the finance ministry secretaries, was staring so intently in my direction.

"Jim-la, I am sorry, but why have you been helping Tibetans for 20 years? It is hard to believe," was the eventual question.

"Jigme-la, I have a nasty little secret that's the key to the whole thing: I don't care one bit that all of you are Tibetans. I do this because we are all human beings and I wouldn't want the Tibetan tragedy to befall me, my family or children. Make sense?"

Jigme nodded in approval, and my answer was as close as I would ever come to saying anything remotely Buddhist, so I was rather impressed with myself. I rose from my chair and headed towards the lecture hall with a small boost of self-confidence.

The rough count in the room was about 90 souls, all Tibetan and all being forced out of their busy day to come and listen to this foreigner. Everyone was thanked for being in attendance, and I spoke my best Tibetan during my introductory remarks and basically said that I can't speak Tibetan very well and must continue in English. For the next hour I pointed to my PowerPoint map of Nepal and described the vaccine smuggling programme, the currency exchange project, all my border trips and a few others I've omitted from this book. I was pleasantly surprised when laughter erupted in the room as I described our UN impersonation caper and I heard audible groans when I showed photos of frostbite victims. Mostly, the talk went smoothly. At the end, I opened the floor for questions and was met with silence until our Tibetan moderator told the crowd it was alright to speak up.

"Sir, tell us what you think of the UNHCR."

"I don't," came my terse reply and I was ready for an argument, but everyone seemed to agree with me.

"If the US and the West have done so poorly, where can we turn for help?" was another question.

Stamping my feet for emphasis, I shouted, "Here! Right here! Right where we're standing! As a Tibetan community, our relationship with India is most valuable and it is the one we should seek to cultivate over the coming years."

The full event was filmed for Tibetan Cable Television or something of that nature, but the presentation was a bit opinionated and controversial so I'm sure it never made it out of editing and the film is languishing in obscurity on a shelf somewhere. No matter, there was a palpable sense in the room that the West was not going to provide answers to the Tibet issue. Still, it was nice to show them that there once was a time when Westerners legitimately thought and acted on behalf of Tibetans, on the ground, where it mattered most.

My last duty was to report back to Lobsang Sangay and tell him the details of the presentation. It would be my last time seeing the *sikyong* and I had a full and heavy heart. To this day he remains an enigma to me, and he is not especially gifted at returning e-mails, but I do genuinely like the guy.

"They asked questions? Tibetans asked questions?" Lobsang seemed genuinely baffled.

"Yep, good questions too," I shot back.

It was getting late in the afternoon and a heavy rain was beginning to fall. I told Lobsang that I needed to get back and pack my bags; he told me there was no real hurry. We both wished we had a pizza at that moment. In truth, I was still thinking about my planned pull-back from the Tibet Movement and was trying to avoid telling him about it when I had an idea:

"Lobsang, I've been doing this forever, as you know. I've got films, photos, documents, articles of clothing, you name it. I think it's time I gave it all to the Tibetan people. It's theirs anyway. I need to close this big chapter of my life and there's no better way of doing it than to give all my notes and archives to the CTA. What do you think?"

"Jim, that's a great idea. I'll put you in touch with Tashi Phuntsok, the director of the Tibet Museum, and you can give it all to him."

Fair enough. I'll deliver as much as I can in the few hours I have left tomorrow, and then I'll be done with the whole thing: chapter closed, lessons learned, life resumed, I thought. I was looking forward now to the cleansing, the catharsis, the closure, and I could not wait to unload what I had on

Tashi and be free, once and for all, of the position, the role and the anxiety I had created for myself over the last few decades.

The next morning I was running behind. I had just a few hours to be down the hill and at Gonggar Airport in order to catch my flight to Delhi. The trip down from McLeod Ganj would eat up 45 minutes, so I had precious little time to speak with Tashi Phuntsok. Still, I was eager to get this over with.

An amiable man with a keen eye for spotting relevant articles of Tibetan history, Tashi Phuntsok is the conscientious director of the Tibetan Museum in McLeod Ganj. He oversees a staff of researchers and is constantly updating and creating new exhibits. He and I spent an hour poring over my photos and records. Tashi showed considerable interest when the subject turned to the frostbite crossing up at the Nangpa La and he hit me with a shocker:

"Jim-la, our young people have no idea any of this happened."

"Are you kidding me, Tashi? These events took place not very long ago. They are also singularly important to understanding the Tibetan's exile experience," I said.

From there we devised a plan to have my materials merge with Tibetan stories of crossing the Nangpa La and to create a comprehensive exhibit detailing Tibetan migration through Nepal for the Tibetan Museum on the grounds of the Dalai Lama's palace in McLeod Ganj. Budgets would now have to be created, approvals won, and extensive research and planning conducted.

It seemed Tibet was not done with me yet.

Chapter 22

At the End of the Day

There is a sense of excitement around the idea of gathering Tibetan thoughts, stories and objects together in an exhibit – it's tangible, necessary and beneficial. In the old days such a project would light a fire underneath me and I would spin off half a dozen peripheral projects to complement the effort. Not now. The world is a different place and my feelings towards Nepal, Tibet and all I've done are evolving as I age. I'm ready to hand over what I know to whoever might find value in it, but perhaps time has changed and diminished the value of what I know.

It's all changing now – as it should, I suppose – but a few ghosts linger. Sudesh still holds court at the New Orleans Café and I just finished what was probably my last night as a musician there, jamming to the old tunes and still trying to fuse the blues with Indian ragas. Deepak is having a rougher time. His trekking empire is on the wane, and if it were not for his considerable and diverse interests – including ownership of a small hotel in Thamel that we both share – he would be in real trouble. I worry about him. Nepal and humanity need people like Deepak Bhandari: Neither, however, seem to appreciate him the way I do.

Kathmandu still possesses its regular lures and diversions, I'm happy to say. Tom and Jerry's is still lively and still full of security and intelligence people. For fun, I still try to pick out the State Department crew; only now, my prey is often less elusive.

One night, for no particular reason, this young American I'd been watching suddenly grabbed his beer and announced to a table full of girls from the local St. Xavier's school teaching staff: "Hey, I work for the CIA. I don't care if anybody knows it – so what?" I do hope he was lying; but if not, he needs to work on his trade-craft a bit more.

Another night, I took notice of a table full of young and serious-looking Chinese patrons and, just for the hell of it, decided to go over and introduce myself. Courteous pleasantries and introductions were passed and shots of cheap whisky were shared all around.

I saw that I was getting the attention of a pretty and well-groomed Chinese girl who was in the company of a perspiring Nepali boy. I made a mental note and kept chatting.

The boy would ask me a small question, I'd give him a small answer and the Chinese girl would whisper something in his ear and he'd ask me again. I caught on.

"Look, *bai*, she speaks perfect English – why doesn't she ask me herself?"

He didn't get to answer before his handler whispered something else into his ear. I think it must have been something crucial and final, as his face turned white and he looked at me like I was Jason Bourne with a toothache. The two of them rose quickly and left. I do tend to fantasise about dynamics that may or may not exist when I'm at Tom and Jerry's, but it was obvious that this poor Nepali boy had found himself in a situation that was beyond his capacities. I remember his face; I hope I get to see it again someday.

*

The US embassy is less overwhelmed these days by visits from bloviating congressmen and State Department officials. The articles that ambassador DeLisi and I wrote helped to change the tone of American scolding on Tibet, but the maddening shift changes at the embassy always bring the possibility of having to start the efforts all over again. At the request of a friend in the embassy, I filed a summary report of the political dynamic involved with official visitors and the damage they may cause to US/Nepal relations when they mention Tibet. It was a rare opportunity to have my opinions heard and I did not waste the chance. I was tired of this shit and the lack of traction caused by all the personnel changes, and I let them have it with both barrels. I outlined simple steps for getting out in front of damaging rhetoric that might cause harm to Tibetans in Nepal, and thoroughly documented all the trouble we had during the "Gentlemen's Agreement" years. Overall, it was made it clear that Tibet must no longer be that great, unmentionable topic that lurks in the US embassy compound in Kathmandu. We risk looking like fools if we do not take a proactive approach. I was thanked profusely for my "thoughtful" report and was told that it would be circulated throughout the embassy, the ambassador's office and USAID. I'm sure that after each individual who had read the report re-emerged from under their desk, they gave it a "thoughtful" dismissal.

In November of 2014, the current incarnation of the special coordinator for Tibetan affairs, Sara Sewall, visited Nepal. The US embassy made the highly unusual choice not to publish her plans or itinerary. My friends in Nepal's national media sphere were furious. I have to assume that the difficulties encountered by previous special coordinator visits played a part in this. To her credit, Sarah Sewall never mentioned the "Gentlemen's Agreement", and for the most part there were no problems as Sewall made her way stealthily around Nepal. This seems to be the new standard. The job of today's special coordinator is to make an obligatory, low-key annual visit to the region and to throw money at the Tibetans – a far cry from the proactive political dynamism that Greg Craig displayed in the same position so many years ago.

In January of 2016, Sara Sewall made her annual visit to India. Her trip to McLeod Ganj was listed, according to this State Department Media Note from January 11th, 2016, as almost an afterthought:

> While in India, Under Secretary Sewall will lead US participation in the US – India Global Issues Forum – the first since 2012 – to review and expand areas of regional and global cooperation. She will meet with civil society representatives to strengthen cooperation around common interests, including countering violent extremism, religious freedom, trafficking in persons, and transparency and governance. She will also deliver a speech, "Democratic Values and Violent Extremism," at the Vivekananda International Foundation in New Delhi.
>
> As the US Special Coordinator for Tibetan Issues, Under Secretary Sewall will also travel to Dharamsala, India, to discuss issues of importance to the Tibetan refugee community.

"Issues of importance" have been distilled down to money, and Sewall's primary – almost singular – function to the Tibetans these days is to announce how much money they get for the year and where the US wants the money to be spent. What started back in 2012 under Maria Otero as a

$2 million grant to the Tibetans known as the "Tibetan Education Project" and was repurposed as a $3.2 million dollar "Health System Strengthening Project" in 2014, has now ballooned to $6 million to be used as an "Economic Support Fund" that will provide money for, yes, entrepreneurship programmes, among other things. I hope I gave Randy some good notes on that.

I've always felt that the USAID/State Department logic when it comes to Tibetans is one of intelligence accumulation and political control. The Americans have no Tibet policy; they just want to keep Tibetans quiet while they deal with China. Ultimately, $6 million buys the US access, control and quiet among Tibetans in India – it's like a big, warm wet blanket designed to smother individual expression and initiative.

The idea of Western control is universal and seems to extend to what remains of the Tibetan Support Group (TSG) community as well. In 2016, the Tibetans finished a series of democratic elections, and Lobsang Sangay was re-elected as *sikyong* of the Tibetan administration. What was remarkable and discouraging was that all the vices of the worst American-style political campaign came into play and left a bad taste in the mouths of many Tibetans hoping for a clean electoral process. Accusations of corruption, tampering with election rules and mysterious Cabinet resignations prevailed. Into this fray, Western TSGs inserted themselves as "election monitors" and voiced their complaints at how imperfect this first real election attempt had been. To their credit, the Tibetans themselves largely ignored the outsiders, but the snub did not go unnoticed. Signed by dozens of TSG luminaries, an "open letter" addressed to the CTA was published that left no doubt that the TSGs collectively felt like a lover spurned:

> His Holiness and the CTA have, on many occasions, requested all the world to help Tibet, and expressed their appreciation for the assistance given by Tibet Supporters and Tibet Support Groups around the world – we who answered the call. That continuing support should not be wholly taken for granted.

It has now been a few years since Lingtsa Tsetan Dorje walked into Tibet. The fact that he has been neither seen nor heard from since troubles me. Also, Spanish courts have completely abandoned their quixotic pursuit of justice under the doctrine of universal jurisdiction and that troubles me for different reasons. Dorje's humanity and desperation stand out, and the thought of his disappearance makes me wonder if there is any hope for those with seemingly pure intentions. Can we be untarnished altruists when it comes to Tibet, or do we need to make our deals with the Devil in order to survive? On the Spanish side, how many more of these bad deals and bungling political ploys do the Tibetans have to endure, and do they have enough time for such futility?

After all these years, I'm not entirely convinced that the US and the West should give up on Tibet outright; they should just learn to shut up. Shut up and get behind India. The West can still offer a lot, they just need to give up the lead and knock off using Tibet as a political pawn to try to get China to act or move in some direction – it hasn't worked and it will not work.

And while I'm trying to keep a positive frame of mind here, there may be some hope yet for those bloated and ineffective TSGs still out there, still clinging to life: Try listening to Tibetans for a change. You owe it to them. You've been making money out of the Tibetan tragedy for far too long. Your poorly attended, token protests have no effect, and all you seem to be able to do these days is "raise awareness" and "monitor" the Tibetan situation. If you cannot listen and take your direction from the Tibetans themselves and work as equal partners under Tibetan leadership, then fold up, close your doors, turn out the lights and go find other ways to make a living.

And what should become of you and me, the individuals looking to help? All of us who are part of countless small efforts to assist Tibetans from our Western perches need a wake-up call as well. All through this book I've heartily endorsed the idea of individual, one-on-one efforts as being the only true means of realising change. Thousands of us have done our well-meaning and unique things for Tibet over the years, but still the problems persist and Tibet is not "free" – far from it. Is the entire premise misguided? What does it really mean for us to "help" a Tibetan?

All of us in the West seem to get this wrong, and it starts with the idea that, at the very least, we want to feel good about what we're doing. This usually means finding an immediate and tangible way to solve a problem. This also usually means throwing a pile of money at a problem unilaterally, so that we can fix it fast enough to get the good feeling that goes along with that. We buy a noodle machine so a Tibetan in India can start a business, or give school money for a Tibetan to study in the West, and we revel in the satisfaction of having done something good. But what have we really done? Are we building unity within the Tibetan community, or are we fostering the idea that Tibetans themselves are a brand with special value?

It is ultimately a question of whether self-determination or foreign dependency offers the best hope of saving Tibet and Tibetan culture. I'll argue that Sarah Sewall's $6 million and all the money you and I have given to Tibetans over the years have created the latter, and it's not a good thing. It's just charity. Charity may be the only way to solve certain problems, but it does not help in forming a cultural identity or a sense of unity of purpose. And I have yet to see it foster a sense of financial responsibility. What I have seen is a competitive free-for-all where individual interests and the scramble for funds trumps community sacrifice and cooperation. The charity I've seen splinters and divides – not the kind of thing that would give hope to an anguished Tibetan who's hungry for a sense of his identity and may be on the verge of doing something desperate.

What then? Should we abandon Tibetans to their own devises and call it "tough love"? Certainly not: Tibetans have been given a tough burden, and as our human brothers and sisters we must, without question, help them. But real, sustained help that is effective is only realised when the people you are trying to help take ownership of their own assistance and development. From my experiences in Nepal I know this ONLY happens when the recipients of our efforts take an active and proprietary role in creating their own direction for the future. We must let the Tibetans build their own programmes their own way, and we must help them as equal partners, not benevolent charity-disbursing masters with a magic cure. This means you and I have to forego the good feeling and instant gratification we get from doing something charitable, dig in for the long haul and prepare to get our hands dirty. So before you buy that noodle machine, find out what that individual recipient wants to do with his life and what risks he is willing to take to see his plans come to fruition. Do some research. You may wind up giving him nothing; you may wind up with a business partner for life and that business may have nothing to do with noodles.

What will "Free Tibet 2.0" look like? My first hope is to see Tibetan leadership and those in the world who advocate on behalf of Tibet issues reflect deeply on the last 30 years. Long ago, the choice was made to internationalise the Tibet Movement, and the international community blew it. With the ever-increasing pressure to assimilate being forced on Tibetans in Tibet and with China aggressively bent on reimagining and controlling all aspects of Tibetan culture and history, Tibetans don't have time to make this type of mistake again. Forget the big gestures; it's time to work in a more focused manner. Next, desperation is cooled by self-determination.

Tibetans need a voice in their own immediate, Indian future, and India needs to keep offering programmes and incentives to allow Tibetan ideas to be heard and to prosper on their own. Private sector expertise and funding must be allowed and encouraged as well. Allow for localised incentives that are attractive enough to keep Tibetan youths from fleeing India to seek their careers abroad. This is the type of approach we in the West should have adopted from the start.

For me, there are still a few things to clean up. I believe more strongly than ever that the crucial battles of "Free Tibet 2.0" will be fought over the absolute preservation and salvaging of Tibetan culture. As China tries just about everything – from increased persecution to the naming of its own Tibetan Lamas and Buddhas – it becomes essential to gather in and document as much Tibetan history, culture and theological practice as is humanly possible. That's why I agreed to work on this final museum project. I want to help define and preserve for history that era of great Tibetan migration and pilgrimage through Nepal. Plus, I'm still trying to get the exact details about the Nangpa La crossing right – I still want to know about every metre, every last detail of that journey, and I'm hoping that the Tibetans who suffered through it will come forward and offer their accounts for this museum exhibit. But the big idea is to have Tibetans start the conversation among themselves and have them tell us how they would like it to be presented.

*

A big obstacle was thrown our way in late April of 2015. Plans that were made for working on the museum exhibit were abruptly cancelled when Nepal suffered a massive earthquake registering at 7.9 on the Richter scale. I was in the US when the first quake hit and I hopped on the first flight to Kathmandu once the news reached me.

For the next month, Deepak, myself and our little staff at Himalayan Aid directed blankets, food, tarps, metal sheeting and medical supplies to the areas identified by Nepalis as being the most immediately in need. Some 80 tons were delivered in all, and when we were through Deepak and I sat back and could not believe how we had accomplished such a feat in just a little over a month. Some weeks later we came to the conclusion that it was our person-to-person, Nepali-to-Nepali effort that helped us identify and focus our efforts efficiently, while the Government of Nepal displayed its staggering yet predictable incompetence, and while the UN and other big aid agencies were bogging themselves down in "cluster meetings" (a term I find only 50 per cent accurate) and heavily bureaucratic and imperiously inefficient aid-distribution schemes.

At the end of November 2015, I did manage to make it back to McLeod Ganj and conduct a few good discussions about the museum project. Ideas were tossed about and we agreed to meet again in the spring to finalise plans. There was also time to see my old friend, the *paljor kalon*, Tsering Dhondup, who was still keenly interested in the entrepreneurship ideas we had discussed before and asked an entirely new set of prepared and informed questions. Tsering-la will be retiring from his post in 2016 – I will miss him greatly.

"Jim-la!" came the call from one of my friends, Khenpo, who worked in the *paljor kalon*'s office. "Jim-la, it is very short notice but you can meet His Holiness tomorrow in the morning if you'd like."

I weighed Khenpo's words carefully in my mind.

Meeting the Dalai Lama is a lifelong dream for many citizens of the world. Not only does he stand for peace, compassion and compromise, but he's one of the most recognised public figures on the planet. Who wouldn't want to meet him if given the chance? Throughout my Tibetan years there had been the odd chance for me to see him, but I had always felt it to be inappropriate. Not only did I want to keep him high on the pedestal where I'd placed him, but the notion ran through me that all the crazy things I was doing on his behalf required a certain degree of separation – I didn't want to be singled out and marked by anyone and potentially have my projects come under unwanted scrutiny. Now, with all the crazy projects behind me, I felt no compelling reason to turn down the offer.

"Sure, Khenpo, let's do it. Pick me up tomorrow."

I have no clear memory of walking back to my room that evening, only the knowledge that my head was racing with un-tethered thoughts.

As might anyone who has the potential for an audience with a world figure, I had rehearsed many times what I might finally say to the Dalai Lama if we ever met. It came down to just one question. I practised the question on Lobsang Sangay at our first meeting, and he immediately went silent and stared off into the distance. It is a question that His Holiness most certainly would have answered diplomatically and graciously in years past, but now I wasn't so sure:

Did we let you down?

Khenpo was waiting by the gates of my hotel first thing the following morning. We exchanged greetings and walked down a steep and narrow driveway that led directly to the Dalai Lama's compound. First security encounter: confirming that my name was on the list of scheduled visitors for that day. After being waved through quickly – Khenpo was a familiar face to the guards – we made our way up to the main waiting lobby where I had to show my passport and fill out a form: my second security encounter. I was led to a seat in the small waiting area with other hopefuls and I inventoried the group: six Western teens and their parents, giddy and laughing, all wearing silk *katas*; a pair of well-dressed and earnest-looking Tibetan businessmen; and a few monks.

The Dalai Lama employed about a dozen plain-clothed Tibetan security agents who were of considerable physical size but unarmed. A few of them quizzed me about my intent and gave me a thorough security scan and pat-down: a third security encounter.

From there, guards led me up a long, paved driveway to the doors of the Dalai Lama's house. I was told to wait in a line and His Holiness would be out shortly. Tibetan pilgrims of all sizes and dress made up a line with Western seekers of all colours and motivations – about 200 in all. A plain white-shirted Indian secret service agent of some sort with his finger poised over the trigger-guard of his AK-47 gave me a menacing glance before turning his attention to a group of about 30 well-dressed Bhutanese pilgrims who had flown directly to Thimphu for the occasion: security encounter number four. This Indian agent was the only armed person on the premises, and as I watched him work the crowd I thought about the perfection of it all. *Yeah, India is into this – they know exactly what they're doing,* I said to myself. And it was true. The government of India was guarding the Dalai Lama, and I couldn't help but think that this was not just for obvious security reasons: they seemed to be protecting an asset.

Everything moved along quickly after that. I was jumped ahead in line a few places as guards asked, "Are you James-la?" and I felt like someone special. Finally, the Dalai Lama walked into the courtyard, smiling and surrounded by his immediate assistants. It had the odd feel of a CNN video and I half-expected subtitles to scroll along the bottom of the scene, but I shook it off and concentrated on my turn with the great man.

"Your Holiness, uh, this is uh, Mr James. He, uh, works in Nepal, I believe."

His Holiness could not care less about the intro his protocol officer supplied: He grabbed my hand warmly and we made small talk for the next few minutes. The conversation consisted of disjointed courtesies and bits of nothing, but just being in the presence of this warm, infinitely human man almost made conversation moot. Still, this was obviously a busy day for him and I didn't want to take up his time, so I uttered a *tu je che* – the Tibetan "thank you" – and he let out a hearty laugh at my foreign audacity.

As I was led down the driveway by a contingent of two Tibetan guards – security encounter number five – the emotions I felt surprised me. No, I wasn't swooning with awareness and compassion as some claimed would happen; rather, a profound and deep sadness came over me, and I didn't know quite what to make of it. I did know that the only thing I wanted the Dalai Lama to do – now and for the rest of his time on earth – was rest. *He's done enough, leave him alone now.* Perhaps my sadness came from watching those crowds waiting for him to appear, and from the knowledge that even in his 80s the Dalai Lama will always have some sort of obligation to see and greet and be seen. The world will not let him rest.

I never asked him my one question.

*

It was mid-spring 2016, and I was in Delhi preparing for my short trip up to McLeod Ganj to meet with the Tibetan administration and the secretary of the Tibetan Museum to push the exhibit into high gear. We had just spent the early part of the year securing the proper approvals from the relevant Tibetan authorities and now, after much delay, we were set to begin. I needed to make sure that the display space was adequately sufficient to hold all the Tibetan stories we were planning to display, and that costs for items like photo enlargements and video screens were kept within budget constraints. Also, quite a few politically sensitive topics needed to be addressed, such as what sort of Chinese retaliation we might expect from the exhibit and what level of Indian media coverage should be allowed. There seemed to be a whirlwind of areas to cover and I had only a few days to get it all accomplished.

"Tashi, I'm afraid I'm going to have to cancel," I texted weakly to my director friend at the museum.

Pumped full of paracetamol, probiotics and every other medicine I could find, I was laid out flat and immobile from a nasty case of food poisoning and who knows what else – I wasn't going anywhere. I had travelled some 30 hours from the US to get to this point and conduct this museum meeting, and it was not going to happen. We were going to lose precious time because of me, as I would now not be able to set the wheels of this project properly in motion.

Anxiety and food poisoning are not recommended as bed fellows, and after Tashi responded to my text with "That is very sad", my condition worsened. I spent the next two days in my room, curtains drawn, in a moping depression punctuated exclusively by mad dashes to the toilet. At one point I was convinced that I was dreaming while fully conscious – go figure that one out. I was out of my body, out of my head and out of my ego, for once, when it all began to turn.

Lying face up in a hotel bed in Anywhere, Delhi, India, it came to me and I coughed through a laughing fog: *You idiot, you really didn't learn a damn thing, did you?*

Preaching the gospel of self-determination for Tibetans had been a banner issue for me, but now my hypocrisy was laid bare. I still could not let go of my need to dictate and control. Bad things were going to happen if I didn't get to that meeting in McLeod Ganj, I had convinced myself. Was it really all for Tibet, or did my hardwired belief in my Western role as saviour of the world still rule all? No matter what high, generous and equitable concepts I espoused, everything still had to be done *my* way. It is a stream of belief that runs so deep in the souls of us Westerners that we are often blind to the duplicity it can engender.

If being deathly ill and stuporous was to be my new precondition for clear thought; it was now leading me to a revelation and found myself sitting upright in bed.

For decades I've been working on this puzzle – with a crusader's quill and ink. I've crossed out answers, built assumptions around my errors and watched as the clues themselves changed. I have saved lives and been branded a fool. I have gathered data and assembled programmes in good faith only to see my efforts politicised. I've both protected and been beaten. I threw myself into this puzzle convinced I could solve it on belief alone.

But Tibetans have no practical use for my beliefs. They play no role in the day-to-day, minute-to-minute struggles of Tibetans trying to survive.

Ultimately, I am a bystander, a mere consultant to this dynamic. Tibet will survive only by its own hand and by working with those partners who understand the most immediate and vital daily needs of the Tibetan people.

There was no spare energy available in my body for these kinds of thoughts, but they persisted and refused to release me until I gave in. As I slid back down beneath the blankets, my thoughts began their journey towards surrender: *Relax, time to let go; you're incidental to the process now. The museum will call you if they need you.* In a day filled with medication and hallucination, an oddly calm and liberating feeling took over; a huge weight of self-imposed responsibility and duty had been shed. As I began to sense my recovery, the departing haze of illness left me with one last truth:

This was not my puzzle to solve. It never was.

Chapter Notes

Chapter 1

The New York Times: Barron, J. (1987 October 5) Chinese Release Two Americans Detained During Rioting in Tibet. *The New York Times,* p. 1, World, Retrieved from http://www.nytimes.com/1987/10/05/world/chinese-release-two-americans-detained-during-rioting-in-tibet.html

"All drops of men and equipment": Knaus, John K. (1999) *Orphans of the Cold War: America and the Tibetan Struggle for Survival.* New York, NY: Perseus Books (p. 155)

"30,000 men by airplane": Knaus, John K. (1999) *Orphans of the Cold War: America and the Tibetan Struggle for Survival.* New York, NY: Perseus Books (p. 186)

Not intended for public use: McCleary, J. (From personal e-mail with the author, February 4, 2014)

"Insufficient to outweigh the almost certain damage": Knaus, John K., with a forward by, Thurman, Robert A. F. Tenzin (2012) *Beyond Shangri-La: America and Tibet's Move into the Twenty-First Century.* Durham, NC: Duke University Press (p. 234)

Chapter 3

Why are We Silent?: This can be found via numerous video sources on the internet. A Youtube.com version is at: GGFilmsChannel (2012, September 27) *Why are We Silent* [Video File]. Retrieved from https://www.youtube.com/watch?v=dJR0dhlr1H8

Glory: Fields, F. (Producer), Zwick, E. (Director). (1989). Glory. [Motion Picture]. United States: Sony Pictures.

"Today, together, let us reaffirm": As cited in Knaus, John K., with a forward by,

Thurman, Robert A. F. Tenzin (2012) *Beyond Shangri-La: America and Tibet's Move into the Twenty-First Century.* Durham, NC: Duke University Press (p. 244)

A breathtaking effort: A lot of the back-room wrangling and legislative successes realized during those days was due in no small part to the tenacity of Mary Beth Markey who later succeeded John Ackerly to the Directorship of the International Campaign for Tibet. A good photo of her and her group can be found at: Knaus, John K., with a forward by, Thurman, Robert A.F. Tenzin (2012) *Beyond Shangri-La: America and Tibet's Move into the Twenty-First Century.* Durham, NC: Duke University Press (p. 238)

"The sky will not fall": Shattuck, J. (2005, October 31) *Freedom on Fire: Human Rights Wars and America's Response.* Cambridge, MA: Harvard University Press (p. 269)

"Human rights are not universal": Shattuck, J. (2005, October 31) *Freedom on Fire: Human Rights Wars and America's Response.* Cambridge, MA: Harvard University Press (p. 270)

Chapter 4

The newspapers thought: Sauer, M. (1998, September 25) On a Limb and a Prayer. *San Diego . Union Tribune* (p. E1). (Also see a copy of page 2 of the article in photo insert section).

Chapter 5

No substantial published procedural arguments: Most articles I've found say there is not much difference between the IM and the SC vector for MMR. Try: Immunization Action Coalition: Measles, Mumps and Rubella, Administering Vaccines (2016) Retrieved from: http://www.immunize.org/askexperts/experts_mmr.asp#top

Chapter 6

Had found favor with the King: If you can find a copy of this "dispensation" given by the King, I applaud you. The best proof of its existence is: Tumbahangphey, A. (2005, September 30). *Manang's Middle Path.* Retrieved from: http://nepalitimes.com/news.php?id=884#.V1iJ8vkrLIU

Chapter 7

There was always some professional doubt: Anderson, P. and Doherty T.M. (2005, August 3) The Success and Failure of BCG-Implications for a Novel Vaccine. Retrieved from: http://www.ncbi.nlm.nih.gov/pubmed/16012514

Chapter 8

Run over the ankles: Accounts of this style of punishment were common from 1999-2003 but I've found no independent verification of the practice as fact. Reports of torture and imprisonment are common, however, and the Central Tibetan Administration in McLeod Ganj ran a Torture and Victims Center back in 2000 that was run by my old Reception Center Clinic boss Tsering Lhamo. I've long since lost touch with her. Today you can check out the CTA's Torture Survivors Program, if it is still running: Tibetan Torture Survivors Program (2014, July 7) Retrieved from: http://tibetanhealth.org/health_programmes/tibetan-torture-survivors-program

Chapter 9

Jumping down from balcony porticos: This was an image that remained inside my head. Film clips from this time are available on the internet, but some of the specific images I remember can be found at: Hagemeister, R. (2008, April 1). *Suppression of Tibetan Protests* [Video file]. Retrieved from: https://www.youtube.com/watch?v=HN9LYniEros

"My eyes are going": "Pema" (personal video interview, March 29,2000).

Chapter 10

We were the longest train of tourists: The porters and staff at Deepak's agency made this assertion, but a blurb on the actual train can be found at: Airline Ambassadors (1999, Summer). Nepal. *Newsletter.* p. 4.

The per capita income of the average Nepali: International Monetary Fund (2003*). Nepal: Joint Staff Assessment of the Poverty Reduction Strategy Paper.* Washington, D.C.: International Monetary Fund. p. 2

Chapter 11

P.J. O'Rourke: I believe the source text for Mr. O'Rourke's sentiments here can be found at: O'Rourke, P.J. (2000). Holidays in Hell. New York, NY: Grove Press.

No explanation about going back: Ironically, one of the few recent articles about the return trip reports how the Chinese are now refusing to allow Tibetans—legally in Nepal or otherwise—to return to Tibet. Sangyal, T., and Tashi, L. (2012, August 30). Tibetans Blocked from Return. Retrieved from http://www.rfa.org/english/news/tibet/blocked-08302012152040.html

I did manage to find one: Tibet Information Network (2000, December 20). TIN News Update. Retrieved from http://tibet.ca/en/library/wtn/archive/old?y=2000&m=12&p=21_1

Chapter 12

Since then, these "Gurkha" warriors: Gorkha Rifles. (2013, April 18). Retrieved from https://www.facebook.com/Gorkha.Rifles/posts/10151555820038754:0

Chapter 14

Taga and his wife Chimi: Most of the information received on the Taga and Chimi story came through a 1999 e-mail chain between myself, Dory Beatrice, who was Director of the San Diego Friends of Tibet, and Rinchen Dharlo, who may have been with the Tibet Fund at that time. We thought it a good idea to have our amputee monk friend Karma visit Taga at the Norbu Linka institute in Dharamsala and compare notes on prosthetics. We had hoped to bring Taga to San Diego for the same re-fitting as Karma, but nothing came of the effort.

People's Liberation Army (PLA) base: So far, and to my knowledge, our team remains the only group to actually photograph this base from a foot approach. There was some argument with the ICT on whether this was in fact a PLA base; a Public Security Bureau (PSB) installation; or a People's Armed Police (PAP) base. A friend of mine with connections to the U.S. Department of Defense Intelligence community speculated that it was a PLA base, but may exist as a utility for multiple force and agency missions. The 2009 shooting of a Tibetan nun crossing the Nangpa-la was, in all probability, conducted by PAP forces originating from this base.

Chapter 15

"Regional security": A recurrent pretext. Ouyang (2015, December 22). China, Nepal strengthen military cooperation. Retrieved from http://english.chinamil.com.cn/news-channels/china-military-news/2015-12/22/content_6827226.htm

To: Immigration Officials See photo section for example of this letter photocopied from original.

For the next eight years: The next reported case of Tibetan repatriation was in 2010, so officially, that was around six years between repatriations. There is always a concern that exposing a problem, the way we did, might force it to go underground; and perhaps this is what happened. Lack of documented cases of forced repatriation simply means a lack of documentation. But the Phayul article here documents a big gap that we, hopefully, triggered with our UN impersonation. Thinly, P. (2010, July 28). Nepal's repatriation of 3 Tibetans leaves UN "concerned". *Phayul.* Retrieved from http://www.phayul.com/news/article.aspx?id=27854

Chapter 16

APF is the newest face of Nepal: Newar, N. (2004, May 21). Peacekeeping away from home. *The Nepali Times*. Retrieved from http://nepalitimes.com/news.php?id=2819#.V2A0_7srLIU

I met the young man: His name was Captain Smith, really. By my estimate, he owes me about $13,000 from all the man-hours and resources I spent assembling his little research paper.

Chapter 17

Human Rights Watch: Human Rights Watch (2014, April 1). *Under China's Shadow*. Retrieved from Human Rights Watch website: https://www.hrw.org/report/2014/04/01/under-chinas-shadow/mistreatment-tibetans-nepal

The UNHCR feigned high disappointment: UNHCR (2000). UNHCR Mid-Year Report 2000. Retrieved from UNHCR website: http://www.unhcr.org/3e6f1b770.pdf

This was the first time such a dynamic was brought to light: I can find no references to any agreement, implied or otherwise, with the Government of Nepal that provides for the safe, guaranteed passage of Tibetans onward to India that employs the description of "Gentleman's Agreement" prior to the *Dangerous Crossing* publication. International Campaign for Tibet (2002, May 1). *Dangerous Crossing* [Pamphlet]. Washington, D.C: The International Campaign for Tibet.

The now defunct Tibet Information Network comes close by referring to an "agreement" between the UNHCR and the Government of Nepal for Tibetan processing; but the right to visit and monitor border areas is refuted and described as informal by a spokesperson for Nepal's Home Ministry. Tibet Information Network (2000, December 20). *TIN News Update*. Retrieved from http://tibet.ca/en/library/wtn/archive/old?y=2000&m=12&p=21_1

In 2010, Mary Beth Markey: Saunders, K. (personal e-mail communication, July 27, 2010).

Nepal has violated the well-established: International Campaign for Tibet (2010, July 27). Nepal police forcibly return three Tibetan refugees across border. Retrieved from https://www.savetibet.org/nepal-police-forcibly-return-three-tibetan-refugees-across-border/

"We have authentic information that our oldest and nearest friend": Ani News (2011, October 22). China in Nepal. *Ani News*. Retrieved from: http://www.aninews.in/newsdetail4/story18699/china-in-nepal.html

"China fears the entry of Western and Tibetan leaders.": Parajuli, K. (2012, November 8). Fearing Tibetans, Beijing closes border with Nepal for Congress.

Asianews.it. Retrieved from http://www.asianews.it/news-en/Fearing-Tibetans,-Beijing-closes-border-with-Nepal-for-Congress-26296.html

"I am impressed by what the Government of Nepal": Post Report (2011, September 30). US Lawmaker lauds Nepal's handling of Tibetan refugees. *The Kathmandu Post.* Retrieved from http://kathmandupost.ekantipur.com/printedition/news/2011-09-30/us-lawmaker-lauds-nepals-handling-of-tibetan-refugees.html

"The 'Gentleman's Agreement' implies": Rinaldi, J. (personal e-mail communication, July 27, 2010).

"We're not just going to cut them": Thapa, D. (2004, November 10). Wolf's Warning. *The Kathmandu Post.* Retrieved from http://kathmandupost.ekantipur.com/printedition/news/2011-11-09/wolfs-warning.html

"ICT had nothing to do with the Wolf statement": Saunders, K. (personal e-mail communication, December 9, 2011).

Pressing Nepal on Tibet Uncalled For: Luitel, G. (2011, November 20). Pressing Nepal on Tibet Uncalled for. *The Himalayan Times.* Retrieved from http://kathmandupost.ekantipur.com/printedition/news/2011-11-09/wolfs-warning.html

The original article is, according to *The Himalayan Times*, found on an old server that can be accessed using Internet Explorer only at: http://thtimes.pugmarks.in/fullNews.php?headline=%27Pressing+Nepal+on+Tibet+uncalled+for%27&NewsID=309875

"My government has long valued the fact": DeLisi, S. (2011, November 21). Rights of Refugees. *The Kathmandu Post.* Retrieved from http://kathmandupost.ekantipur.com/printedition/news/2011-11-20/rights-of-refugees.html

"It has been a difficult time for Nepal": Rinaldi, J. (2011, December 5). Rash of Criticism: Nepal Deserves an Apology. *The Himalayan Times.*

Again, original article can be found using Internet Explorer only at: http://thtimes.pugmarks.in/fullNews.php?headline=Rash+of+criticism+&NewsID=311700

"Personally, I believe that Nepal has actually done a very good job": Post Report (2011, December 12). The World is Bigger than India and China. *The Kathmandu Post.* Retrieved from http://kathmandupost.ekantipur.com/news/2011-12-12/the-world-is-bigger-than-india-and-china.html

"Did you talk about refugee law and Gentleman's Agreement": Embassy of the United State; Nepal(2012, April 5). Transcript of the Press Conference. Retrieved from U.S. Embassy, Nepal website: http://nepal.usembassy.gov/sp-04-05-2012.html

"I don't consider that we are dealing differently": Embassy of the United State; Nepal(2012, April 5). Transcript of the Press Conference. Retrieved from U.S. Embassy, Nepal website: http://nepal.usembassy.gov/sp-04-05-2012.html

Chapter 18

"The United States is deeply concerned": Office of the Spokesperson (2012, December 5). Statement by Special Coordinator for Tibetan Issues Maria Otero. Retrieved from U.S. Department of State website: http://www.state.gov/r/pa/prs/ps/2012/12/201594.htm

"The EU is profoundly saddened": Council of the European Union (2012). *Declaration by the High Representative, Catherine Ashton, on behalf of the European Union on Tibetan Self-immolation.* [Press Release]. Retrieved from http://www.consilium.europa.eu/uedocs/cms_Data/docs/pressdata/en/cfsp/134378.pdf

Canada: Baird, J. (2012, December 14). Canada Concerned about Rash of Tibetan Self-Immolations (2012, December 14). *Global Affairs Canada.* Retrieved from http://www.international.gc.ca/media/aff/news-communiques/2012/12/14b.aspx?view=d&lang=eng

Went to work by saying how "strong" the statements were: Twitter clucked that there was, perhaps, a united voice forming among nations and the buzz was one of self-congratulatory back-slapping for a while; but eventually, the residue washed out and everyone seemed to settle on the idea that the statements were "strong." James, J. (2012, December 31). Human Rights in Tibet—the World Responds, part 2. *Contact.* Retrieved from http://www.contactmagazine.net/articles/december-2012/human-rights-tibet-world-responds-part-2/

John Ackerly and Blake Kerr: Kerr, B. (1993). Sky Burial. Chicago, IL: Nobles Press. (Chapter 7).

Does the West Still Want to Free Tibet?: Keating, J. (2012, May 7). Does the West Still Want to Free Tibet? *Foreign Policy.* Retrieved from http://foreignpolicy.com/2012/05/07/does-the-west-still-want-to-free-tibet/

Todd Stein: The Keating article above was also noteworthy in that Mr. Stein rebutted its assertions in the comments section, and I, subsequently, followed with a rebuttal of Mr. Stein's rebuttal. The comments section has now, mysteriously, disappeared from this article. Perhaps they are still available to *Foreign Policy* (FP) subscribers. E-mails sent to "Ken" at FP requesting the transcripts or content of the comments section were returned with ad-spam from FP. Contact FP at FP@cambeywest.com if you'd like to try your luck at dislodging these comments.

"Institutionalized": The ICT's preference for an "institutionalized" Tibet movement can be alternatively documented in a few places. Stein, T. (2012, September 8). Tibet Ensconced in American Politics. *Tibetan Political Review.* Retrieved from https://sites.google.com/site/tibetanpoliticalreview/articles/tibetensconcedinamericanpolitics

International Campaign for Tibet. (2013, May 30). Message from the Board of Directors of the International Campaign for Tibet. Retrieved from http://

www.savetibet.org/message-from-the-board-of-directors-of-the-international-campaign-for-tibet/

Madeline Albright: Knaus, John K., with a forward by, Thurman, Robert A. F. Tenzin (2012) *Beyond Shangri-La: America and Tibet's Move into the Twenty-First Century.* Durham, NC: Duke University Press (pp. 265-268).

Dianne Feinstein and her husband: Knaus, John K., with a forward by, Thurman, Robert A. F. Tenzin (2012) *Beyond Shangri-La: America and Tibet's Move into the Twenty-First Century.* Durham, NC: Duke University Press (pp. 272-276).

The entire TPA can be found online: The best version I can find is at: Bureau of East Asian and Pacific Affairs (2003, May 16). Tibetan Policy Act of 2002. Retrieved from http://2001-2009.state.gov/p/eap/rls/rpt/20699.htm

Tibet: Problems, Prospects, and U.S. Policy: Dumbaugh, K. (2008, July 30). Tibet: Problems, Prospects, and U.S. Policy. Congressional Research Service. Retrieved from https://www.fas.org/sgp/crs/row/RL34445.pdf

George Stromboulopoulous: Strombo (2008, May 12). *Lhadong Tethong on The Hour with George Stroumboulopoulos.* [Video File]. Retrieved from https://www.youtube.com/watch?v=ob9xh-MEWd4

Joel McCleary: Knaus, John K., with a forward by, Thurman, Robert A. F. Tenzin (2012). *Beyond Shangri-La: America and Tibet's Move into the Twenty-First Century.* Durham, NC: Duke University Press (pp. 216-218, 230-231).

Chapter 19

CNN felt the need to drag a camera crew: Sidner, S. (2012, February 22). Is China Pushing Nepal to Crack Down on Tibetans? *CNN.* Retrieved from http://www.cnn.com/2012/02/21/world/asia/china-tibet-nepal/

A Facebook exchange from January: International Campaign for Tibet. (2016, January 13). What are we asking our representatives to do for Tibet? [Blog Comment]. Retrieved from https://m.facebook.com/events/1670711013211093?view=permalink&id=1682662465349281

"Gangnam Style": SFTHQ (2012, November 7). *Tibetans vs China's Xi Jinping: Gangnam Style.* [Video file]. Retrieved from https://www.youtube.com/watch?v=NxxEo6lEC_U

Avaast.org petition: Is this Tibet's big chance? (2013, November). Retrieved from https://secure.avaaz.org/en/stand_with_tibet_loc/?pv=120&rc=fb

Giant Tibetan skeleton puppets": Tibet Coalition, AVAAZ To Rally For No Vote In China's Election to the UN Human Rights Council (2013). Retrieved from https://www.studentsforafreetibet.org/news/tibet-coalition-avaaz-to-rally-for-no-vote-in-china2019s-election-to-the-un-human-rights-council

China has its own agenda: Jacques, M. (2009, April 12). Epinions—When China Rules the World. From the Martin Jacques website. Retrieved from http://www.martinjacques.com/when-china-rules-the-world/when-china-rules-the-world-7/

Western democracies have recently resolved to strike ISIS: Woeser, T. (2014, December 30). Faith in Addition to Face—To Facebook, Inc. *China Change.* Retrieved from https://chinachange.org/2014/12/30/faith-in-addition-to-face-to-facebook-inc/

ICT had its hands all over it: *ICT testifies in Spain's National Court on Chinese leadership policies in Tibet.* (2012, December 30). Retrieved from https://www.savetibet.org/ict-testifies-in-spains-national-court-on-chinese-leadership-policies-in-tibet/

Henry Kissinger hates the concept: Kissinger, H. (2002). Does America Need a Foreign Policy? New York, NY: Touchstone/Simon and Schuster. (pp. 277-281).

Remarkably and stunningly: United States Commission on International Religious Freedom annual report. Retrieved from http://www.savetibet.org/united-states-commission-on-international-religious-freedom-annual-report/

"Jim, we went into a tea house": (Personal conversation with intern J.P., Kathmandu, 2012).

"Bureaucratic hurdles, geo-political instability": Shrestha, S. (2016, January 22-28). Big delays in big projects. *The Himalayan Times.* Retrieved from http://nepalitimes.com/article/nation/delay-in-big-projects,2838

Chapter 20

China is stripping away at large, heaping chunks: Virtually every pro-Tibet site will use the language I've used to describe this change. Trying to make the same point without the political emotion of such sites is difficult. Supplied here is a relatively tone-free accumulation of ideas and sources that re-inforces the point being made in the text. Compiled by Hays, J. (2013). Chinese Government in Tibet. Facts and Details. Retrieved from http://factsanddetails.com/china/cat6/sub37/item202.html

"Systematic foreign aid creates": Watkins, T. (2010, April 21). Haiti doesn't need foreign aid money—it needs a better development strategy. *The Christian Science Monitor.* Retrieved from http://www.csmonitor.com/Commentary/Opinion/2010/0421/Haiti-doesn-t-need-foreign-aid-money.-It-needs-a-better-development-strategy.

A village revolt in Wukan: Patience, M. (2011, December 15). China's Wukan village stands up for land rights. *BBC News.* Retrieved from http://www.bbc.com/news/world-asia-china-16205654

$6 million: Paljor, Y. (2015, December 22). *US Sanctions $6 Million for Tibetans in Nepal and India for Fiscal Year 2016.* Retrieved from http://www.tibetanjournal.com/index.php/2015/12/22/us-sanctions-6-million-for-tibetans-in-nepal-and-india-for-fiscal-year-2016/

"In 127 BC": Roy, J.N. and Braja, B.K.(2007). *India and Central Asia.* Delhi, India: Concept Publishing Company. (p. 95). Retrieved from https://books.google.com/books?id=-lJI9avHstYC&pg=PA95&dq=%22In+127+BC,+the+inhabitants+of+Yarlung+valley%22&hl=en&sa=X&ved=0ahUKEwjk-bnas6_NAhUHxmMKHbYQDc0Q6AEIHjAA#v=onepage&q=%22In%20127%20BC%2C%20the%20inhabitants%20of%20Yarlung%20valley%22&f=false

G. Niranjan: *Tibet Campaign Concluded with a Public Event in Hyderabad.* (2013, January 12). Retrieved from http://www.thetibetpost.com/en/features/press-and-statements/3167-tibet-campaign-concluded-with-a-public-event-in-hyderabad

On May 15 of that same year: Bisht, G. (2014, June 2). Tibetan refugees to be given benefits of welfare schemes. *The Hindustan Times.* Retrieved from http://www.hindustantimes.com/chandigarh/tibetan-refugees-to-be-given-benefits-of-welfare-schemes/story-2AqbgUwlFM2S8VsGfEzShL.html

"Middle way": A pragmatic approach that rejects Tibetan independence in China while seeking autonomy and cooperation. Try: http://www.dalailama.com/messages/middle-way-approach

"Tibetans may have wearied from the plodding" Rinaldi, J. (2014, June 23). Tibet and its cause: A Mission and a Message. *The Tibet Post.* Retrieved from http://www.thetibetpost.com/en/outlook/reviews/4111-tibet-and-its-cause-a-mission-and-a-message

"Shut up and stay in the refugee camps": Refers to a stipulation in that initial USAID $2 million project introduced by Maria Otero whereby educational opportunities were given to Tibetans staying in refugee camps throughout India. Otero found it somehow beneficial to "encourage youth to remain in the settlements." Otero, M. (2011, July 13). *Roundtable on "The Dalai Lama: What He Means For Tibetans Today."* Retrieved from U.S. State Department Website: http://www.state.gov/j/168181.htm

"Rangzen": A Tibetan word meaning "freedom." Rangzen Movements, which are present within the Tibetan community, advocate Tibetan independence from China.

Chapter 21

U-Tsang Tibetan: Spoken in Lhasa and generally indigenous to the central U-Tsang region of Tibet.

His 5/50 idea: This concept was formally introduced in May of 2016, so it seems I had knowledge of it long before he made it official. http://tibet.net/2016/05/sikyong-announces-five-fifty-strategy-for-second-term/

"The right place for us to struggle is inside Tibet": *Vanished Activist Vows 'Peaceful Struggle' Inside Tibet* (2013, July 22). Retrieved from http://www.rfa.org/english/news/tibet/vanished-07222013150101.html

Chapter 22

The U.S. Embassy made the highly unusual choice: (Personal conversation with K. Koirala, in Kathmandu, November, 2014).

While in India, Under Secretary Sewall: Sewall is very careful, during her question and answer session in this briefing, to not offend China and sticks rigidly to referring to U.S. interests in Tibet as being "humanitarian" and for "refugees." *Under Secretary Sewall Travel to India* (2016, January 11). Retrieved from U.S. State Department website: http://www.state.gov/r/pa/prs/ps/2016/01/251099.htm

"His Holiness and the CTA have, on many occasions": *An Open Letter to the Sikyong, Kashag and Election Commissioner of the Central Tibetan Administration, Dharamsala* (2015, October 13). Retrieved from http://www.jamyangnorbu.com/blog/2015/10/13/an-open-letter-to-the-sikyong-kashag-and-election-commissioner-of-the-central-tibetan-administration-in-dharamsala-india/

Its own Tibetan Lamas and Buddhas: Beech, H. (2015, December 11). China's Database of 'Living Buddhas' is the Latest Attempt to Control Tibetan Affairs. *Time.* Retrieved from http://time.com/4145552/china-tibet-living-buddha-dalai-lama/

SELECTED BIBLIOGRAPHY

Buckley, M. (2014). *Meltdown in Tibet.* New York, NY: Palgrave Macmillan Trade.

Collier, P. (2007). *The Bottom Billion.* New York, NY: Oxford University Press.

Crow, D. (2000). *In Search of the Medicine Buddha.* New York, NY: Penguin Putnam Inc.

Dalai Lama XIV. (2014). *Cultivating a Daily Meditation.* Dharamsala, India: Library of Tibetan Works and Archives.

Dawkins, R. (2010). *The Greatest Show on Earth.* London, UK: Transworld/Black Swan.

Dolma, K. (2013). *A Hundred Thousand White Stones.* Somerville, MA: Wisdom Publications.

Easterly, W. (2013). *The Tyranny of Experts.* New York, NY: Basic Books.

Easterly, W. (2007). *The White Man's Burden.* New York, NY: The Penguin Press.

French, P. (2003). *Tibet, Tibet.* New York, NY: Alfred A. Knopf.

Gandhi, M. (1957). *Gandhi: An Autobiography.* Boston, MA: Beacon Press.

Green, J. (2010). *Murder in the High Himalaya.* Philadelphia, PA: Perseus Books Group.

Jacques, M. (2009). *When China Rules the World.* New York, NY: Penguin Press.

Kerr, B. (1997). *Sky Burial.* Ithaca, NY: Snow Lion Publications.

Khentse, D. (2007). *What Makes You Not a Buddhist.* New Delhi, India: Timeless Books.

Kissinger, H. (2002). *Does America Need a Foreign Policy?* New York, NY: Touchstone/Simon and Schuster.

Kissinger, H. (2011). *On China.* New York, NY: The Penguin Press.

Knaus, J.K. (2012). *Beyond Shangri-La.* Durham, NC: Duke University Press.

Knaus, J.K. (1999). *Orphans of the Cold War.* New York, NY: Public Affairs/ Perseus Books Group

Mayhew, B., Brown, L., Butler, S. (2015). *Lonely Planet Nepal.* Oakland, CA: Lonely Planet Publications.

Moyo, D. (2009). *Dead Aid.* New York, NY: Farrar, Straus and Giroux.

O'Rourke, P. (2000). *Holidays in Hell.* New York, NY: Grove Press.

Pistono, M. (2011). *In the Shadow of the Buddha.* New York, NY: Dutton/ Penguin Group.

Rinzler, L. (2012). *The Buddha Walks Into a Bar.* Boston, MA: Shambhala Publications, Inc.

Sharma, R. (2016). *The Rise and Fall of Nations.* New York, NY: W.W. Norton and Company.

Sharma, S. (2001). *Procuring Water.* Kathmandu, Nepal: Nepal Water conservation Foundation.

Shattuck, J. (2003). *Freedom On Fire: Human Rights Wars and America's Response.* Cambridge, MA: Harvard University Press.

Shrestha, N. (1997). *In the Name of Development.* Lanham, MA: University Press of America.

Sirolli, E. (2012). *How to Start a Business and Ignite Your Life.* Garden City Park, NY: Square One Publishers.

Smith, C. (1990). *Travels in Nepal.* London, UK: Penguin Books.

Tsering, Y. (1987). *Tibetan Phrasebook.* Ithaca, NY: Snow Lion Publications.

Woeser, T. (2016). *Tibet on Fire.* London, UK: Verso.

INDEX